Understanding Organisations

Organisational Theory and Practice in India

MADHUKAR SHUKLA
Associate Professor
Xavier Labour Relations Institute
Jamshedpur

Prentice-Hall of India Private Limited
New Delhi - 110 001
2006

Rs. 195.00

UNDERSTANDING ORGANISATIONS: Organisational Theory and Practice in India
by Madhukar Shukla

ISBN-81-203-1122-1

Sixth Printing ... ... October, 2006

Published by Asoke K. Ghosh, Prentice-Hall of India Private Limited, M-97, Connaught Circus, New Delhi-110001 and Printed by Syndicate Binders, A-20, Hosiery Complex, Noida, Phase-II Extension, Noida-201305 (N.C.R. Delhi).

Contents

Preface

Organisations are an inescapable part of modern life. Our whole life is a continuous process of traversing from one organisation (e.g. family, school, college, company, office, etc.) to another. Even if we do not work or live in these Organisations, we constantly get affected by them as the beneficiaries (or victims) of their actions. We travel in trains, buses and planes, use telecommunication facilities, go to restaurants, stay in hotels, maintain accounts with banks, invest in company shares and schemes, buy commodities and pay for services, and so on. None of these would be possible without Organisations to manage and provide them.

Despite such all-pervasive influence of Organisations on human lives, it is surprising how often people (even the practising or potential managers) tend to view Organisations as distant, abstract entities unrelated to one's day-to-day experience. Most people seem to be blissfully unaware of the extent to which Organisations *organise* their lives (as well as those of others) and, therefore, are unable to relate to organisational realities.

The aim of writing this book was to assist the practising and potential managers to learn how to make sense out of organisational realities. A number of reasons have prompted me to write 'yet another' book on Organisational Theory (OT). The problem with most books on OT (a few exceptions apart) is that they deal with the issues of organisational design in a rather dry and lifeless manner. While the aim of such books is to provide a better understanding of organisational reality, often the residual feeling after reading them is that Organisations really are difficult entities to comprehend. I have strived to provide and easy-to-read, yet exciting, account of what an organisation is and how it operates. Further, I was motivated by my experience with my MBA students, and with the practising executives in my training and consultancy assignments. I found that these people were magnanimous in sharing their enthusiasm and thrill, once the OT concepts were presented to them in a simple and an interesting manner.

Another reason for bringing out this book is to give an Indian background to organisational theory. For, the books written by authors from abroad lack the Indian flavour and the students find it difficult to comprehend the concepts of organisation theory without real-life examples of Indian companies. I have tried to remedy this situation by providing examples from well-known Indian Organisations.

Perhaps the most important reason for writing this book is its specific focus and content. Most books on OT limit their focus on organisational design issues to certain mechanical and tangible principles. Sometimes, these principles are even offered as a panacea for designing an effective organisation. Such an approach, however, misses out the complexity and richness of the ever-changing organisational life. The reality of the Organisation is not only tangible and explicit but also intangible and implicit. In fact, one can develop a deeper insight into the formal aspects of organisational design (i.e., departmentation, strategy, span of control, etc.) only if one develops a sensitivity for the intangible processes (i.e., power issues, culture, interpersonal processes, etc.). Moreover, Organisations are not static entities, which remain same over a period of time. They are dynamic: capable of growing, changing, failing or transforming themselves.

This rich and complex organisational reality that embodies various perspectives in and approaches to understanding, designing and managing Organisations is described in detail in Chapter 1.

The chapters that follow are sequenced in an inductive and exploratory manner. Before converging (in Chapter 7) on the various ways in which an organisation can be designed, Chapters 2–6 describe the building blocks and the numerous influences (e.g., environment, strategy, technology) which determine that design. One common theme running across these chapters is the *contingency approach* to organisational design, viz., the 'ideal' organisational design is one that is adaptive to its specific circumstances. These chapters also focus on the tangible and explicit aspects of organisational design.

These obvious and manifest features of the organisation, however, only describe *what* an organisation is, not *how* it functions. This 'how'—the operating process-based reality of the Organisation—is discussed in Chapters 8–10. Here, the reader will find insights for understanding some of the common experiences of organisational life, such as how decisions are taken, how conflicts and power issues mould organisational activities, how values and norms influence performance, and so on. In discussing these processes, I have tried to establish their links to the formal and tangible aspects of Organisations.

Any discussion of organisational design would be incomplete without understanding how it changes and how it can be changed. The last three chapters (11–13) focus on the issues related to organisational change: how Organisations change or are transformed, why they do not change, and the emerging issues in designing Organisations. I believe that this a critical area which is often neglected in discussions on OT.

This book is designed for the practising managers, management students, consultants, and teachers. Though the text describes various OT theoretical frameworks in detail, an underlying assumption in these discussions is an old dictum: *There is nothing as practical as a good theory.* I have also attempted to link the theory to practice by including a section at the end of each chapter, which discusses the implication of the ideas for managers.

While I was writing this book, I had experienced it essentially as a solitary activity. However, I now realise how many people directly or indirectly assisted me during the course of writing this book. Two persons who have immensely supported and tolerated me during this period are Geeta Saxena—my friend, colleague and wife—and Manasi, my daughter. Without their patience, encouragement and constant support, this book could never have been written. There are a number of other individuals also whose contribution to this book is invaluable. I would like to express my gratitude to my friends and colleagues for their sustained support and encouragement: to Professors Sharad Sarin and Pramod Kumar for their valuable comments and suggestions; to my students who enthusiastically used the initial drafts of the chapters (in the form of class handouts) and unknowingly encouraged me to expand them into book form; to Mr. Jagan Rao (*the* Jagan) for patiently teaching me *how* to use (and not use) the computer; to Ms. Gracy Sebastian and Ms. Lizamma James for painstakingly keying-in portions of the text: and to Mr. S.K. Tiwary for assisting me in tackling numerous problems. I am also grateful to the authorities of XLRI, not only for the support and facilities they provided, but also for the enriching experiences which helped me refine many ideas and examples which went into the making of this book.

Writing this book has been an exciting venture. I hope this thrill of discovery and adventure will also be experienced by the reader while going through the pages of the book.

Madhukar Shukla

1 Interpreting Organisational Reality

The (anti-)hero of Franz Kafka's *The Castle* is a wanderer, searching for a sense of identity. His name is K, no more than that. Wishing to escape from his lonely rootlessness, he tries desperately to seek acceptance from the ambiguous authority structure of the castle. But his attempts to make a meaningful contact with the authorities turn out to be frustrating. He is unable to fathom the vagueness and ambiguity, not to mention the stark impersonality of the echelons of the castle. Their procedures seem arbitrary, devoid of any humane, or even meaningful, content. At times he feels he is being unfairly treated and so responds with ineffectual defiance. But a more common feeling is of self-doubt, a sense of guilt, that it must be his own fault. If there is a rule, it has to have a rationale, some meaning, even if one finds it difficult to comprehend it. In his isolation and his inability to make a confident response, he senses that the problem must be with him only, not with the authorities.

He feels indecisive, and that he must keep on trying. There must be some way of satisfying the unclear requirements of the authorities, to behave satisfactorily so that they will accept him. If he could only figure out the rules, he would follow them.

In many ways, the allegory of *The Castle* is an archetypal version of the contemporary individual in an organisation. Of course, organisations are not as unpredictable as the castle. But they are complex enough systems to create a bewildering array of inconsistent images, and bring out our most deep-seated anxieties, predispositions and biases. For K, unable to comprehend how the authorities of the castle functioned, the castle became the canvas on which his personal inferiority, his need to belong, his loneliness could be projected; like most of us, K lived in a world of his own making; more so, because he (again, like many of us) lacked the conceptual options of viewing and interpreting his world in any other manner. The tragic consequence was his loss of individuality and an abject dependence on the authorities. This probably is the single most important reason for any practising or potential manager to develop an insight into the organisational reality.

Psychologists have long been aware that when confronted with a complex and ambiguous situation [such as a Thematic Apperception Test (TAT) or Rorschach card] people tend to interpret it in a way which reflects their own intra-psychic reality, which may range from neurotic obsessions to professional biases. Also, that the personal effectiveness and creative potential of the individual lies in his ability to view and make sense of the situation in more than one way. But to do so, the person must have the necessary concepts which can help him in interpreting the reality. In a famous experiment conducted by Jerome Bruner (1957), when a King of Red Spades was flashed before a group of persons for a split second, they perceived it as a King of Hearts or a King of Diamonds. What they visualised was not because of defective eye-sight, but because of an inadequate set of mental pigeon-holes in which Red Spades did not figure.

What we perceive as our concept of the reality, is often restricted by the mental categories and the concepts, which we carry in our minds. Reality, it seems, is not unlike the complicated elephant of the six blind men!

I. IMAGES OF ORGANISATION

You may wonder what all this has got to do with the study of organisations? Plenty. Because organisations, complex and complicated realities as they are, are far from a unified whole, and do not convey a common meaning to everyone. This complexity allows people to interpret the organisational reality in ways convenient to them. Interaction with members of any organisation (be that an industrial organisation, a government office, an advertising agency, or an educational institution), makes one appreciate the richness and variety of ways in which people view the realities in which they live and work. A conversation with them would bring out various types of responses:

- "We're so very efficient here. Our systems are absolutely impeccable. Everything works with clockwork precision. We ensure that every job is properly defined, and our employees do exactly what they are supposed to do."

- "There is no rationality, no recognition of merit here. You are rewarded not for what you do, but whom you know. Do you know, department X got a larger budget allocated, because they pulled the right strings? Decisions are taken here on the basis of political interests, not on what is technically right."

- "We have strong traditions which are deeply ingrained. In fact, their impact is noticeable in all aspects of our corporate life — the way decisions are taken, in the interactions among departments and people, even in the way our employees dress or the way they greet each other. In fact, sometimes I feel that these unspoken values which we share, determine almost everything we do."

- "Of course, we are very much a part of the larger socio-political system. If you see how quickly we respond to the environment — our pricing policy, purchases, marketing strategy — you will be amazed. I think one of our strengths is that we quickly convert any piece of information into a business opportunity."

- "This is an amazing place. Although it is an organisation with a nice sounding name, yet it could even be called a prison or an asylum which houses misfits, neurotics and perverts. Look at our sales people! They are aggressive, highly competitive and would resort to any practice to bag an order. But for the fact that they are selling our products, if you were only to look at their behaviour, you would say they are psychopaths!"

- "Do you know our annual turnover is more than the combined annual budgets of the five states in which we have our units? The economies of the cities where our units are located are totally dependent on us. Would you say we're unjustified if we want to influence what happens in these states and cities? After all, we also have to look after our interests."

Such diversity of perspectives is not only characteristic of the laymen, but also of the researchers and organisational theorists. Theories and conceptualisations, explaining the realities of organisation, have also used a variety of paradigms and metaphors to capture the essence of how organisations function (Morgan, 1986). The following are some of the prominent images of organisation which recur across the literature on organisational theory.

A. Organisations as Machines

The term 'organisation' derives from the Greek, *organon*, meaning a "tool" or an "instrument". And a good tool is one which has precision, efficiency, reliability, and predictability built into it.

These, in fact, are the most obvious features of any organisation. Organisations are built around systems and procedures which create conditions of efficiency and reliability of performance. Fixed working hours, production schedules, maintenance schedules, financial control systems, quality control systems, sales targets, code of conduct, clear job descriptions and reporting procedures, etc., are all natural corollaries of viewing the organisations as machines. The aim of these efforts is to routinise the activities and reduce uncertainty of operations. Organisations often even go to the extent of mechanising those aspects of behaviour which are otherwise interpersonal and spontaneous. For example, many pharmaceutical companies train their medical representatives to deliver extremely standardized sales-talk to physicians. These talks are standardised to the extent of phrases and gestures. Similarly, the on-board announcements made by the air-hostesses of any airline (e.g. welcoming passengers aboard, imparting safety information, wishing a safe landing), are stipulated to be read out from a standardized manual and the air-hostess is not supposed to add or delete even a single word. Even in their internal communications, organisations insist that grievances, leave applications, indents, etc., be submitted in prescribed formats and only then would they be responded to.

Many classical theories of organisation and management are characterised by the mechanical view of the organisation. In 1776, the Scottish economist Adam Smith in his book, *The Wealth of Nations* noted that division of labour, relying on breaking the total task into small specialised atomistic units, helped in increasing efficiency by replacing the discretion of workers with controls exerted by machines or supervisors. German sociologist Max Weber was the first person to provide a comprehensive definition of a highly mechanical form of organisation, *Bureaucracy,* which achieved high precision, reliability, orderliness, and efficiency through division of tasks, hierarchical supervision and detailed rules and regulations (see Exhibit 1.1). Weber noted that bureaucracy helped in routinising the administrative process in the same way as machines standardized the manufacturing process. (In passing, one must also mention that Weber was far from comfortable with the idea of bureaucratic organisations. While, as a sociologist, he described in detail the logic of bureaucratic forms of organisations, which were the offshoot of Industrial Revolution, he also suspected that these forms had the potential of suppressing human spontaneity and democratic norms of human interactions.)

Exhibit 1.1

Weber's Principles of Bureaucracy

For many people, bureaucracy means red-tapism, paper work, wastage of efforts and so on. But Weber, in using the term bureaucracy was defining a particular structural configuration, which not necessarily meant only inaptitude. Weber ascribed the following characteristics to bureaucracy (Robbins, 1989):

- **Division of Labour:** Each job is broken down into simple, routine, and well-defined tasks.
- **Well-Defined Authority/Hierarchy:** There is a multi-level formal structure with a hierarchy of positions or offices. Each lower office is under the supervision and control of the higher one.
- **High Formalisation:** To ensure uniformity and to regulate the behaviour of job holders, there is a heavy dependence on formal rules and procedures.
- **Impersonal Nature:** Sanctions are applied uniformly and impersonally to avoid involvement with individual personalities and personal preferences of members.
- **Employment Decisions based on Merit:** Selection and promotion decisions are based on technical qualifications, competence, and performance of the candidate.
- **Career Tracks for Employees:** Members are expected to pursue a career in the organisation. In return for this career commitment, employees are given permanent employment; that is, they are retained even if they "burn out" or their skills become obsolete.
- **Distinct Separation of Members' Organisational and Personal Lives:** To prevent the demands and interests of personal affairs from interfering with the rational impersonal conduct of the organisation's activities, the two are kept completely separate.

Other theorists, e.g. Henri Fayel, F.W. Mooney, Lyndall Urwick and F.W. Taylor, who proposed theories espousing more mechanistic form of organisational and managerial functioning, were less of theorists and more of practitioners. Their contribution was in the form of documenting what they practised to solve real-life problems of management. Underlying their writings was a view that efficient management is a process of planning,. organising, coordinating and controlling. Together, they also established the foundations for many modern management techniques which were to follow, such as Management-by-Objectives

(MBO); Project Evaluation and Review Technique (PERT); Planning, Programming, Budgeting System (PPBS); Time and Motion Study, etc. Their writings also refined and codified the tenets of classical organisation theory (see Exhibit 1.2). Obviously, if managing an organisation consists of a set of rational and segmented practices, the supporting organisational structure has to be equally rational and mechanistic. The result is the bureaucratic organisational structure designed along functionally and hierarchically divided tasks.

Exhibit 1.2

Principles of Classical Management Theory

- **Unity of Command:** An employee should receive orders from only one superior.
- **Scalar Chain:** The line of authority from superior to subordinate should be used for communication and decision-making.
- **Span of Control:** The number of people reporting to one superior must not be so large that it creates problems of communication and coordination.
- **Staff and Line:** Staff personnel should provide advisory service without violating the authority of the line functions.
- **Initiative:** This should be encouraged at all levels of organisations.
- **Division of Work:** Management should aim to achieve a degree of specialisation designed to achieve the goal of the organisation in an efficient manner.
- **Authority and Responsibility:** Responsibility should be appropriate to the authority given to complete a task.
- **Centralisation of Authority:** Centralisation of authority must aim at optimising the use of faculties of personnel.
- **Discipline:** Behaviour of personnel must be in accordance with agreed rules and customs.
- **Subordination of Individual Interest to Common Interest:** This must be achieved through firmness, setting examples and constant supervision.
- **Equity:** Fair remuneration must be paid for an individual's performance.
- **Stability of Tenure of Personnel:** This must be implemented to facilitate the development of abilities in particular line of work.
- **Espirit de corps:** This must be encouraged to facilitate harmony as a basis of strength.

The image of an organisation as a machine is the most popular and widely perceived one. However, despite the efficiency and control they provide, there are a number of limitations. These are:

1. Mechanistic organisations are suited for stable environments, and have difficulty in adapting to changing circumstances.

2. They promote unquestioning dependence on fixed rules and regulations, and thus dampen the problem-solving capacities within the organisation.

3. They have a dehumanising and alienating effect on people.

4. Since they often create situations in which individuals are at cross-purposes with the organisation, they tend to promote unanticipated and undesirable political behaviour.

B. Organisations as Living Systems

For all the rules and procedures of organisations—which are the hallmark of a mechanistic view of organisation—they do not merely keep on repeating their activities in an identical manner over time. That would be possible if organisations were insulated from external influences, but since that is not the case, they have to change and adapt in response to demands from external environment. In one of the classic studies, Burns and Stalker (1961) found that regimented and bureaucratic organisational structures were primarily useful in dealing with regulated and predictable environments. But in an unstable and complex environment, organisations need to develop more loose and flexible structures to cope with adaptive demands. Their findings also highlighted a crucial aspect of organisational functioning, which was altogether ignored in the machine image of organisation, viz., the importance of interface between the organisations and their environment.

This characteristic of adapting to the environment also makes organisations similar to living systems. In fact, not only do organisations continuously interact with their environment, but they also undergo the phenomenon of growth, maturity and decline. Katz and Kahn (1978) defined organisation as an open system (see Exhibit 1.3). This image of organisations as a living or open system has an important bearing on our understanding of the organisations. The most important being that, organisations are influenced by the environment. This commerce between the organisation and its environment is not only confined to the inputs (men, machine, material) and output (services/products), but changes in the environment also determine corresponding changes in the organisational strategy, structures and system. For example, in the 1970's, ITC Ltd. found its business environment changing with the implementation of FERA and MRTP Acts. This change necessitated a change in corporate strategy and ITC's diversification into the Hotel industry.

The open systems approach highlights survival and environmental adaptation as the primary goal of the organisation. Depending on the demands emanating from the environment, organisations tend to develop strategies and structures to help them in achieving this primary goal (we will discuss this point in detail in Chapter 4). The principle of equifinality suggests that there can be more than one way of achieving this goal. This contingency view of organisational functioning (Kast and Rosenzweig, 1973) makes it possible to appreciate the wide variety of organisational forms. A hotel, for instance, cannot be structured like an auto-assembly plant, because of the differences in the nature of environmental demands. (This view, one will notice, is markedly different from the mechanistic view discussed earlier, which stipulated that only a single organisational form could be considered effective.)

Exhibit 1.3

Some Characteristics of Open Systems

The concept of open system was developed by biologists to explain some of the salient characteristics of living systems. One will notice how well these characteristics also apply to organisations. These characteristics are:

- Open system take **inputs** from the environment and transform them into **outputs** which are again pumped back into the environment.
- The processes or pattern of activities, which perform these transformations are called **throughputs.** The throughput processes are **cyclic** in nature, in the sense that once completed, they return to the point of origin and tend to repeat themselves.
- In the input-throughput-output cycle, open systems tend to import more energy than they expand. As a result they are characterised by **negative entropy,** that is, they grow and become more **differentiated.**
- Open systems are receptive to **information inputs,** which provide a feedback to the systems about the direction of their growth.
- Open systems tend to maintain a balance or **steady state,** which is dynamic in nature.
- Open systems are characterised by **equifinality,** that is, they tend to reach the same goal (i.e. survival and growth) from differing initial conditions and by a variety of paths.

Studies also reveal that there is a logical connection between the environment and the organisational forms. Lawrence and Lorsch (1967), for example, found that organisations dealing with a more complex environment tend to become more differentiated, i.e., they develop diverse functions and task-segments. Moreover, like complex organisms, they also develop more sophisticated integrating mechanisms to deal with the diversity within the organisation. Similarly, Mintzberg (1979) identified five organisational forms, each suited for a particular kind of operating environment (see Chapter 7 for a description of these structural forms).

The open systems' view also brings into focus the crucial role of strategy in organisational functioning. Given the primary goal of survival and adaptation, organisations need to devise an appropriate strategy for dealing with the environment. Asian Paints, for example, at its inception, encountered a highly competitive and dominating environment, captured by multinational companies. Since the multinationals primarily focused on the urban markets, the company decided to create a niche for itself in the rural market. This strategy, which laid the foundations of its success, also resulted in creating a wide base of dealer-network, an efficient (and probably the earliest) computerised information system for planning product schedules to match the market demands, and even in determining the appropriate size of paint containers to suit the needs of rural markets (Bhattacharya, 1989).

Since organisations resemble living beings, they also grow and mature like living beings, that is, they show a predictable sequence of growth. Organisations do appear to change and evolve through reasonably consistent transitional stages. Greiner (1972), for example, proposed a five-stage model to explain organisational growth sequence (refer to Chapter 12 for more detail). This model described the various predictable crisis with which an organisation must cope with in its life-cycle. For example, an organisation may start as an entrepreneurial venture, relying on informal control and coordination mechanisms. But as it grows, it may encounter a need for a clear direction, without which its efforts would flounder and its energies would get dissipated. The shift may be from growth-through-creativity to growth-through-direction. However, as the organisation grows, the same leadership which provided the direction may precipitate problems of autonomy for the members of the organisation. Resolution of this crisis will pave the way for growth of the organisation through delegation and decentralisation. Such a life-cycle perspective (Kimberly and Miles, 1980) provides useful insights into the structural and systemic changes that take place in the course of an organisation's growth and change.

While the open systems' view is quite popular among organisational theorists and practitioners, it also has certain limitations. The main drawback of this model is that the operating environment of the organisation is not as objective and concrete, as the model makes it out to be. The interpretation of the environment depends on the subjectivity of the decision-makers. Thus, organisational adaptation to the environment is not automatic, but is moderated by the cognitive acumen of its members.

It is, of course, difficult to identify exactly what comprises the organisation's operating environment. Normally, operating environment is defined as those segments of larger environment with which the organisations directly interact (suppliers, vendors, market, government, etc.). But on many occasions, apparently unrelated events in the environment have a significant influence on the organisation. For example, coming together of OPEC nations had a totally unanticipated repercussion on many companies, particularly on the western coast of India; organisations had to cope with the mass flux of skilled manpower who left for lucrative assignments in the Gulf.

Moreover, it is only partly true that organisations "adapt" to their environment. They also select their operating environment and are often able to change it. In the earlier example of Asian Paints, the company selected its own marketing environment, and in the process of doing so, changed the very structure of the paint market. Similarly, many large companies, by promoting feeder ancillary units, tend to stabilise their environment which may have been unstable otherwise.

Finally, while organisations do grow in a predictable sequential manner, by no means is this pattern invariant in all cases. In fact, unlike human beings, organisations rarely die and disintegrate; even when they do go into decline, they have a remarkable ability to survive. Often they renew themselves and make a comeback. Such turnarounds which are a normal business reality, are often difficult to explain in terms of the life-cycle perspective.

C. Organisations as Brains

We have seen that organisations are not merely reactive entities, which passively adapt to the environmental demands. They are also proactive in their stance, in that they deliberately select their operating environment, and consciously plan their strategies and internal design. This means that the changes in the organisational strategies, structures and systems do not occur automatically in response to external environment, but depend on the manner in which the organisations receive, process and act upon the information emanating from internal and external environment.

An interesting example of this information-processing activity is BHEL's corporate planning exercise (Chaudhury, 1979). In 1974, BHEL envisaged a three-fold increase in the country's power requirements in the coming decade. Correspondingly, the company developed a corporate plan, which focused on larger volumes, import substitution through indigenisation, diversification into related areas. The implementation of this plan involved restructuring and designing of new organisational systems. In doing so, BHEL was not responding to the current environmental demands, but was gearing itself to meet the requirements of an anticipated future.

This ability of organisations to anticipate and plan for a "non-existent" (though future) requirement, makes them similar to complex information-processing systems, which are capable of problem-solving, learning and innovating. Galbraith (1977) observed that organisational designs primarily aim at meeting the information-processing requirements emerging from routine and exceptional circumstances. Rules and procedures, hierarchy and target-setting processes can be understood as the "problem-solving mechanisms" which help the organisations in dealing with recurring problems, and thus help in achieving coordination and control. For example, for any problem faced by an employee, he/she can refer to the rule-books or consult a senior official to find a solution. But often (particularly in a fast-changing business environment), the nature and number of these exceptions (i.e., problems) increase much beyond the problem-solving capacity of the existing rules, hierarchies and managerial processes (something similar, incidentally, also happens to the human brain under conditions of stress). In such situations, Galbraith suggested that organisations resort to one of the two major design strategies. These are:

(a) *The organisation may reduce its need for information-processing*: This can be done by creation of *slack resources,* e.g. by increasingly extending dead-lines, lowering standards, and other such measures. Though costly, these measures provide the organisation with surplus time and resources for meeting unprecedented problem-solving demands. Alternatively, the organisation may choose to create *self-contained tasks*, so that each unit needs only the information which is relevant to its functioning. For example, an organisation may shift from a functional structure to a divisional structure based on the product, market segment or geographical location.

(b) *The organisation may increase its capacity for processing information*: If the organisation has to deal with too many exceptions, there is a continuous need for necessary information to reach the decision-makers. Organisations often meet this need by designing and implementing *vertical information systems,* which help the management in collecting and processing relevant information. Alternately the organisation may create *lateral relations*, allowing the decision-making process to move downwards in the hierarchy. The formation of committees, task-forces, problem-solving forums, etc., help in solving problems through interdepartmental contacts and reduce the need for hierarchical intervention in the problem-solving process.

These design strategies, one would have noticed, also imply reformulation of rules, hierarchical relationships and target-setting processes. That is, organisations, in the process of responding to the environment, also reflect upon, challenge and change their basic operating norms and procedures. Argyris and Schoen (1978) termed this process as "double-loop learning".

Double-loop learning can be understood by comparing an organisation with the thermostat of an oven. The thermostat also responds to environmental demands. It senses changes in the environment, compares these changes with desired standards, and corrects deviations from these set standards. This was termed by Argyris and Schoen as "single-loop learning" (see Figure 1.1). But suppose, there is an intelligent thermostat. It would not only respond to the

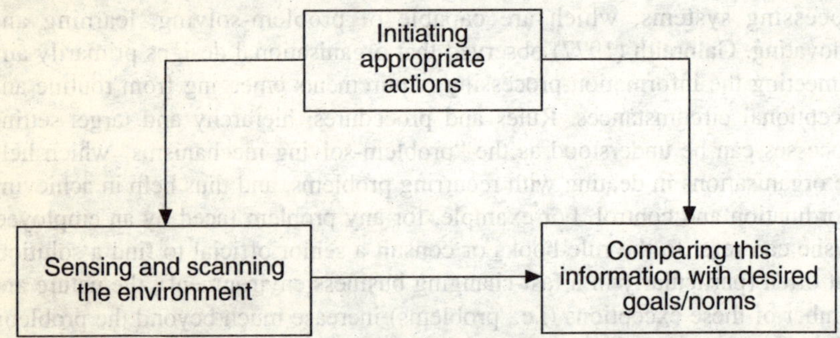

Figure 1.1 Illustration of single-loop learning cycle.

environmental temperature, but also change the desired standard depending upon the need of the situation (i.e. whether a cake is being baked, or chops are being roasted). This ability to question the existing standards and arriving at different norms of what and how things should be done is the ability of any system to *learn how to learn* or double-loop learning (see Figure 1.2, also Chapter 13 for a fuller elaboration on organisational learning). At the individual level, our habitual or reflex-based actions emerge from single-loop learning, while double-loop learning is involved in any process of personality change which affects our assumptions, beliefs and values.

Interpreting organisational reality as a complex and sophisticated information-processing system has far reaching implications. A system capable of learning how to learn is also capable of innovation and self-renewal. Of course, not all organisations are innovative. This is because of the bureaucratic constraints which they impose upon themselves. But potentially, even highly

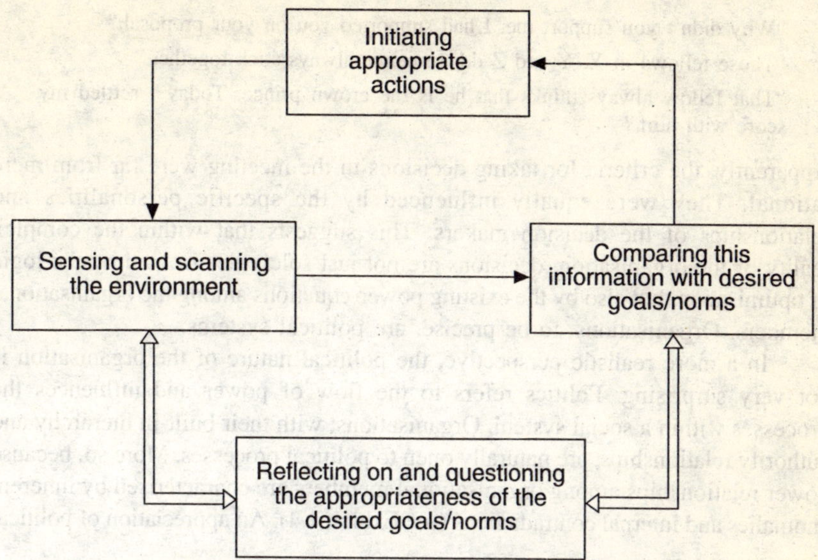

Figure 1.2 Double-loop learning cycle.

bureaucratised organisations are capable of becoming highly innovative. Some of the recent changes in many of the financial and banking organisations in our country are ample proof of this potential.

The Brain model suggests a more interactive and proactive stance of the organisation vis-a-vis the environment, which has implications for our understanding of the strategic management. The traditional models of strategy formulation highlighted the role of long-range planning. The organisation would set goals and targets, and then set out to achieve them. In contrast, an innovative organisation would set broad directions for itself and then engage in a continuous process of matching the environment and its own targets, thus revising its own strategic choices.

But the Brain model of organisation has a serious drawback. It ascribes a certain conscious and deliberate rationality to the organisation, while ignoring its "irrational" human contents. While most practising executives and theorists would like the organisations to behave in a healthy rational manner, this may not always be possible as organisations consist of human beings who may not always behave rationally in terms of their values and ambitions. A comprehensive understanding of the organisation would remain incomplete without considering these factors.

D. Organisations as Political Systems

Observe senior executives coming out of the boardroom after any meeting on important organisational issues (e.g., budget allocation, strategy formulation, restructuring, etc.), and one is struck by the comments one overhears:

> "Of course, his point of view will be accepted. After all, he is boss's bridge partner."

> "Why didn't you support me. I had supported you on your proposal."
>
> "Those fellows in X, Y and Z departments, always stick together."
>
> "That fellow always thinks that he is the crown prince. Today I settled my score with him."

Apparently, the criteria for taking decisions in the meeting were far from mere rational. They were equally influenced by the specific personalities and relationships of the decision makers. This suggests that within the complex reality of the organisation, decisions are not just solely determined by the logic of optimisation, but also by the existing power-equations among the organisational members. Organisations, to be precise, are political systems.

In a more realistic perspective, the political nature of the organisation is not very surprising. Politics refers to the flow of power and influences the processes within a social system. Organisations, with their built-in hierarchy and authority relationships, are naturally open to political processes. More so, because power relationships among organisational members are characterised by inherent anomalies and internal contradictions (see Exhibit 1.4). An appreciation of political

---

Exhibit 1.4

Why Organisations are Political Systems

- Organisational members enjoy power from various sources (e.g., due to position, expertise, group-support, seniority etc.) which help them in influencing each other. This creates complexity and contradictions in relationships, for instance, when a senior executive faces a trade union leader. Both have power, but from different bases.
- The decision-maker has to contend with and balance diverse and often contradictory demands arising from different constituencies (subordinates, colleagues, superiors, etc.). Since satisfying each of these groups is essential for the effective implementation of decisions, the decision-making does not remain a mere rational and objective exercise.
- By virtue of their role, certain people/departments are more important for achieving organisational goals as compared to others. Thus, while on paper, all people/departments are equal, some are, actually, more equal than others.
- In any organisation, people differ widely in terms of their need for power and control. It would be natural for those with high need for power to interpret and respond to situations in ways which maximise their power.
- Most organisations work on the principle of resource optimisation. Thus, for an organisation to function like a clockwork mechanism, the demands and resources have to be suitably matched. This is easier said than done, and so, lobbying for resources becomes a practical necessity for any well-meaning executive.
- Lastly, any viable decision needs to satisfy three kinds of goals: corporate goal, departmental goal and individual goal. These three, in most situations, are not congruent with each other, and therefore, call for political skills from the decision-maker.

---

nature of the organisation is important, besides other reasons, for understanding the organisational goal-formation process. Pfeffer (1978) commented that:

> It is difficult to think of situations in which goals are so congruent, or the facts are so clear-cut that judgement and compromise are not involved. What is rational from one point of view is irrational from another. Organisations are political systems, coalitions of interests, and rationality is defined only with respect to unitary and consistent ordering of preferences.

This being the case, the goal-formation process is open to influences from vested and dominant coalitions. But organisational politics is not always dysfunctional to the achievement of organisational goals. Mayes and Allen (1977) defined organisational politics as "the management of influence to obtain ends not sanctioned by organisation or to obtain sanctioned ends through non-sanctioned influence means." The legitimacy of political behaviour, in the organisational context, is, therefore, also a function of the goals being sought. Moreover, unlike common functional bureaucratic organisations, certain organisational forms (e.g., adhocracies, divisional structures etc.) tend to give greater legitimacy to political behaviour.

Studies (e.g., Hickson et al. 1971; Kanter, 1979) have also identified contingency factors which enhance or decrease the organisational power of departments and people. Hickson et al. (1971), for example, found that those departments which are able to deal with environmental uncertainty, whose activities cannot be substituted by others, and which are central to the work-flow of organisational activities, stand to enjoy greater power and influence as compared to others. Similarly, Kanter (1979) identified a list of job characteristics which determine the experience of power or powerlessness among the incumbents. These factors play a significant role in intra-organisational decision-making, with the more powerful departments exerting greater influence than the others (see Chapter 8 for details).

In viewing organisations as political systems one also acknowledges a real (though to some, uncomfortable) fact about the nature of organisations; namely, there are limitations in understanding organisations as rational systems. The political sub-terrain deals with those impolite realities of organisational life, which are universally experienced but rarely talked about. Understanding organisational politics is also the point of entry into that rich, humane and unconscious reality of organisation—the organisational culture.

E. Organisations as Cultures

A young MBA joined an organisation, and after the brief induction period, was assigned to a certain department. He was informed that everyday at 11 a.m. there was a coffee break, when coffee was served in the lounge. Not being very keen on the 11 o'clock coffee, the young man kept to his room, using his time for work-related purposes. Within a month, however, he sensed that he was not receiving adequate help from his colleagues, and there was a certain aloofness in their attitude towards him. He was taken aback, when one day his boss pulled him up and asked him why he was so uncooperative, and what made him think he was superior to his other more experienced colleagues.

Of course, the young man was neither actually uncooperative nor did he think himself as being superior to others. He was, however, ignorant of the value of certain rituals which determine the nature of interactions in every organisation. His staying away from the coffee-break was an innocent act. But so is reading novels unless someone insists on doing it during a party or at a business meeting.

And that precisely is the point: every social situation, whether a party or an organisation, has certain implicit norms of behaviour, certain shared values and ways of doing things. It is these rituals, values, and interpretative systems which constitute the organisational culture. The American Heritage Dictionary (1976) defines culture as "the totality of socially transmitted behaviour patterns, arts, beliefs, institutions, and all other products of human work and thought characteristic of a community or population." Or more simply, in the words of Marvin Bower, the managing director of MacKinsey and Company, "the way we do things around here."

This way of doing things is an important dimension for understanding organisations, because these ritualistic behavioural patterns signify the dominant (and often implicit) values and assumptions which people hold regarding their work, relationships and organisation. Moreover, the influence of these values and assumptions is not just confined to apparently trivial behavioural patterns like meeting each other during the coffee-break.They also determine behaviours which have crucial implications for organisational performance and effectiveness. If, for example, one of the implicit organisational values is *interpersonal trust,* it will have positive consequences for collaborative decision-making, information sharing, reduction in paper work, etc.

The significance of organisational culture in determining organisational effectiveness has been highlighted by a number of studies. Peters and Waterman (1982), observed that successful companies were characterised by strong cultures. That is, these organisations had core values which were intensely cherished, clearly stated and widely shared among its employees. In another study, Deal and Kennedy (1982) studied 80 companies. They found that only 18 out of these had clearly articulated values and beliefs. Significantly, these eighteen companies were also outstanding performers. Among the other 62 companies, there were companies which had clearly stated financially oriented goals, but there was no consistent relationship between the clarity of goal statement and the company's success. It seems that widely shared values more than widely shared tangible goals, contributed to organisational success.

But how are these values learned, sustained and shared? For the management to formally proclaim quality as an organisational value is, after all, not the same thing as people actually being quality conscious in their behaviour and performance. Organisational researchers (e.g., Peters, 1987; Pfeffer, 1981; Boje et al. 1982, etc.) have identified metaphors, stories, corporate myths and symbols as powerful tools for managing organisational culture. For example, in successful and achieving organisations, it is normal to find people exchanging organisational anecdotes with consistent themes of achievement, risk-taking and being rewarded for their initiative. What counts in these stories is not the accuracy of details but the fact that they represent an effective manner in which "elements of organisational culture are conceptually organised into a system or organisationally relevant logic (Boje et al. 1982)."

Viewing organisation as a cultural system has some significant implications. First, it means that managing is more than mere formal processes of planning, directing, controlling and coordinating. Rather, the task of a manager is, to use Smircich and Morgan's (1982) term, "management of meaning". They noted that "successful corporate leaders who give direction to the organisation in a strategic sense frequently do so by providing an image or pattern of thinking in a way that has meaning for those directly involved." The viable role of a manager, thus, is to manipulate the symbolic meaning which he conveys to his subordinates through his actions.

The cultural perspective also helps one in focussing on the significant role of basic human processes (e.g., motivation, perception, and leadership) in determining how organisations function. Organisational cultures, while integrating the prevalent beliefs about the "appropriate" nature of transactions, also include beliefs about organisational purpose, criteria of performance, hierarchical relationships and nature of success. People express the elements of culture in their relationships and day-to-day working, and in doing so, also influence the more tangible organisational arrangements. Quinn and McGrath (1985) described how different kinds of organisational cultures correspond to differences in technologies, organisational forms and strategic orientations adapted by the organisations. For example, an organisational culture characterised by high value for security and predictability is likely to emphasise closer hierarchical controls, routinised functioning and a conservative strategic orientation which focuses on traditional and tested markets/products.

Probably, the most significant contribution which the cultural perspective makes to our understanding is regarding the nature of organisational change and adaptation. If the process of organisational adaptation to change (whether planned, e.g., through OD or unplanned, e.g., due to mergers, takeovers, market collapse, etc.) is to be effective, the change must take place in the perceptions, motivations and relationships of the organisations members. This means that effective structural and strategic changes have to be rooted in the processes of cultural change in the organisation (Berg, 1985). Understanding cultural dynamics, therefore, is an essential prerequisite to planning and implementation of change.

The concept of organisational culture provides an insight into the crucial interface between the organisation and societal culture. Apart from the organisational determinants (e.g., founder's legacy, operating environment, strategic orientation), organisational culture is also an extension of the larger culture of the society. An appreciation of this fact also helps explain why two units of the same organisation (e.g., TELCO, Jamshedpur and TELCO, Pune) have such different ways of operating. In his study of forty cultures, Hoefstede (1980) found four dimensions (power distance, individualism-collectivity, masculinity-feminity, and tolerance of ambiguity) that made one culture different from others. He also found that these differences influenced the way in which people responded to organisational and work-related demands.

F. Organisations as Psychic Prisons

One of the seven ordeals of the *Thief of Baghdad* was to pass through the enchanted cave. The sides of his path were strewn with stone statues of earlier unwary travellers who had violated the basic condition for a safe journey through the cave—they had lost touch with their internal calling (the *vocation*) and had strayed away from the path. The cave offered numerous lures (from illusions of enchanting damsels to frightening ghostly images of one's own making) to distract the traveller from his path. Only those who remained anchored in their deep sense of purpose could pass through the cave unharmed. Others, who lost this control over themselves, were turned into stone by the cave and imprisoned.

In many ways, organisations are similar to the enchanted cave. Short of turning people to stone, they do funny things to them. While on the one hand, they provide a canvas on which people can live out and realise their potential for growth and self-actualisation, on the other, they also stimulate and bring out our most pathological tendencies into play. To appreciate this aspect of organisational reality, consider the following examples:

- The Chief Executive of one of the largest political organisations of the world was a man of deep sensibilities. He was deeply attached to his mother; in his younger days, he was a talented artist; he loved wine and dogs. On the evening of the collapse of his organisation, he committed suicide; but before doing so, he was romantic enough to get married to the woman he loved (who also committed suicide along with him); and was considerate enough to take his dog out for his evening walk. The man, of course (!), was Adolf Hitler. The fact that this same person could also send countless innocent Jews to torture and death (the orders being followed by normal people with family and children), is an ironic comment on the evil potential of organisational life.

- In an interesting experiment, Milgram asked his subjects to administer electric shocks to a group of individuals (the purported aim of the study was to observe limits of human tolerance to pain). The subjects, of course, did not know that the persons behind the glass screen, whom they saw screaming and writhing were actually not receiving any shocks, and were confederates of the experimenter. What was revealing was the fact that the subjects, who were otherwise normal sensible people, went to the extent of "administering" shocks of 440 volts, simply because the experimenter asked them to do so. Such is the power of the authority!!

- Edvin Sutherland in his book *The White Collar Crime* quotes the first-hand experience of a young man who got into business of selling used cars: "I learned that this business had more tricks for fleecing customers than any other I had tried previously. Cars... with everything wrong were sold as "guaranteed". When the customer returned and demanded his guarantee, he had to sue to get it and very few went to that trouble and expense: the boss said you could depend on human nature. The thing that struck me as strange was that all those people were proud of their ability to fleece customers. They boasted of their crookedness and were admired by their friends and enemies in proportion to their ability to get away with a crooked deal: it was called shrewdness. Another feature was that all these people were unanimous in the denunciation of gangsters, robbers, burglars, and petty thieves. They never regarded themselves to be in the same class and were bitterly indignant if accused of dishonesty: because for them it was just good business."

The unfortunate part is that these examples are not as extreme and rare as they may seem to some: one only has to think about the bridges which collapse due to adulterated cement, spurious killer drugs, carcinogenic edible products, working conditions which are known to produce fatal diseases, cut-throat vengeance which ruins the lives of the people, and so on. What is striking in these everyday happenings is that people involved in committing such ignoble deeds are otherwise respectable, mentally healthy and normal persons.

But how do innocent people get trapped into things which are obviously unethical and pathological? There are numerous researches and theoretical perspectives which highlight the pathological potential of the organisations. Classical psychoanalytic theories, in fact, viewed the whole civilisation, its institutions and norms, as neurotic defenses against the repressed, hostile and sexual impulses. That is, organisations provide an opportunity to people for working out their neurotic impulses in an acceptable form. Kets de Vries (1980) noted that "the dividing line between pathological developments and corporate success is a rather thin one." Zalzenik (1970), found in his studies that unconscious anxiety often has a decisive influence on coalition building and power politics of organisational life. A leader who is unable to form close interpersonal relationships due to unconscious fears, may deal with the anxiety by enforcing more mechanistic rules and procedures, which avoid opportunity for more spontaneous interactions.

In an organisational context, people facing similar dominant influences (e.g., market, environment, corporate history, culture, top-management, etc.), also tend to experience similar anxieties and develop coping mechanisms for dealing with them. What may appear as common values and styles that bind the organisation often are rooted in shared collective intra-psychic concerns which lurk beneath the surface of conscious awareness. In their studies, Kets de Vries and Miller (1987) identified five organisational pathological configurations. Each of these type of organisations (dramatic, paranoid, detached, compulsive, and depressive) emerge out of unconscious themes commonly shared among the members of the organisation. As a consequence, these organisations tend to develop consistent, though maladaptive, strategies, structures and cultures to deal with the dominant concerns (see Chapter 11 for a detailed discussion on neurotic organisations).

Of course, not all organisations promote and perpetuate pathological behaviours. Pathology in organisations, as in human psyche, occurs when the system becomes out of tune with the demands of the objective reality. The greater the flexibility and responsiveness of an organisation, the lesser are the chances of its trapping itself (and its members) into pathological patterns. In fact, more and more organisations are moving away from fixed rigid patterns to more flexible ones (Tannenbaum and Davis, 1969). One can say that the whole purpose of understanding organisations is to develop working environments which are more humane, healthy and flexible.

II. RECONSTRUCTING THE ELEPHANT

So what is an organisation? Is it a rational objective entity, or a subjective projection of its members' psyche? Is it a strategic system, which rationally responds to the environment or do organisational actions emerge from the internal political contingencies? And if organisations are all these (and more) how does one integrate and construct a unitary view of the organisation?

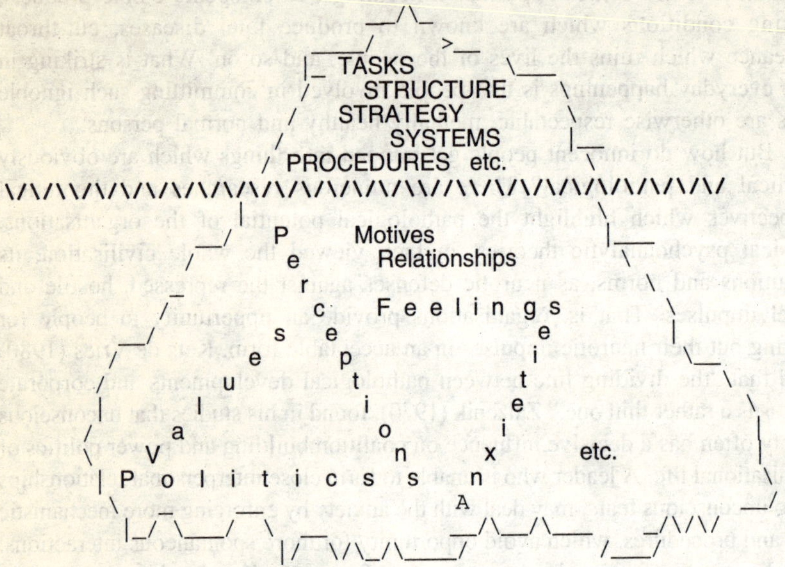

Figure 1.3 Illustration of organisational reality as an ice-berg.

Unfortunately, there are no clearcut answers to these questions. Managers are doomed (or privileged) to live in a pluralistic and ambiguous world. There are, however, at least three critical implications which one can draw from the preceding discussion:

1. Organisations are complex entities. Their complexity lies in something far more than just the number of variables which influence and determine what happens in an organisation. Rather, they are complex because they are made up of multiple realities, which simultaneously contradict and complement each other. Each of these views is correct, yet incomplete. A comprehensive understanding of organisations must draw from each of these and seek to integrate them.

2. Most managers tend to take their view of organisation for granted. After all being "practical" means avoiding theory (such as the ones we will be discussing in the following chapters). But, to be effective, it is useful to be aware that most of our understanding of organisations is based on personal "theories" (or metaphors) which we carry in our minds. For the manager, it is essential to be aware of these taken-for-granted views of the organisation. It is these underlying assumptions in our understanding which determine what "organising" would mean in terms of practical decisions.

3. Lastly, what is visible and tangible about an organisation (e.g., its structure, systems, strategies, etc.), is only a part of the total reality. There is also a large part of organisational reality which is non-tangible, informal, and subjective. One may, thus, look at the organisation in the classical imagery of an iceberg, in which a large part of the totality—its cultural norms, power-politics, pathologies, etc.—is submerged and hidden (see Figure 1.3).

The organisation exists in a given environment, and it interacts with this environment to optimise its goals of survival and growth. It selects a strategy, and evolves corresponding structure and technological systems to effectively adapt and respond to the environmental demands. Most often (though not always) one finds an optimum fit among these variables, which follows a rational logic. This is the visible reality of the organisation.

The invisible reality of an organisation is that of a human system, and so, for various human reasons (e.g., non-availability of information, limited rational decision-making skills of the people, and the all-too-human motives and fears, etc.), the rationality of the organisation is, to use March and Simon's (1958) term, a "bounded rationality". To start with, the operating environment of any organisation (whether stable or changing, simple or complex) is what its members *perceive* it as. Moreover, the strategies, structures and systems which the organisation develops to deal with this environment are what its significant members *consider* as appropriate. And, of course, the very process of arriving at decisions about these issues is a human, interpersonal process, in which the outcome is strongly influenced by the personalities of the members involved. Any understanding of organisation would, therefore, remain incomplete without relating the visible and invisible parts of the organisation.

2 Organisational Design

In Chapter 1, we have seen that organisations are complex realities. Their totality can be grasped through a number of images and metaphors, each of which highlights a unique feature of the organisational reality. For the practicing manager however, the term 'organisation' refers to a concrete and tangible entity, which describes the manner in which men, machine and material resources are or should be organised and interrelated. While the metaphors of organisations (e.g., machine, brain, culture, psychic prisons, etc.), help us in understanding what an organisation is, managerial role requires converting this understanding into practical decisions about what an organisation should or can be. In their day-to-day functioning, managers tackle many problems which require such a decision. For example:

- If the department has fifteen steno-typists, who serve about forty executives, should each steno-typist be directly attached to two or more executives, or should they be organised as a common pool under a supervisor?
- In a large department, how many people should be directly reporting to the departmental head?
- Should the maintenance crew be given a definite schedule every day/week, or should they be alloted the total number of jobs in a time-frame, allowing them to plan their own work?
- Can the five units of the organisation evolve their own norms of functioning, or should the corporate office define identical norms for all the units?
- What should be the limits of financial decisions which can be taken by a particular level of executives? etc.

Such decisions highlight the need for an organisation to evolve a rational and consistent method of structuring its activities. It is important to note that the need for designing the organisation does not exist only at the level of large corporate setups (e.g., whether or not the organisation should have a divisional structure). Rather, even at the sectional/departmental levels, managers have to take many designing decisions.

Designing an organisation or developing a viable organisational structure focuses on two essential problems:

1. How to integrate the various behaviours and activities across the parts of organisation, so that they are coordinated towards a common goal; and,

2. How to facilitate the flow of information within the organisation, so as to minimise the uncertainty in decision-making at various managerial levels?

If, for instance, the manager intends to organise his department by delegating the decision-making authority at different levels, he/she must also think of mechanisms to insure that relevant information is available at these levels for taking appropriate decisions. Moreover, it is also essential for the manager to devise mechanisms for coordinating these decisions, so that they don't contradict each other, or clash with the departmental goal. An effective design of the organisation would, naturally, be one which provides suitable and consistent solutions to both these issues. In this Chapter we will discuss some of the basic choices and constraints which a manager must consider in the search for a useful organisational design.

I. WHAT IS ORGANISATIONAL DESIGN?

If one takes a closer look at various organisations, they appear to be as diverse and unique as different species. Some organisations have a large number of hierarchical levels, while others have just three or four; in some organisations all major strategic and operational decisions are taken at the top levels, while in others, decision-making authority is decentralised down the line; or, some organisations encourage working in a more routinised and regimented way as compared to many others. Similarly, organisations also differ in terms of size of operating units, interdependence among various jobs, the manner in which decisions are taken, the nature and extent of formal transactions among departments/jobs, and so on.

Such differences exist because organisations are, after all, only instruments to achieve certain ends; and like instruments, they need to be moulded to achieve these objectives. For example, if the objective is to cut down the cost, stringent measure for cost control would need to be implemented. On the other hand, if the aim is growth and innovation, more decentralisation and flexibility in operations may be called for. Thus, the design of any organisation has a specific goal-based logic. The goals set forth while designing an organisation may be as varied as increase in profits, survival, better utilisation of human resources, greater efficiency, public image, etc. That is why, decisions regarding organisational design are an important aspect of a manager's job and responsibilities. An appropriately designed organisation provides a basis for performing the job in a planned manner. Clark (1972) stated that:

> ...organisation design is concerned with making decisions about the forms of coordination, control and motivation that best fit the enterprise. In making these decisions, it is necessary to consider external factors like market, and internal factors like the needs and aspirations of the members of the enterprise.

> Organisational design is intimately concerned with the way in which decision-making is centralised, shared or delegated and with the way the enterprise is governed.

A point which needs to be highlighted is that the design of an organisation is not a mere description of the organisation chart. Organisational structure, as depicted by the organisation chart, describes the existing divisions and clusters of tasks and people within an organisation. It identifies the responsibilities, span of control and reporting relationships of people and departments. But this is only a partial view of the organisation as it only describes what an organisation is, not what it does or how it operates. In fact, in confining organisational design to mere drawing up of a 'good' organisation chart, there is a danger of making the organisation rigid and inflexible (many of the highly successful organisations, such as IBM and Apple Computors, in fact, consciously avoided developing an organisation chart during their growth phase). As Reddin (1987) pointed out: "To take a psychoanalytic view, an organisation chart is a defense against anxiety. What you do in formalising your organisation is to defend yourself in what you secretly believe to be its weakest parts."

An effective designing process, therefore, besides delineating the clustering of positions and hierarchies, must also identify the "design of the organisational processes of work, in particular the decision process, whose features are as structural in their implications as those more usually recognised in the organisational chart (Newman, 1973)." Similarly, Duncan (1979) noted that the organisational structure "is more than boxes on a chart; it is a pattern of interactions and coordination that links the technology, task and human components of the organisation to ensure that the organisation accomplishes its purpose."

One can look at the designing process as dealing with the development of two interrelated, but superimposed, "structures" (Newman, 1973). One aspect of the organisational design deals with the static description of the various positions, hierarchies and formal reporting relationships. This is the *situational structure*, which is the mechanical and tangible aspect of the organisational design and can be captured on the chart. On the other hand, the *process structure* describes the somewhat intangible forms of organisational processes, viz., the communication and decision-making patterns, nature of coordination and control mechanisms, the flow of power and influence processes, the cultural implications of a particular way of working, etc. A comprehensive organisational design takes into consideration, and aims at integrating, the two kinds of structures.

Thus, for example, if an organisation is planning to start a new department (say, quality assurance), there are numerous design considerations which need to be taken into account. The most obvious and mechanical decisions would be regarding issues such as the size of the department, the required level/seniority of the HOD, who the HOD should report to, posts and designations within the departments (and their internal reporting relationships), etc. In addition to these, the designing process must also address itself to various other important issues such as the objective of the department, the criteria for evaluating its performance, the information system required for it to function effectively, the extent of the influence it can exert on other departments, etc. Even the decisions regarding manning, budgeting, and other such aspects, require careful reflection, since they would influence the effectiveness of the design in due course. For example, if the new department is to be manned by experienced people drawn from the already existing departments, it would generate a different kind of cultural dynamics, than if new professionals are recruited to form the department.

II. DETERMINANTS OF ORGANISATIONAL DESIGN

Compare an advertising agency with an assembly-line shopfloor of a manufacturing organisation. Both are forms of organisation, and yet are very different from each other. Whereas in the advertising agency, the functioning is informal and democratic, reporting and control systems are loose, and people enjoy a fair amount of freedom in doing their work, the assembly-line shopfloor, is characterised by routinised jobs, clear-cut job descriptions, and close control and monitoring of activities. It is not very difficult to discern and appreciate the reasons for differences in these two organisations. While both organisations are similar in that they employ people to achieve a common organisational objectives, they differ in a number of ways, such as the nature of their objectives, the nature of their output, the methods required for working, etc. It is factors such as these which determine the logic of the designing process. In the following sections we will consider some of these salient determining factors.

A. Environment

One of the most obvious determinants of organisational design is, of course, the environment in which the organisation operates. The external environment subjects the organisation to a complex set of forces. The environmental influences on an organisation are diverse in nature and include the competitors, suppliers, consumers, trade unions, technological breakthroughs, governmental regulations, etc. These affect the organisation both directly and indirectly. The entry of a competitor in the market would directly affect the organisation, while it would be indirecly influenced by the changes in the socio-political environment (for example, the reunification of Germany and the opening of the European market in the 1990's created new opportunities for exports for many Indian companies).

The open systems view of the organisation (Katz and Kahn,1978) implies that the effectiveness of the organisation would largely depend on its ability to develop mechanisms for coping with these environmental influences. Organisations sometimes deal with such environmental demands through non-structural means, such as advertising, public relations or changes in the organisational goals. Often, however, the coping strategies are structural in nature, and result in changes in the organisational design. For example, in the late 1980s, Eicher Goodearth reorganised their operations and the manufacturing setup, to cope with increasing competition (Skaria, 1991). The three plants of the company, which were all making tractors earlier, were converted into three specialised plants manufacturing tractors, gears, and engines, respectively.

In general, the studies on organisation-environment interface (e.g., Burns and Stalker, 1961; Lawrence and Lorsch, 1967) suggest a relationship between the amount of environmental uncertainty and the extent of flexibility in the organisational design. For example, industries dealing with products related to the fast changing areas of society (e.g., computers, fashion garments, advertising, etc.) tend to develop more flexible structures to cope with the changing environmental demands. On the other hand, industries in the traditional core sector (e.g., steel, coal, fertilizers, etc.) exist in a relatively stable environment, and, therefore, are more likely to have an inflexible (and often rigid) organisational design.

B. Objective/Mission

The objective or mission of the organisation is a critical factor which influences its design. In a way, the organisation's objectives determine which particular segment of the environment it is prepared to interact with. For example, a polyclinic housing specialist doctors may pursue the objective of providing highly personalised total health-care to its clientele. This objective automatically implies greater amount of attention to the patient (and not just to his symptoms), more coordination and communication among specialists, and greater informality. On the other hand, a hospital following the objective of providing basic health-care to a large population at minimal cost would need to be designed so as to allow a high and quick turnover of patients. To achieve this, the hospital may introduce formal routines to ensure the operating efficiency. It may also break up the total job into a number of smaller routine jobs (e.g., the specialist doctor may recommend an injection, but it would be administered by the nurse, so that the doctor's time is saved).

A clear statement and understanding of an organisation's mission or objective has a critical influence on its functioning. Many public sector banks, for example, look at their objective of developmental banking as a mere lending function. In contrast, the Industrial Credit and Investment Corporation of India (ICICI) redefined this objective in the 1980s, and conceptualised its task as that of working with the borrower-entrepreneur as a business partner. To accomplish this objective, the ICICI went ahead to develop professional managerial structures and systems which were more market-oriented and less bureaucratic (Bhattacharya, 1989).

Within an organisation also, the departmental missions and objectives (often defined by the departmental head) have a decisive influence on the way the department is organised and how it operates. For example, if the finance department defines its objective as that of controlling the financial resources, it will design for itself various systems, procedures, and jobs to ensure close control and monitoring of finances. On the other hand, if its objective is to provide financial support to the on-going activities in other departments, its systems will be more open and interactive.

C. Strategy

While the objective or mission of the organisation defines what the organisation wishes to do, the strategy focuses on the manner in which it will go about accomplishing it. Chandler (1973) defined strategy as:

> ...the determination of the basic long term goals and objectives of an enterprise, and adoption of courses of action and the allocation of resources necessary for carrying out these goals. Decisions to expand the volume of activities, to set up different plants and offices, to move into new economic functions, or to become diversified along many lines of business involve the definition of new basic goals.

Based on his studies of different organisations, Chandler also concluded that *structure follows strategy*, that is, the structure or design of an organisation is determined by its choice of strategy. For instance, in 1993, the strategy adopted by Voltas to pull out of trading in favour of manufacturing, led to a restructuring of its thirteen divisions, and the formation of its three strategic business units. Many other studies (e.g., Channon, 1972; Dyas and Thanheiser, 1976) have also supported Chandler's contention.

One must note that strategy formulation involves an act of choice regarding how the organisation intends to deal with the environmental opportunities and threats. One obvious way it would adopt would be to develop appropriate structural mechanisms. For example, in responding to increased competition in the business environment, an organisation has a choice between two strategic courses of action: (1) it can diversify into different product markets, so as to spread out its risks, or (2) it can concentrate and protect its market niche, and try to counter competition by decreasing its overall operating costs. Clearly, the first strategic option will necessitate development of a complex and decentralised structure, while to implement the second option, the organisation will have to create a structure with tighter controls and greater accountability of roles.

D. Technology

Another important influence on organisational design comes from the nature of technology used for transforming the environmental inputs into organisational outputs. Some theorists (e.g., Newman, 1971) have defined technology as an intervening variable between the strategy and organisational design. Newman noted:

> We cannot jump directly from strategy to management design because we have not yet classified the array of actions that will be necessary to execute the strategy. Thinking of technology helps us to elaborate the work implications of strategy...

Sufficient research evidence exists to support the *technological imperative* hypothesis (e.g., Woodward, 1965; Harvey, 1968; Perrow, 1967, etc.). The essential logic of these research findings is that since different technologies (mass-production, batch-processing, craft, etc.) call for different kinds of control systems, they give rise to different structural mechanisms.

There is, however, considerable confusion regarding the definition of the term "technology". Technology, as a term, is normally used to describe the manufacturing process. But then, what about service organisations (e.g., hospitals, advertising firms, banks, etc.) ? Moreover, different researchers have defined technology in different ways, often making it difficult, if not impossible, to integrate the research findings.

One way of getting over this confusion is to understand technology as the process used by the organisation for transforming the inputs into outputs. The input can be raw materials, capital, labour or information, while the output can be a product or a service. Defined in this manner, technology refers to, in Newman's words, the "work to be done". Thus, for example, if the organisation is using a customised technology (e.g., as in an advertising agency, a construction firm, or a tailoring shop, etc.), there is a greater need for integration and coordination of the marketing, designing and manufacturing functions. This would necessitate the development of a loose and flexible matrix structure. On the other hand, an organisation aiming to offer a standardised product or service in large quantity (whether railway transport or cigarettes) would need to standardise its operations, and so, is likely to evolve a formalised structure.

E. People and Culture

It would be too naive to assume that any specific organisational structure (whether it is centralised or decentralised, formalised or flexible, tall or flat, etc.) is an automatic and inevitable consequence of its environment, objectives, strategy, and technology. A more realistic perspective would recognise that any organisational structure is an outcome of a managerial decision-making process. After all, somebody (a person or a group) has to decide as to, what particular structure is most appropriate for the organisation in a given situation. It is, therefore, but natural that the personal preferences, needs, aspirations and anxieties of these people would play a dominant role in the development of the specific organisational design.

One person, who has a decisive influence on the choice of organisational design is, of course, the CEO (or the departmental/divisional head, in the case of the organisational subunit). Based on their study of a number of "troubled" companies, Kets de Vries and Miller (1987) concluded that the "strategy, organisational structure, and culture will often reflect the personality and fantasies of the top manager." For example, if the top manager is autocratic by nature, he/she would prefer an organisational arrangement which would allow him/her to have closer control over people and operations. On the other hand, CEOs predisposed to taking risks would favour the selection of opportunity-based diversification strategies, which may result in less centralised divisional structures.

Besides the chief executive, another major influence on the outcomes of organisational decision-making process, comes from the dominant coalitions within the organisations (Pfeffer, 1978; Hackman, 1985; Medcof, 1985; Stevenson et al. 1985, etc.). Robbins (1987), summarising this aspect, noted that the organisational structure is:

> ...the result of a power struggle between special-interest coalitions, each arguing for a structural arrangement that best meets its own needs instead of organisational interests—all the time, of course, couching its arguments and preferred criteria in terms of organisational effectiveness....A coalition's location in a structure will determine such things as its influence in planning, its choice

of technology, the criteria by which it would be evaluated, allocation of rewards, control of information, its proximity to senior executives, and its ability to exercise influence on numerous decisions in which it has a stake in the outcome.

The nature of people employed by the organisation (and the consequent culture which they evolve) also influences the choice of organisational structure. Organisations, through their history, recruitment policies and socialisation processes, tend to inculcate similar orientations among its employees. These orientations influence the choice of organisational design in that they make certain designs more acceptable to people as compared to others. For example, an organisation which houses entrepreneurial and innovative employees would find it very difficult to implement a structure which relies on formalised behaviour and close monitoring of activities.

F. Age

The age of the organisation is another factor which makes certain choices of organisational design more appropriate at one time as compared to others. Some organisational theorists (Cameron and Whetten, 1981; Quinn and Cameron, 1983) have suggested that the criteria of organisational effectiveness changes during the course of its life-cycle. This is so because as the organisation grows and matures, it has to cope with different kinds of environmental demands. Correspondingly, each developmental stage of the organisation will favour specific structural mechanisms for coping with these demands. A young organisation, for example, is more likely to be informally structured with loose control mechanisms, since it is still vulnerable to even minor fluctuations in its environment, and must deal with them swiftly. On the other hand, an old well established organisation would need to maintain its successful levels of performance, and so, would need to streamline and formalise its structure and systems.

G. Size

While the size of an organisation is often related to its age, it is useful to consider it as an independent influence on organisational design. Many organisations, in fact, do not evolve from a small to large size, as is assumed by the life-cycle theorists. Rather, with huge initial capital investments, they start with the advantage (or disadvantage) of being large. Many studies have identified recognisable relationships between the size and structure of the organisation. Blau (1970), for example, found that organisations become more structurally differentiated with increase in size. Similarly, Pugh et al. (1969) concluded that "an increased scale of operation increases the frequency of recurrent events and the repetition of decisions". Such a condition favours standardisation of activities. Another study (Child, 1973) supported these findings and concluded that "larger organisations are more specialised, have more rules, more documentation, more extended hierarchies, and a greater decentralisation of decision making further down such hierarchies." In comparison, the smaller organisations would be more amenable to centralised control, which is exerted through informal contacts.

III. IMPLICATIONS FOR MANAGERS

The preceding discussion amply highlights the complexities involved in the organisational design process. Designing an effective organisation seems to be far from a straightforward linear activity. It appears more like an act of balancing the diverse influences and forces. Before proceeding to the next chapter, let us briefly consider what implications this discussion holds for practising managers:

1. One must recognise that the specific design of an organisation is not an arbitrary arrangement. Rather, it emerges out of the influences of many diverse factors. The relationship between the organisational design and its determinants is somewhat complicated by the fact that these various influences on the organisational structure are also interrelated with each other (see Fig. 2.1). A change occurring in any one factor (say, the influencing coalition or the environment) is bound to create pressure for corresponding changes in the others. An effective organisational design (and the managers) must, therefore, be cognizant of such interdependencies and should evolve mechanisms for coping with the pressures arising from change.

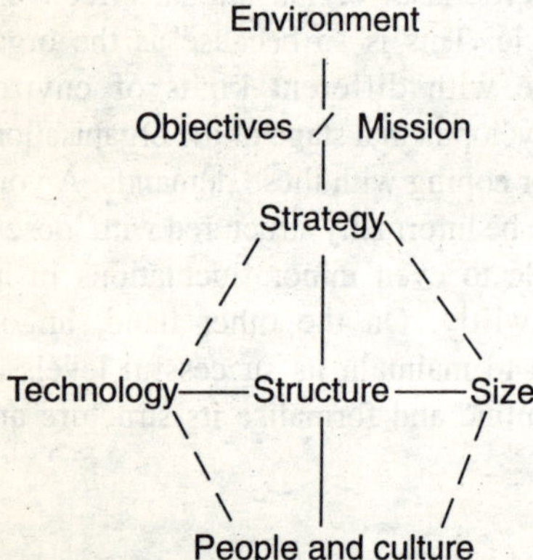

Figure 2.1 Illustration of interdependencies among the determinants of organisational design.

2. One needs to appreciate that designing an organisation requires dealing with both the tangible and the intangible aspects. An effective organisation structure takes as much care of the formal business requirements as it focuses on the underlying human processes. As Newman (1971) pointed out:

> Some managers make a change in their formal organisation and assume everything else will fall in place. To be effective, ...these changes must be incorporated into informal behaviour, and supporting adjustments must be made in other facets of management.

Thus, for example, implementation of an organisational design incorporating decentralisation of decision-making is not merely a matter of formal documentation of delegation of powers across different hierarchical levels. To be successful it would also require upgradation of decision-making skills across different levels, as well as the development of an organisational climate supportive of such change. During the mid 1980s, due to the liberalisation of economy (and the consequent boom in the consumer durable market), many organisations floundered due to the inconsistencies in their efforts. Various organisations changed their strategic posture and introduced structural changes to meet the strategic requirements. They failed because these changes were resisted by their own culture. On the other hand, organisations which could effectively deal with changes were those which adapted a more integrated view of these contingencies.

3. Lastly, while the various determinants of organisational design are interrelated, the designing process almost always has to cope with certain constraints. An ideal design would, of course, be one which is totally consistent with the different requirements of the various influences (see Table 2.1). For

Table 2.1 Required Consistencies among the Determinants of Organisational Design

Determinants of organisational design	Required design options	
Perceived environment	Simple, stable	Complex, changing
Required organisational response	Slow and conventional	Quick and flexible
Appropriate organisational structure	Mechanistic, formal and decentralised	Organic, informal and centralised
Appropriate technology	Routine, mass-production	Non-routine, customised
Culture and people	Conservative and formal	Innovative and informal

instance, an ideal situation would be when the strategic requirements call for a flexible decentralised design, which matches with the cultural orientation of the employees, as well as with the influences arising from the nature of required technology. Such a happy situation, however, rarely exists in reality. One may find oneself, for instance, saddled with a technology which cannot be changed without sacrificing the basic operating efficiencies (e.g., even if the strategy calls for greater autonomy and flexibility, the highly routinised assembly-line still remains the cheapest alternative for mass-producing automobiles). Such mismatches, while posing a major constraint on the logic of the designing process, are also a challenge to the ingenuity and creativity of the manager.

3 Components of Organisational Design

For any practicing manager, designing the organisation would involve converting his/her understanding of the influences discussed in the previous Chapter, into tangible organisational structures. An effective structure would be one which can successfully cope with these demands and constraints. But in order to design such an organisation, the manager must also be aware of the building blocks of an organisational structure. It is necessary, therefore, to consider what constitutes the organisational structure.

There is, by no means, much agreement among the organisational theorists about the components of organisational structure. Different researchers have proposed different factors (often with differing definitions) as constituting the organisation. Research on Organisational Theory abounds with terms such as *Autonomy* (Reimann, 1974), *Centralisation* (Hage, 1965; Hage and Aiken, 1967; Thompson, 1967), *Professionalisation* (Hall, 1968), *Span of Control* (Ouchi and Dowling, 1974), *Formalisation* (Reimann, 1974); *Differentiation* (Weber, 1974; Lawrence and Lorsch, 1967), *Integration* (Perrow, 1970; Lawrence and Lorsch, 1967), *Specialisation* (Payne and Mansfield, 1976), etc. Identification of factors which would be relevant to organisational design (in that they are predictive of the performance and effectiveness of the organisation) is somewhat complicated by the fact that many of these components lack empirical support. Dalton et al (1980), after reviewing more than 100 research papers concluded:

> The literature on structure-performance relationship is among the most vexing and ambiguous in the field of management and organisational behaviour. Evaluations and generalisations concerning the nature and directions of these relationships are tenuous... our review has illustrated not only a lack of consistency but also a paucity of research in essential areas with respect to associations between structure and performance.

While acknowledging this ambiguity and inconsistency, it is still possible to identify some of the significant, and empirically verified components of the organisation. Even though, the terms used by the researchers have varied, there are sufficient overlaps in their definition to make it possible to integrate the findings under three major components: *Complexity, Formalisation* and *Centralisation*.

I. COMPLEXITY

Complexity refers to "the degree of differentiation that exists within an organisation (Robbins, 1987)." It focuses on the number of specific jobs, roles, hierarchical levels, work-centres, etc., in the organisation. The greater is there such a differentiation in the organisation, the more complex would be the organisation.

The relevance of complexity as a component of the organisational structure can be appreciated by considering the following example. Imagine a typing pool section in an organisation, employing 50 typists. They all do similar work, which includes typing letters, reports, cutting stencils for cyclostyling, etc. The complexity of this section is low. It would be simpler to control them (use identical performance norms), coordinate their activities (use them interchangeably for different jobs) and communicate with them. But suppose, these 50 typists were grouped into different speciality services (e.g., letter-typing, stencil-cutting, report-typing), each under the supervision of a senior typist, this would make the process of managing (control, coordination and communication with) the section a somewhat more complex activity.

The more complex an organisation, the greater is its need for devising more complex mechanisms for control, coordination and communication. When an organisation is not very complex, the activities of its members can be controlled and coordinated through simple mechanisms, such as informal communications and a few rules and procedures, etc. With increasing complexity, these simple mechanisms become ineffective. To reduce uncertainty in decision-making, more sophisticated and often expensive mechanisms are required by the organisation. One finds highly complex organisations using a variety of such control and coordination mechanism, e.g., coordination committees, computerised information system, policy manual.

Organisations can be complex in three ways: *Horizontally* (the degree of differences in the nature of jobs in the organisation), *Vertically* (the number of hierarchical levels, or the depth in the structure) and *Spatially* (the degree of geographical separation among the work-units).

A. Horizontal Complexity

Horizontal complexity refers to the degree of differentiation between the organisational units/subunits in terms of nature of work, requirements of skills and knowledge, and employees' orientations. Other terms used to describe horizontal complexity in research literature are *differentiation, division of labour, departmentation* and *functional specialisation.*

Horizontal complexity is often an organisation's way of coping with increase in the quantum and complexity of its total work-load. As organisations grow in terms of size and complexity, they tend to break up their total task into specialised jobs and functions, which are then manned by personnel with specific expertise and skills. For example, at some stage the organisation may only have an administration department, which looks after a variety of functions such as personnel, training, transport, security, salaries, etc. With an increase in the work-load on this department, the management may decide to create separate departments to manage these different activities. However, this division of functional activities would also create differences; each department would have different goal emphasis, time orientation, and even work attitudes and vocabulary. The training manager's job is clearly different from that of the transport manager. The diverse nature and orientation of these specialised personnel would not only create communication problems among them, but would also pose difficulties for the management in coordinating their activities.

A most common division of functional activities which exists in many organisations is between the *line* and the *staff* functions. An organisation, very broadly speaking, has two types of tasks: those which contribute to the main objective of the organisation (the line functions), and those which support the line functions by developing and maintaining relevant systems for organisational working (the staff functions). For example, in a manufacturing organisation, functions like production, sales, etc. are the line functions, while functions such as personnel, finance, data processing, etc., would be the staff functions. Given the different nature of job responsibilities of the line and staff functions, these departments behave in very different manners, often conflicting with each other. Hodgetts (1980) noted that the line functionaries are mostly action-oriented as they work with clear-cut short-term targets, and prefer simple, quick and practical solutions. In comparison, the staff functionaries most often, work for long-term targets, are more theoretical, and prefer more sophisticated methods for solving problems.

While it is apparent that greater specialisation of functional activities and division of labour calls for more sophisticated and expensive coordination and control mechanisms, one may wonder as to why at all organisations opt for becoming more complex. There are, in fact, many efficiencies inherent in implementing functional specialisation and division of labour. Some of the most obvious ones are:

1. A complex and sophisticated job involves a variety of skills and expertise. It is normally not possible for one person to possess all such skills in the required degree.

2. Division of labour favours efficiency of operations. Repetition of activities not only increases one's skills at performing that task, it also reduces time required for changing from one task to another.

3. Any job would have both the high and low skill components. If the same person is to do the complete job, most of the time he/she would be operating below his/her skill level. This would be an inefficient use of resources.

4. The recruitment and training costs are less for the organisation if the nature of job is specific and repetitive.

5. If the job is simple, specialised and repetitive, it is easier to develop performance standards for appraisal and control purposes.

B. Vertical Complexity

Vertical complexity refers to the number of hierarchical levels which exist between the top management and the lowest level operators in the organisation. Increase in vertical complexity is often the organisation's response to increase in the horizontal complexity. When organisational activities become more and more segmented and specialised, it becomes more difficult for the different organisational subunits to understand the part they play in the achievement of the total organisational goal. Somebody is required to integrate and coordinate these otherwise separate efforts, and to supervise that the work is being performed according to plan. This need for supervision and coordination results in increased vertical complexity.

One factor which determines the number of hierarchical layers in the organisation is the *Span of Control*. Organisations with same number of employees can have different number of levels, depending on the span of control (see Figure 3.1). If the span is narrow, it will result in a tall organisation, whereas if the span is wide, the organisation will have a flat structure. A tall organisation would employ many more managerial personnel at different levels for managing the same number of operators. While this can be considered to be an inefficient use of managerial resources, it also has the advantage of decreasing the load of routine supervision for the managers, so that they can spend their time more profitably on planning and problem-solving activities

Organisational hierarchical levels	Personnel at each hierarchical level: Span of control = 3	Span of control = 9
1	1	1
2	3	9
3	9	81
4	27	729
5	81	
6	243	
7	729	
Number of operators	729	729
Number of managerial staff	364 (Level 1–6)	91 (Level 1–3)

Figure 3.1 Comparing organisations with different spans of control.

If the number of hierarchical levels is more, the problems involved in managing the organisation also increase: there is greater potential for distortion of communication across hierarchies; there is greater demand for coordinating the managerial decisions taken at different levels, and the senioı levels of management become more distant from the operating core. On the other hand, the flat organisational structures have their own problems, such as more managerial pressures on the executives, lesser promotional opportunities, etc. Whether an organisation should opt for a tall or flat structure would depend upon a number of factors. These are listed in Table 3.1.

Table 3.1 Comparison of Tall and Flat Organisational Structures

Tall organisational structure (Narrow span of control)	Flat organisational structure (Wide span of control)
Needed when:	
• Closer control and monitoring is required.	• More autonomy and self-control is required.
• Mistakes are likely to be costly.	• Flexibility and innovation is required.
• Tasks/roles are clear; require specialisation.	• Ambiguous tasks and roles; specialisation doesn't work.
• Routine technology.	• Non-routine technology.
• Inexperienced subordinates.	• Experienced subordinates.
• Placid, stable environment.	• Unstable, turbulent environment.
Dysfunctional consequences:	
• Discourages initiative; encourages centralisation.	• Lack of proper control; encourages laissez-faire.
• Bottlenecks, distortion of vertical communication.	• Too much demand on the manager for coordinating.
• Slow promotion.	• Reduced promotional opportunities.

C. Spatial Complexity

Spatial complexity refers to the degree to which the subunits and personnel of an organisation are geographically separated. An organisation may continue to have the same number of occupational roles and departments (horizontal complexity) and hierarchical levels (vertical complexity), but if it decides to geographically separate its activities, this would introduce additional requirements for control and coordination of these activities. These requirements arise out of increased spatial complexity.

For example, many consumer product companies have their marketing offices dispersed around the country. While they engage in essentially identical activities, this geographical distancing creates many problems of communication. On the contrary, if all managers, involved in a project were staying in the same location, it would make the decision-making process much simpler.

Many organisations cope with the spatial complexity by having their own corporate courior service, wireless system or hotlines. The advent of more efficient telecommunication systems and computor technology has also helped the organisations to overcome the problems of communication and coordination. The use of such corporate mechanisms, however, does not mean that the complexity induced by spatial separation can be eliminated. Rather, in devising methods to counter spatial complexity, organisations become more complex (e.g., a new department would have to be setup to look after the courior service).

II. FORMALISATION

Formalisation refers to the degree to which jobs in an organisation are standardised. Greater formalisation would reduce the employees' discretion in dealing with their work. By introducing detailed rules, meticulous work-procedures and clear job descriptions, organisations ensure that any input is handled in a standard manner so as to produce a uniform output. On the other hand, less formalisation would mean that the jobs are less programmed and provide sufficient discretion to the employees to exercise choices in dealing with their work.

There can be various reasons for an organisation to introduce formalisation:

1. Formalisation of jobs reduces the variability of outputs. By protecting the output from human and incidental variations, the organisation can ensure that its quality standards are maintained. As mentioned earlier, in most pharmaceutical companies, the sales presentation made by the medical representatives to the doctors is standardised to the extent of sales talk and even the gestures and intonations. This ensures that the representative is able to effectively communicate maximum information about the products to the doctors within the short appointment time.

2. Formalisation is one way of dealing with the complexity of management problems. If the work-process involves a number of specialised, but interdependent jobs, the need to coordinate these activities also increases. For example, a typical assembly-line consists of a number of specialised operations which are linked with each other serially. By formalising the activities for each work-centre on the assembly line, the organisation achieves coordination among these activities.

3. Formalisation reduces the need for direct supervision and control. This helps by ensuring more time available to the manager for other planning and problem-solving activities. Once the specific jobs/activities have been standardised, the manager need not get directly involved in routine supervisory activities; these can be safely delegated down the line. Thus, formalisation leads to more efficient use of the managers' time.

4. By reducing the discretions in doing the job, formalisation also reduces the chances of mistakes occurring in the execution of the job. Mistakes, after all, mean loss of money.

5. Lastly, the greater the discretion in the performance of the job, the greater would be the need for exercising a judgement by the incumbent. Obviously, a job which entails a greater degree of professional judgement would cost the organisation much more in terms of the employees salaries, perks, benefits, etc. For example, if the job is to recruit and organise a work-force for manning a newly commissioned plant, without any formal guidelines whatsoever, finding the right incumbent might cost the organisation a lot of money. On the other hand, if there are comprehensive guidelines for recruitment policies and procedures, this job can be handled by a less experienced person—naturally, at a lesser salary.

Of course, not all jobs can be formalised. Certain kind of organisational work is more amenable to formalisation as compared to others. It is easier, for instance, to standardise the operations of an unskilled job as compared to a skilled job. Thus, one normally finds greater formalisation at the lower levels in the organisation, where jobs are more likely to be repetitive, unskilled and not requiring much discretion. As one goes up in the hierarchy, one has to deal with many more unique problem situations, which cannot be standardised. Moreover, the nature of the work itself also influences the extent of formalisation. For example, it is far easier to standardise the jobs on the production floor, than it is to formalise the work of a public-relations executive, receptionist, or a salesperson.

A. Organisational and Professional Formalisation

One must, however, also note the exceptions to the above discussion. Formalisation of behaviour does not always involve implementation of rules and procedures; neither does it always apply to routine unskilled jobs only. Standardisation of behaviour also exists in many highly professional jobs. For example, in an operation theater, the surgeon, the anaesthesist and the nurse often perform a delicate operation, without even exchanging a single word; their behaviours are standardised and well coordinated, based on a professional understanding of each other's role. However, these behaviours are not written down in any organisational manual. Similarly, the behaviours of many other professionals, e.g., engineers or accountants, are also formalised due to their training.

To understand this difference, it is useful to differentiate between *organisational formalisation* and the *professional formalisation*. Perrow (1972) noted that the "organisation can either control (employee behaviour) directly through its own procedures and rules, or else it can achieve indirect control by hiring duly trained professionals." Catering and Hotel Management Institutes, for example, train their students not only in techniques relevant to hotel management, but also in behavioural skills in matters such as greeting the customer, table service, arranging a dish, and so on. Similarly, a trained management graduate from a business school not only learns specialised management techniques, but the training also moulds him/her to think and behave in certain manners, appropriate for a corporate setting. Even though organisations, by and large, achieve similar goals through both kinds of formalisations, the two are, obviously, quite different in nature and complex (see Table 3.2).

Table 3.2 Comparison of Organisational and Professional Formalisation

Organisational formalisation	Professional formalisation
• Usually achieved through rules, procedures, job-descriptions, etc.	• Usually achieved through years of professional training.
• Focuses primarily on moulding the external behaviour of the individual.	• Focuses primarily on the internal attitudes and orientations of the person.
• Based on extrinsic rewards and punishments.	• Based on internalised values and socialisation.
• Most often used for routine, unskilled work.	• Most often used for skilled, non-routine work.
• Usually found in more complex organisations.	• Usually found in less complex organisations.

B. Formalisation Techniques

Organisations have a variety of choices for achieving formalisation. Let us look at some of these formalisation techniques.

1. Selection and recruitment. The hiring practice adopted by the organisations is one of the most widely used method for controlling discretion and formalising employee behaviour. Organisations select their employees on the basis of certain well-defined criteria. Besides assuring themselves that the person has the required technical skills and qualifications, organisations also assess the candidate through interviews, group discussions, background investigations, etc. to check how well the person will "fit" into the organisation. The person is screened for his attitude, manners, work and social habits, even dress and appearance.

Many highly professional organisations, for example, invite the short-listed candidates for a live-in interview. The candidates are evaluated not only on the basis of how well they fare before the interview board, but also on their display of general etiquette and how they socialise. Such a detailed selection procedure automatically eliminates those who the organisation thinks would not fit in their corporate culture. Those finally hired, are the ones who behave and exercise their discretion within limits acceptable to the organisation.

2. Role/Job descriptions. The specificity with which jobs are defined in the organisation plays a crucial role in regulating employee behaviour. Organisations make a considerable effort to create job descriptions which spell out the do's and don't's of any job. These role definitions not only describe what the job entails, but often also how the activities required for the job are to be performed. The job descriptions are further reinforced by an appropriate appraisal system. If an employee does not fulfil his role expectations, he is adversely affected in the matter of reward systems, viz., promotions and increments. On the other hand, those who conduct their jobs in a manner required by their role get rewarded for their performance.

3. Rules and procedures. Rules and procedures constitute a detailed programme for guiding, moulding, and regulating the employee behaviour. Rules are explicit statements of what an employee can or cannot do, whereas the procedures explicitly describe the sequence of behaviours an employee must go through to get anything accomplished within the organisation. For example, if an employee wants to draw a tour advance for an official out-station visit to a customer, the rules would dictate the amount he can draw, whether he can travel by air or train, the type of accommodation he can avail, etc. The procedure, on the other hand, would guide him to fill up the required forms, obtain necessary sanctions, etc. If the employee violates either the rules or the procedures, he will be in a difficult situation, and his task remaining unaccomplished.

It is important to note that organisations have rules and procedures, not only for organisational work, but also for issues relating to the employee's personal life. For instance it is the rules that govern when and how the employee can go on leave, whether or not a salary advance can be sanctioned, what the duration of the lunch hour will be, etc. More detailed organisational rules and procedures restrict the possibilities of variations in employee behaviour, and so encourage greater standardisation of activities in the organisation. Less formalised organisations, on the other hand, have fewer rules and procedures to govern employee behaviour.

4. Training. One of the most widely accepted methods adopted by the organisations to instill desired behaviour patterns among their employees is through conducting training programmes. Many organisations expect their freshly inducted employees to undergo an induction programme before allocating specific work assignments. This involves familiarising them with the company's philosophy, history, systems, procedures, personnel policies, etc. Such an induction programme aims at communicating the opportunities as well as the constraints, which an employee can expect to encounter while working for the company. The interaction which the new entrant has with other employees during the programme (e.g., presentations made by senior executives, discussions with HODs, briefings given by the course coordinator) also communicate messages about the desired norm of behaviour in the organisation.

Besides the induction programmes, many organisations also expose their employees to various technical skills and management development programmes. By developing relevant managerial and technical skills, organisations aim not only at ensuring uniformity of behaviour among the employees in various situations, but also at attaining similarities in the thinking and attitudes of their employees.

5. Culture and organisational socialisation. It is interesting to note how persons working together in the same organisation (or organisational sub-unit), over a period of time, tend to start adopting almost similar attitudes and displaying similar behaviour patterns. It is almost as if they implicitly agree on the norms of desirable and undesirable behaviour. These implicit norms or "rules of the game" constitute organisational culture (Van Maanen, 1976). Schein (1985) defines organisational culture as:

> ...a pattern of basic assumptions—invented, discovered, or developed by a given group as it learns to cope with its problems of external adaptation and internal integration—that have worked well enough to be considered valid and, therefore, to be taught to new members as the correct way to perceive, think and feel in relation to those problems.

Organisational culture and the informal process through which organisational members get acculturised is one of the most subtle, but enduring, method of formalisation. Organisations use a variety of symbolic rituals and tokens to create cultural pressures on the individual to conform to certain codes of conduct. For example, many organisations in our country (e.g., CMC Ltd., Maruti Udyog) have done away with the concept of cabins in the offices. Instead, staff and executives sit in an open hall. In doing so, the organisations also manage the level of formalisation. Similarly, organisations use methods such as uniforms, separate canteens for workers and executives, informal gatherings, etc., for sustaining their culture, and through that, reinforcing the desirable behaviour among the employees.

III. CENTRALISATION

The third building block of organisational design is the level of centralisation (or decentralisation) in decision-making. Centralisation/decentralisation is an important dimension of organisational effectiveness, since it refers directly to how appropriately and swiftly the organisation is able to deal with critical issues and arrive at relevant decisions. Hage (1965) defined this dimension as the proportion of jobs whose occupants participate in decision-making and the number of areas in which this participation takes place. Similarly, Reimann (1974) described centralisation as reflecting the locus of decision-making, with respect to major and specific policies, the degree of information sharing between levels, and the degree of participation in long-range planning. One of the most comprehensive definitions was offered by Robbins (1987) who defined centralisation as:

> ... the degree to which the formal authority for making discretionary choices is concentrated in an individual, unit, or level (usually high in the organisation), thus permitting employees (usually low in the organisation) minimum input in their work.

In the light of the above definitions, it is important to qualify our understanding of this concept with a few salient points:

1. Centralisation/decentralisation refers to the *distribution of formal authority* within the organisation. It is quite likely that there are informal coalitions and leaders in the organisation who may have influence over the decisions. This, however, cannot be interpreted as affecting the level of centralisation in the organisation.

2. Centralisation of decision-making may be with a single person, unit or level. This single point, however, should be placed at a higher level in the organisation.

3. If decision-making is delegated down the line, but there are elaborate formalised policies, systems and rules which constrain the discretion of the lower level employees, this cannot be understood as decentralisation. On the other hand, many organisations provide discretionary powers to the lower levels, but also develop information-systems to keep the top management aware of the decisions that are taken. If the information-system only helps the top management to monitor without hindering with the decision-making authority of the lower levels, it cannot be understood as centralisation. Thus, the centralisation-decentralisation issue needs to be understood in terms of the amount of *discretion available with the decision-maker*, rather than be seen as merely the point at which the decision is being taken.

A. Organisational Decision-Making Process

Decision-making is traditionally defined as an act of making choices. A typical manager, for example, is required to make choices about the budget allocation and its utilisation, job distribution amongst the personnel, methodology to be adopted to execute work etc. The decision maker considers and evaluates various alternatives for a given problem and then selects the one which seems most appropriate to him/her. While from the point of view of an individual, such a definition seems adequate, it represents only one step in the organisational decision-making process.

Paterson (1969) described the various steps involved in the organisational decision-making process (see Figure 3.2). One would observe that each of

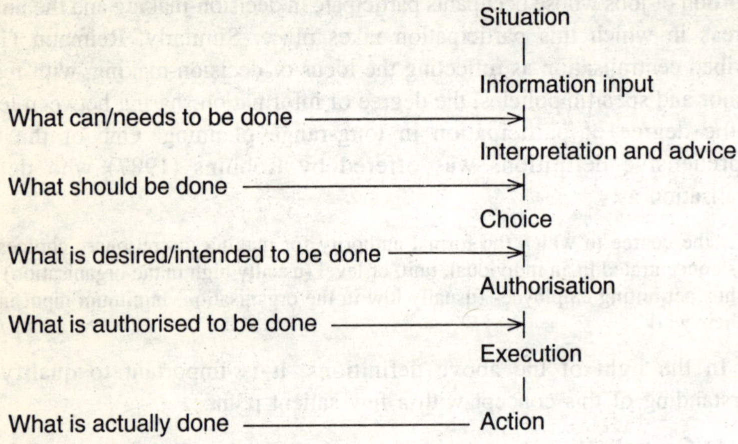

Figure 3.2 The organisational decision-making process (based on Paterson, 1969).

these steps provides opportunity to influence the decision. The process starts from information input, which is normally fed by the lower levels to the decision-maker. Even at this stage the subordinates have an opportunity to screen and pass on only such information that they consider relevant. Once the information is made available, it is to be interpreted to decide what should be done. For example, if the information highlights that sales are falling, the interpretation would pin point whether it is because of product quality, demotivated or inadequate sales force, increased competition, or due to lacunas in distribution network, etc. The decision-maker's choice would largely depend on these interpretations. The choice, however, merely highlights the desire of the decision maker. In order to be executed, it has to be authorised. For instance, in the above example, based on the interpretation, the General Manager (Marketing & Sales) may take a decision for awarding incentives to the sales force to increase their motivation level. The implementation of this decision may require authorisation of many others, some of whom may even be at the lower levels (e.g., the Regional Marketing Manager or the Regional Accountant). If there are many layers between the decision-maker and the level at which the decision has to be executed, the final outcome may get influenced by the intervening levels and may turn out to be very different than the original decision (e.g., awarding an incentive may involve so many complicated requirements, that it may create dissatisfaction instead of motivation to the sales force).

It is clear that decision-making would be absolutely centralised if the decision-maker controls all the steps. Very often, the decision-making process in a small entrepreneurial firm is characterised by such a pervasive control. In larger organisations such an extent of centralisation is, by and large, practically not possible. Often, the decision-maker only controls the process of making choices, while all other steps are controlled by others. This leads to a more decentralised decision-making. In extreme decentralisation, even the choices are decided by the incumbents at lower-levels. In many organisations (e.g. clubs, political organisations, educational institutions), the organisational leader is more of a figure head, whereas the actual strategic and operational decisions are taken at lower-levels.

B. Centralisation and Decentralisation

It would be too simplistic to treat centralisation and decentralisation as an either/or choice in organisational design. As we saw in the previous section, there are various shades and levels of centralisation (or decentralisation). Thus, there is no totally centralised or decentralised organisation. Rather, in practice, the designing decision focuses on the specific activities and decision areas which need to be centralised or decentralised, and the extent to which this would be appropriate for organisational effectiveness.

In order to take such designing decisions, one must be aware of the relative advantages and disadvantages of centralisation and decentralisations. Classical organisational theorist, Fayol, argued for a balance between the two, which of course, is a truism. The critical issue is the side towards which the balance should tilt. Many recent writings (e.g., Toffler, 1981; Huber, 1984; Naisbitt and Auberdene, 1985, etc.) point out the need for greater decentralisation in the coming times. They argue that with the increasing complexity of demands on the organisation, it would no longer be feasible to centralise the decision-making process. Organisational decisions would require more heterogenous inputs, swifter implementation and greater flexibility. The advances in computers and communication technology would not only make decentralisation easier, but also imperative (we will discuss these issues in greater detail in Chapter 13).

Such environmental changes notwithstanding, centralisation still offers numerous advantages. Certain situations require centralisation, while others require decentralisation. Table 3.3 summarises the comparisons between these two design variables.

IV. IMPLICATIONS FOR MANAGERS

It is important to appreciate that the three components of organisational design, viz., complexity, formalisation and centralisation, are by no means, mutually unrelated and independent. Change in one is likely to create the necessity of change in others. For example, if an organisation increases the horizontal complexity by segmenting the jobs and creating division of labour, it may also

Table 3.3 Relative Advantages and Disadvantages of Centralisation and Decentralisation

Centralisation	Decentralisation
Advantages:	
• Uniformity of policies, standards and actions.	• Greater flexibility and appropriateness in responding to local situations.
• Enables closer control and coordination.	• Allows top management to focus on policy issues.
• Maximises economies of scales; eliminates duplication.	• Facilitates intra-unit communication.
• Reduces risk-factor in decision-making by less informed or less skilled subordinates.	• Increases opportunity for on-the-job training for subordinates.
	• Increases morale and commitment.
	• Creates healthy competition among units.
Disadvantages:	
• Top much decision load on top management.	• Causes problems of control and coordination.
• Causes alienation and lack of initiative.	• Causes conflicts of goals and interests among units.
• Inappropriate response to local requirements.	• Loss of economies of scales; duplication of efforts.

become necessary to introduce greater formalisation to control and coordinate this complexity. However, the exact nature of relationship among these components is far from clear-cut, and may not always be the same. In the above example, if the horizontal complexity has increased because of multiplicity of professional specialisation (e.g., in a multi-disciplinary task-force), the organisation may actually require less formalised systems and procedures. Thus, it is useful to treat these three components as independent, though related, factors.

As one would also have noticed, an appropriate choice of the design components is an essential prerequisite for organisational effectiveness. A large corporation aiming to increase its responsiveness to the environmental demands would flounder if it continues with its centralised structure for decision-making. Similarly, after a high-growth period (during which organisations often over-extend themselves) certain amount of formalisation may by required for consolidation of activities and resources. A mismatch between what an organisation is supposed to achieve, and how it structures itself to do so, is likely to produce many dysfunctional consequences for both the organisation as well as its members. Let us look at some of these consequences:

1. An inappropriate organisational structure blocks the relevant information from reaching the decision-makers. The structure establishes the lines of communication between different levels and parts of the organisation. In the absence of right communication channels, the decision-makers would receive too little, too much or even distorted information about what is happening in the

organisation. Consequently, one may find that (a) the organisation tends to make the same mistakes again and again, (b) there is a decline in the organisation's capacity to anticipate problems and take necessary action, or/and (c) the organisation's response to internal and external problems is slow and inappropriate.

2. The lack of proper information not only affects the decision-making process, but also disrupts the control and coordination of activities within the organisation. Too many hierarchical levels, for example, may totally distort the intent of a directive emanating from the top. Similarly, lack of proper information flow may make it difficult for the manager to synchronise and integrate the efforts of different inter-linked departments and sections.

3. Lastly, a bad choice of organisational structure contributes to increase in the role stress. Inappropriate structure creates organisational contradictions, in that the activities and decisions of one organisational subunit start contradicting the efforts of other subunits. These are stressful experiences for the organisational members. When, for example, the financial controls implemented by the accounts department become a reason for delay in project implementation, it puts pressure on the project manager. Moreover, if the structure does not properly communicate clear expectations to individual role incumbents, it increases ambiguity for the person.

4 Organisation—Environment Interface

1. In January, 1992, Living Media India Ltd. launched a new business fortnightly, *Business Today*. The company offered a lucrative discount if one paid an year's subscription within the first few months of the launch. Against the news-stand price of Rs. 25, the subscription rate worked out to only Rs 10 per issue!! It was not surprising to find that within a few months the new business fortnightly became an equal rival to the well-established Business World and Business India, the other significant entities in the same field.
2. With a gradual reduction in the defence budget since 1991-92, ordnance factories (government-owned, solely manufacturing items for armed forces), slowly started finding their capacity underutilised and their operations financially non-viable. Solution: Many of them diversified into manufacturing items of civilian use, such as industrial fabrics, spare parts, etc. This, of course, meant that these companies had to start doing something they had never done before viz. marketing of their products.
3. How did Skypak, the forerunner of courier services in India, create a market in an environment which was completely unknown? And that too while keeping the investments in infrastructure to a bare minimum. The offices of Skypak during these earlier days were single rooms with frugal bearings, manned by a single person on the company's permanent payroll. The company gave this person only two things: a challenging and tough target, and immense autonomy and freedom.

The above represent just a few random instances of organisations interacting with (modifying and getting influenced by) their environments. Organisational effectiveness is largely (though not solely) determined by how well it is able to assess and manage its business environment. Organisations, as we noted earlier, are similar to living systems, in that to survive they have to continuously interact, influence and respond to the environment. In this Chapter, we will discuss some of the frameworks for understanding the environment and its impact on the organisations. We will also look at the various options organisations exercise for managing their environments.

I. WHAT IS ENVIRONMENT?

Obviously, all that is not a part of the organisation. Miles (1980) said about the organisational environment as: "Just take the universe, subtract from it the subset that represents the organisation, and the remainder is environment." Simple as this definition seems, there are two problems with it, specially, if one wants to derive practical guidelines from it for dealing with the environment. Firstly, it is not so easy to define the "subset that represents the organisation." It is difficult, for example, to decide whether the shareholders of a company should be considered a part of the organisation, or a part of the environment which influences the organisation's operations. Similarly, would one consider the trade unions (or the dealers) a part of the environment or of the organisation? As we shall later see, much depends on one's own perception and understanding of organisational boundaries. Secondly, such a definition makes the environment composed of so many things, that it becomes too general for any meaningful managerial analysis and action. There may be many influences in so broadly defined an environment which would have no bearing on the goals and activities of the organisation. It is meaningless, for example, for the manager of a software firm to be concerned about the recession in the passenger car market.

It is for this reason, one needs greater analytical rigour for understanding the organisational environment. The above definition describes the general environment, which includes a wide array of factors, ranging from the state of economy to such influences as the state of technology, cultural factors, etc. Table 4.1 lists out these diverse factors which have potential for influencing organisational activities and functioning. One would also notice that some of these factors have a more direct bearing on organisational decision-making than others.

Table 4.1 Factors Comprising the External Environment of the Organisation

Socio-political
- Governmental policies and regulatory controls
- Socio-cultural attitudes towards the industry and its product/service
- Stability of government and economy
- State of trade union movement
- State of consumer and environment protection movements
- Availability of relevant manpower

Market
- State of competition (demand and supply) in the industry
- Competitors for suppliers
- Competitors for customers
- Distributors and dealers
- Actual users of product or service
- Availability of supply of raw material, equipment, etc.

Technology
- Advances in technology relevant for the industry
- New/substitute products
- New and more efficient production technologies (e.g., Kanban, JIT, etc.)
- Developments in information and communication technology

Of more relevance to the manager is the operating or task environment, which is composed of those elements of the general environment which have a specific and direct bearing on organisational goals and activities. Duncan (1979) noted that the "task environment constitutes that part of environment defined by managers as relevant or potentially relevant to organisational decision-making." For example, disruptions in power supply is a specifically relevant environmental factor for many manufacturing organisations because it directly affects their operations (though, it would not have much significant impact on the banking organisations).

The operating environment of an organisation depends on the domain it chooses to operate in. An organisation's domain determines the specific points at which it depends upon its environment. It defines the organisation's niche, and identifies those portions in which the organisation prefers to interact with the environment. Thus, certain changes in the environment are likely to influence some organisation more as compared to others. Import restrictions, for example, would affect organisations in those sectors more, which rely on imported technology/raw material. Similarly, floods and droughts would have greater impact on those organisations which operate in or depend on rural economy (e.g., IFFCO, Eicher Tractors, consumer goods companies producing basic necessities, etc.), than, say, on the Oberoi Group of Hotels.

The distinction between general and operating environment, however, is far from clear-cut. Often, changes which appear to be unrelated to the organisation's operating environment turn out to have major consequences for the organisation. The political changes in the former Soviet Union, for example, may not appear to have any direct connection with tea gardens in Assam. But indirectly, they created a crisis for the Indian tea industry, when in 1991, Russia put a freeze on the import of tea—a major portion of which was exported from India.

It would be too simplistic to assume that similar kind of environmental factors always influence the organisations, directly and in the same manner. Organisations are, of course, influenced by the *actual* environment; but they are also influenced by the environment as it is *perceived* by the managers who influence organisational decisions. The same environmental changes can be perceived differently by different people and organisations (e.g., in our previous example about import restriction, managers of a company not relying on imports can perceive it as an irrelevant change as far as their operations are concerned, or they may also perceive this change as a strategic opportunity, which can be utilised for a competitive advantage). Obviously, what managers perceive in a situation would be influenced by their personality, background, education, specific location in the organisation, etc. If these personal factors bias the managers in their assessment of the environment, it would, naturally, lead to faulty organisational decision.

II. ENVIRONMENTAL IMPACT ON ORGANISATIONS

Inspite of the complications which one faces in trying to define what exactly would constitute an organisation's environment, different kinds of environments do have a more or less discernable, even predictable, influence on the organisation (its structure, control systems, culture, etc.). Organisations have a tendency to mould themselves to adapt to the environment. An organisation which is operating in a relatively predictable and unchanging environment (i.e., assured supply of raw material, adequate demand of the product/service, little or no competition, etc.) is not likely to experience any need for a swift and innovative response to the environment. It is, therefore, more likely to routinise its activities and operations (through clearly defined rules and procedures), and exercise strict controls to maintain these routines. On the other hand, an organisation existing in an uncertain and changing environment would need to be more flexible in order to cope with the environmental demands. In this section we will discuss three important frameworks which enrich our understanding of the manner in which environmental forces influence and mould the organisations.

A. Burns and Stalker: The Mechanistic and Organic Organisations

In 1961, T. Burns and G.M. Stalker published a book, *The Management of Innovation*, which was based on their study of about twenty British and Scottish firms in the electronics industry. Their findings demonstrated that organisations operating in stable environment are very different from those which have to face a changing and dynamic environment. They coined two terms, 'mechanistic' and 'organic' systems of management, to describe these differences (see Table 4.2).

Table 4.2 A Comparison of the Characteristics of Mechanistic and Organic Organisations

	Mechanistic	Organic
Nature of environment	Relatively stable, simple and predictable.	Relatively dynamic, complex and uncertain.
Task definition	Tasks are segmented from each other and isolated from the overall organisational goal; rigidly defined into specialities.	Tasks are loosely defined in context of overall organisational goal; need redefinition through continuous interaction among members.
Communication	Vertical, primarily to communicate decisions and give instructions.	Lateral, primarily to share information and solve problems.
Authority	Position-based	Expertise-based
Control mechanisms	Hierarchical and impersonal (through rules, procedures, etc.)	Reciprocal; through interpersonal negotiations and contracts.
Decision-making	Autocratic, programmed, computational	Participative, non-programmed, judgemental.
Formalisation	High	Low
Centralisation	High	Low

The mechanistic organisations, they found, are suited for relatively stable and placid environmental conditions. Such organisations are neatly programmed, strictly controlled and hierarchically structured. Organisational tasks are typically broken down into specialised activities. Individuals are responsible for their specific functions, in a relative isolation from the overall organisational goal. There is a great emphasis on the procedural precision and maintenance of functional boundaries. The underlying assumption is that it is the superior who knows what the total task is, and it is his responsibility to see that these separate functional efforts add up to achievement of the organisational goal. Correspondingly, vertical channels of communication are more frequently used, "with information flowing upward through a succession of filters, and decisions and instructions flowing downwards through a succession of amplifiers."

The organic organisations, on the other hand, are more likely to exist under unstable environmental conditions in which "new and unfamiliar problems and requirements continually arise that cannot be broken down and distributed among specialists roles within a hierarchy." Given these conditions, it becomes necessary to review and redefine the responsibilities, methods, inter-role relationships, and even goals, on a continual basis. Moreover, the organisational members need to conduct their jobs with full knowledge of overall organisational goals and context. This calls for a greater information-flow among the members, and a need to rely on those who are more informed and competent to tackle the problem at hand. To meet these requirements, such organisations are more loosely structured, emphasise lateral rather than vertical communication, are less formalised, and give more value to expert-based authority than to position-based authority.

One must note that Burns and Stalker's classification describes a polarity and not a dichotomy. Their descriptions of the mechanistic and organic structures corresponded to two "ideal" types. Most organisations actually face environments which are either relatively stable or relatively changing, and therefore, contain characteristics which are typical of both types. Their study, however, did help establish a cogent rationale for the environmental fit hypothesis. It also highlighted the basic tenet of managerial wisdom that there is no ideal organisational form to suit all environmental contexts.

B. Lawrence and Lorsch: Differentiation-Integration Theory

Another significant study to demonstrate the relationship between environmental characteristics and effective organisational structures was conducted by P.R. Lawrence and J.W. Lorsch (1967). They studied ten firms in three industries: plastics, food and containers. These industries represented differing degrees of environmental uncertainty. At one extreme, the plastics industry operated in high environmental uncertainty: high competition, short product life-cycle, new products and process developments, etc. The container industry, which represented the other extreme, was characterised by slow and steady growth, more or less assured market, no new products in last two decades, etc. Food industry fell somewhere in between, coping with an environment which was less uncertain than plastics industry and more uncertain than the containers industry.

Lawrence and Lorsch sought to identify the influence of uncertainty in an organisation's external environment on its internal environment. They expected that successful and effective organisations would be able to better match their internal environments with the demands of the external environment. The level of environmental uncertainty was assessed by looking into such factors as how fast the environment is changing, how much information the management has about the environment, how quickly and how frequently does the organisation gets a feedback from the environment on its actions, and so on.

To assess the internal organisational environment, Lawrence and Lorsch postulated two dimensions, *differentiation* and *integration*. They defined differentiation as both the degree of horizontal complexity, as well as the diversity of attitudes, perceptions and interpersonal orientations among the organisational members. Thus, highly differentiated organisations will be characterised by more number of functional departments, more jobs requiring specialised skills, high task segmentation, and so on. Moreover, this complexity would also encourage the individuals in different segments (departments) of the organisation to develop and hold different values, attitudes, norms of behaving and relating, and even different perceptions of what constitutes the legitimate organisational goal. For example, in a differentiated organisation, the marketing executives may see taking initiative and risks, and working through informal contacts, to increase market share/sales volumes as valued norms of their job; on the contrary for people in the production function, the relevant job-related values may consist of operational efficiency, predictability of performance and a more methodical approach to problems. Such differences would also make it more difficult for people in different segments of the organisation to observe and understand issues in the same way.

The other dimension, integration, described the degree to and manner in which different organisational units and departments collaborate to achieve a unity of efforts. A well integrated organisation would show a high degree of consistency and coordination in the efforts of its various units. On the other hand, a low level of integration in the organisation would show itself in mutually contradictory efforts among the units, interdepartmental conflicts and lack of synergy. For example, the finance department may follow its goal of controlling costs by striking down an important investment decision taken by the production department, which would have increased its operating efficiency.

Lawrence and Lorsch found a striking relationship between the environmental uncertainty, and the way in which organisations manage their internal environment. The significant implications of their findings can be summarised as follows (see Table 4.3):

1. The greater the environmental uncertainty, the greater is the differentiation within the organisation. Organisations tend to deal with the environmental uncertainty by adding or developing new functions and roles in their structure. This is done by creating new departments, or sometimes, by splitting existing functions into divisions with a more specialised focus (e.g., during the 80s in India, as the business environment became relatively uncertain, organisations responded by adding new departments, such as HRD, Quality controls, Market Research, Business Development, etc., in their structures). Correspondingly, members in these different functions also develop a variety of sub-cultures, which get represented in the differences in their interests, perceptions and interpersonal orientations.

Table 4.3 Significant Findings of Lawrence and Lorsch's Study (1967)

	Plastics	Food	Container
% New products in last 20 yrs	35%	15%	0%
Environmental uncertainty	High	Moderate	Low
Actual differentiation	High	Moderate	Low
Actual integration	High	Moderate	Low
Typical integrative devices	Integrating departments and roles, teams, hierarchy, plans, rules and procedures	Integrating roles, task-forces, hierarchy, plans, rules and procedures	Hierarchy, plans, rules and procedures
% Integrating personnel	22%	17%	0%

2. These differences in the interests and orientations of the organisational members/units also create difficulties in achieving collaboration and consensus among them. This creates a need for integration. That is, a need to have a unity of efforts among interdependent units and departments. Lawrence and Lorsch found that effective organisations are able to develop integrative devices and mechanisms which match their level of differentiation.

3. Organisations can have a variety of integrative mechanisms. Hierarchy, rules, and procedures are the most basic means of achieving unity of efforts. By formulating rules and procedures (e.g., manual of personnel policies, financial control systems, standard operating procedures, documenting the delegation of powers), organisations ensure that members of different departments and units behave in a uniform, or at least in a coordinated, manner. However, as organisations become more and more differentiated, these simple devices become inadequate to serve the purpose. Highly differentiated organisations supplement these devices with more sophisticated and process-based methods for achieving integration. These methods include the formation of interdepartmental coordination committees, liaisoning mechanisms, integrating the departments, etc. Many companies which have a multi-product, multi-divisional structure use other integrative devices, e.g., inter-divisional transfers, strategic planning meetings or multi-divisional task forces.

4. Lawrence and Lorsch also found that as the need for integration becomes more important for an organisation, more managerial manpower is required to look after integration as a function. For example, National Dairy Development Board, as it expanded and diversified, found it necessary to create a new group to look after Regional Coordination. Similarly, the corporate staff in many highly diversified organisations with a divisional structure (e.g., Eicher Goodearth, Hindustan Ciba-Geigy, HMT) also includes the HR/OD personnel, besides the traditional finance and legal functionaries. Their task is to build a common

organisational identity across different divisions through training, culture-building exercises, etc. This is in contrast to less differentiated organisations, which achieve integration through formalised rules and procedures.

C. Duncan: A Model for "Right" Organisational Structure

In 1979, Robert Duncan published an article in *Organisational Dynamics,* proposing a comprehensive framework for understanding the design options one has for coping with different types of environments. Duncan's thesis was based on his own research work, and integrated earlier works of Lawrence and Lorsch (1967), Galbraith (1978) and Thompson (1967), to develop a heuristics for taking decisions about the appropriate organisational structure. He viewed organisational structure as an information-processing device, which "links the elements of organisation by providing the channels of communication through which information flows." Viewed in this manner, an effective organisational structure would be one which is able to cope with the information-processing demands of its environment.

The framework of Duncan (1979) was based on a conceptualisation of environmental uncertainty as consisting of two, more or less independent, dimensions: environmental change and environmental complexity. He proposed that the interaction of these two dimensions provides a heuristic framework which can be used to assess the state of the task environment of the organisation (see Table 4.4).

Table 4.4 Four Task Environments and their Organisational Structures (based on Robbins, 1987)

CHANGE			
	Dynamic	**3. Moderately high perceived uncertainty** Complexity : Low Formalisation : Low Centralisation Example: Small entrepreneurial firms	**4. High perceived uncertainty** Complexity : Low Formalisation : Low Decentralisation Examples: Advertising firms, R &D units, Task forces
	Stable	**1. Low perceived uncertainty** Complexity : High Formalisation : High Centralisation Examples: Mass production manufacturing companies, Bureaucracies	**2. Moderately low perceived uncertainty** Complexity : High Formalisation : High Decentralisation Examples: Multiproduct firms, Hospitals
		Simple	Complex
		COMPLEXITY	

Environmental Change may range from purely static to dynamic. A static environment would be characterised by little or no change in the environment over time. Such environments call for information-processing in a routinised manner from the organisation, and therefore, provide opportunity to regulate the behaviour of the members through formalisation and standardisation. If the amount of information is large, and of different types, it is also possible to deal with such environments through increased complexity of structure (e.g., division of labour, functional segmentation, span of control). On the other hand, it is essential for organisations existing in dynamic and unpredictable environments, to provide the employees with enough freedom and information to enable them to deal with unforeseen demands. Also the need to give swift responses does not allow the organisation to structure itself into functional segments (that would increase information-processing time). Therefore, organisations coping effectively with changing environments are likely to be characterised by a low formalisation and low complexity.

The other dimension of Duncan's framework, i.e. environmental complexity, refers to the number of environmental elements that can affect an organisation's operations. Some organisations operate in a relatively simple and homogenous environment, with few environmental factors which can influence its operations. For example, a single product company, which has an assured supply of raw materials, and which has a monopolistic base in a localised market, has fewer information-processing demands on itself. In such a case, it is possible for one or a few persons to take all major decisions, thus creating a centralised structure. In contrast, an organisation, dealing with different kinds of products/services, and operating in diverse regions has to cope with more complex environmental demands. In order to be effective, it would require use of diverse kinds of expertise and information-processing skills. Therefore, its organisational structure must permit decentralisation of organisational decision-making.

Duncan proposed that the structure of an organisation would depend on the information-processing demands placed on it by the environment, and the design strategy adapted by the organisation to cope with these demands. His thesis can be summarised as follows:

1. If the environment is simple (not many factors to be considered in decision-making) and stable (no significant change in the environmental components), an organisation's need for information and coordination would be low. These can be easily met by specialisation of functional expertise, simple standardised decision-making, and centralisation of authority. A functional structure would be appropriate to meet these requirements.

2. As the environmental uncertainty increases, the functional structure becomes inappropriate for meeting the greater demands for information-processing and coordination. One of the ways in which the organisations can cope with this situation is by structuring themselves in such a manner that they reduce the requirement of information for decision-making; they need to decentralise or divisionalise themselves around products, projects or geographical regions. Each of the division would be considered a self-contained unit, giving members of

each unit the autonomy and responsibility to focus on their own products or market areas. This strategy is particularly useful when the environment is complex, and, therefore, each segment can be treated separately.

3. Even divisional structures become problematic in a situation where the very texture of the environment is undergoing a change. Changes in customer psychographics, fluctuations in supply, politico-economic turmoils, breakthroughs in product development and technology, etc., may place demands for greater coordination among divisions. To cope with such uncertainty, the organisational structure would need to increase its information-processing capacity. That is, the structure must make more information available to more persons, so that the staff is more directly involved in coordinating its activities. This can be accomplished through developing matrix structures.

III. STRATEGIES FOR MANAGING ENVIRONMENT

The frameworks discussed in the previous section highlight the role of organisational structures in reducing the uncertainty created by the peculiarities of the environment. As we have seen, a viable structure either helps the organisation in dealing with the environment in a systematic and segmented manner (as in the case of functional and divisional structures), or provides for a more effective, flexible and optimum utilisation of existing skills in the organisation to cope with the environmental demands (as in the case of task-forces and matrix structures).

There are, however, numerous other strategies which the organisations use for uncertainty reduction. While some of these do get translated into structural changes, many of these don't. In fact, organisations often evolve these strategies for managing their environment so as to avoid making structural changes. Let us consider some of the most popular options:

A. Domain Choice

Organisations can, and often do, change their domain of operations to change their operating environment. In doing so, they also avoid facing the uncertainties inherent in the previous domain. Many organisations move into markets where there is lesser competition, select products/technologies for which raw material is easily available, or go into areas which invite less stringent government regulations, and so on. For example, Asian Paints' strategy, in its initial years, to cater primarily to the rural segment of the market had the obvious advantage of avoiding competition from the multinationals, which were the major players in the paint market at that time.

It is, of course, not always possible for the organisations to change their domain. What most organisations do is to enlarge their operations to cover many domains. Such a strategy helps the organisations in spreading their risks evenly. Moreover, it also provides for greater flexibility in use of diverse resources. For example, since the seventies, ITC Ltd. has consistently followed a strategy of enlarging its domain of operations, and reducing its total reliance on cigarettes (that market being most vulnerable to governmental regulations). As a result, now ITC operates, besides cigarettes, in many other market domains (e.g., hotels, paper, oil seeds and edible oils and financial services).

Similarly, many consumer product companies increase their brand range (e.g., regular to premium brands of soap, tea, cigarettes, liquors, biscuits, etc.) to cater to the lower as well as the upper ends of the market. This strategy takes care of fluctuations in demands across different market segments, without drastically affecting the organisation's profitability. Obviously, a company which has some product to sell to different classes of people (poor-rich, young-old, men-women, rural-urban, etc.) has a better chance of survival in an environment where customer choices are changing, than the one which has only a few products, targeted at a selected segment of customers.

B. Recruitment

Recruiting the right kind of people is a popular and effective method employed by organisations to counter the environmental uncertainty. Obviously, an organisation which has competent and skilled persons manning its key positions, would have an advantage in dealing with the environment. For example the Essar Group, in its drive to professionalise itself, inducted for its key positions, persons who had vast experience of managing core-sector projects. Similarly, the manning pattern of Pepsico Food (India) at the senior management positions has shown a remarkable bias towards ex-Lever Group employees. The reason is obvious, since Lever is well known for its professionalism and ensures a thorough grooming of its managerial cadres.

Organisations, however, do not always recruit people only for their professional competence. Hiring employees from the competitor's organisation, for example, has the additional benefit of access to strategic information (which may, in fact, be more important than the hired person's competence). Likewise, it is quite common to come across employment advertisements for senior financial and administrative posts, inviting applications from people retired from government service or financial institutions. The 'contacts' these people bring would be valuable for the organisations for influencing some of the key elements in their environment.

C. Vertical Integration

This strategy refers to extending organisational control over the input and/or output ends of the environment by incorporating them into organisational boundaries. If the company decides to start manufacturing its own raw materials, instead of relying on the suppliers for the inputs, it is known as **backward integration.** Many manufacturing companies, for example, set up their own captive power plants. This helps in reducing their dependence on the unpredictability of power supply from the electricity boards. Similarly, a company producing non-perishable food items (e.g., sauces, jams, wafers, etc.) may backward integrate by opening its own farms for producing the required raw material. This way it would ensure the supply of raw material on a regular basis at the minimum cost.

Likewise, if the organisation decides to control the output end it is known as **forward integration.** A company would have a better control over its sales, if instead of going through dealers, it opens its own retail counters (e.g., Modern Textiles opening its own showrooms, *Amadeus,* in metro cities). Likewise, an organisation may also integrate forward by going in for manufacturing value-added finished products from its own produce. Essar Gujarat's project for making HR steel coils from its own produce, sponge iron, would be one such example of forward integration.

D. Buffering

Vertical integration requires high investments, and it may not always be possible for the organisation to use such a costly method for controlling environmental fluctuations. An alternative is to create buffers at the input and output ends to take care of the variations in the demand and supplies. Buffers protect the basic operating functions, e.g., production, from getting affected by environmental changes. For example, organisations maintain high inventories of raw material and spare parts, so that market fluctuations in their availability do not hamper with the core manufacturing process. Similarly, many organisations, which operate in a seasonal market (e.g., fertilisers or textbooks), maintain an inventory of finished goods to offset these seasonal fluctuations.

E. Smoothening

This is yet another strategy which helps the organisations to level out the impact of environmental fluctuations. The example of Business Today, given at the beginning of this Chapter, is one such instance of smoothening. By offering a heavy discount on the annual subscription over the newsstand price, the magazine attracted a large number of annual subscribers, and thus, smoothened the demand. Moreover, by capturing enough subscribers, this strategy would have helped the publishers to maintain economies of scales, as well as attract more advertisers.

Smoothening is often an effectively used strategy to counter an environment where fluctuations in demand are predictable, but extreme. That is, the organisation has to deal with overload at one time, and under-utilisation at another. By offering attractive incentives to the customer, the organisation manages to even out the load between extremes to manageable limits. The differential rates at different times of the day for long-distance calls, offered by the telephones department, is one such example of smoothening strategy. Similarly, one finds that organisations dealing in seasonally used items fridges, air-conditioners, heaters, and even the hotel industry, offering off-season discounts to smoothen out the demand fluctuations.

F. Advertising

Advertising is an effective and popular way of coping with, and even influencing, the environment. Effective advertising aims at luring the customers to buy the product/service, and thus, helps in creating brand loyalty, reducing competitive pressure, and thereby stabilising demand. For example the success of *Pan Parag* (which increased its sales from a mere Rs. 43 lacs in 1984-85 to more than Rs 70 crore in 1989-90), is largely attributed to its Rs. 2 crore annual expenditure on advertising. Moreover, effective advertisements also help in creating awareness by educating the existing as well as potential customers about the products/ services being offered by the organisation. The three advertisements of Skypak in 1984, for instance, when the company was merely a Rs. 35 lacs enterprise, helped the company in creating a new market for courier service in the country. By the end of the year, the organisation's turnover had increased to about Rs. 1 crore.

In recent years, advertising has also been used for corporate image building, examples being, Tata Steel's "We also make steel" advertisements and ITC's "Made in India" media campaign. Effectively used, such advertisements can significantly influence the environment. Not only do they build loyalty among the customers by projecting an appropriate image of the organisation (professional, humanistic, quality conscious, innovative, etc.), they also increase the investors' confidence, and help in raising financial resources.

G. Contracting

In many situations, it is possible for the organisation to control key elements of the environment by entering into a contract with them. Long-term fixed contracts, either for purchase of supplies or for sale of outputs, protect the organisations from the vagaries of the environment. For example, the yearly contract which many offices have with an agency for the printing and supply of stationary items, helps them to operate within their budget since price fluctuations in the market do not affect their supplies. Similarly, many organisations, in the business of soaps, confectionaries, paper napkins, etc. enter into long-term contracts with different hotels as suppliers. This not only stabilises the supplies for the hotels, but, for the supplying organisations also, it makes the demand pattern more predictable and stable. In fact, contracting a dealership network, which is a popular strategy with most consumer product organisations, is itself a way of reducing part of environmental uncertainty. Through entering into a contract with the dealers, organisations ensure that their output would reach the customers on a regular basis.

H. Mergers/Acquisitions/Strategic Alliances

These strategies, which can be generally termed as **coalescing** (Robbins, 1987), are becoming more and more popular in our country, particularly so since the changes in government policies have lessened the monopoly restrictions. Such methods definitely give a strategic advantage to the organisations, in that they help in supplementing lacking organisational resources and competencies. Through mergers, acquisitions and strategic alliances, organisations get an opportunity to widen their customer base, offload or utilise the surplus capacity, integrate vertically, use each other's strengths, and so on. For example, the acquisition (or "merger", as the business press reported it) of Tata Oil Mills Company Limited. (TOMCO) by Hindustan Lever Limited (HLL) in March, 1993, gave an obvious strategic advantage to HLL. Not only did HLL eliminate a major competitive factor through this deal, but it also acquired TOMCO's stronghold on the southern Indian market, which included its four manufacturing plants, 2400 stockists and about a million retail outlets. For the Tatas too, it was a beneficial deal, since they could sell off a loss-making unit, which in any case did not fit with their core business strategy.

Similarly, the strategic alliance between Godrej Soaps Limited and Proctor and Gamble India Limited in January 1993 was aimed to give both companies a competitive advantage. On the one hand, it helped Godrej Soaps Limited to offload its unutilised manufacturing capacity, use the research facilities provided by Proctor and Gamble, and to focus primarily on plantation, chemicals and biotechnology. For P & G India, on the other hand, it opened up the opportunity to use the marketing and distribution network of Godrej Soaps (which covers over 2 million outlets), along with the use of Godrej soap brands, which had a 25 per cent market share in the premium segment. Besides, this partnership gives both companies greater strength to compete with their common rival in the soap and detergent market, Hindustan Lever Limited.

I. Lobbying

To many, lobbying carries a somewhat negative and unethical connotation. It is, however, a much practised method of managing environment, used by most industries. By attempting to get a favourable treatment from the government (in terms of concessions, financial support, quick clearances, etc.), organisations are able to exercise a certain amount of control over the environmental uncertainties. While individual companies are known to have varying amount of political/government connections, a fair degree of lobbying effort is above-board and quite normal. In many industrial sectors, organisations join together to form federations, consortiums and associations as a means of influencing the environmental elements which they have to face together. For example, in 1992, the central sector power corporations decided to form a consortium to bargain with the banks and financial institutions on the issue of interest rates on their taxable bonds. Likewise, many business forums, e.g., FICCI, CII and ASSOCHEM, are the usual means through which a group of industries try to mould the environment.

Often, these associations serve another purpose, besides endeavouring for changes in the environment, external to a particular industrial sector—they also help in stabilising the business environment within that sector. Many such forums evolve agreements on the internal business practices and codes of conduct, which become binding on all member organisations. For instance, the Advertising Association of India does not permit its member organisations to handle the account of a client if he is in dispute with another member of the association. Such codes and agreements keep the unhealthy competition in the industry under check, and thus, reduce the environmental uncertainty for the member organisations.

5 Organisational Strategy and Structure

1. The product portfolio of the Transelektra group of companies is a curious mix. Known more for its insect and mosquito repellents, *GoodKnight* and *Hit,* Transelektra is in a variety of businesses, which include making films; publishing magazines; making and selling baby diapers; manufacturing paper products like packaging paper, greeting cards and leisure stationary; producing PTC resistors and exporting textiles and wire ropes. All these ventures have been successful too. From its inception in 1984 till the year 1991, the turnover of the group increased from Rs. 1 crore to Rs 33 crores.
2. Despite its growth and dominance, Bajaj Auto Ltd has chosen not to diversify. It remains an engineering-based company in the two-wheeler market, where, inspite of the increased competition, it enjoys a 48 percent market share (figures for 1991-92). The company is known for its strength in product quality, and to keep the costs of engineering design low, it has relied on larger volumes to give it economies of scales. This focus on an efficient production process and upgradation of technology can be seen at all levels in the company.
3. For a long time the Pune based company, Alfa-Laval was known as a specialised manufacturer of dairy machinery equipment. During the later part of the 80's, however, the company diversified into many new activities, such as project engineering, designing and engineering custom built plants for the beverages and oil-processing industries, manufacturing centrifugal separators and heat exchangers for power and steel plants, and producing pilot fermenters for pharmaceutical and biotech industries. Through these diversifications, the company has also grown, increasing its turnover from about Rs 50 crores in 1987 to Rs 145 crores in 1992. However, while spreading its risks across various activities, the company still retains its basic aim of maintaining its leading edge in technology.

Organisations, apparently, can be successful in different ways. The above examples highlight the fact that not only do different organisations pursue their goals and objectives in their individualised idiosyncratic manner, but they also have a number of options in designing strategies for responding to the environment. In the previous Chapter, we mentioned that the environment does not directly influence the organisation; rather, the environmental influences are tempered by the managerial perceptions and choices. In this Chapter we will take a look at the choices and options, which managers exercise in formulating strategies, and their implications for organisational design.

I. WHAT IS STRATEGY?

The origins of the concept of strategy do not lie in management. but in the field of military sciences. In fact, the term strategy derives from the Greek term *strategos,* which means "the art of the general", i.e., the behavioral and psychological skills required for the role of a general. Its inclusion in the management sciences is as recent as about three decades back, when, possibly the growing competition in business (and therefore, the possibilities of winning and losing) gave rise to the metaphor of business as a battle-field. Quinn (1980) analysed how certain features of successful strategies (e.g., clarity, maintaining the initiative or surprise) are common, "whether in business, government or warfare."

To grow and prosper, an organisation not only needs objectives, but also a plan of action to achieve these objectives; it needs a well-defined scope, direction and methodology of growth. To quote Ansoff (1965), "concept of the firm's business" is commonly known as strategy. Glueck (1972) defined the corporate strategy as:

> an integrated functional plan in response to a problem perceived to be thrust upon the company by the environment, or in response to initiations of the corporation to change the impact the company wishes to have on the environment.

One must note three critical features in this definition: (i) a strategy refers to an integrated organisational response affecting the whole organisation, and not to an isolated decision, (ii) it is a consistent response to environmental demands and opportunities, and/or (iii) it is an initiative by the organisation to change the environment.

Viewed in this manner, strategic decisions intervene between the organisation and its operating environment, with the purpose of finding a fit between the two (which may also include redefinition of either the operating environment or the nature of organisation itself). Andrews (1972) noted that an organisation's strategy can be seen as an optimal match between the environmental opportunities and threats and the organisational strengths and weaknesses. This matching expresses itself in the form of a definition of organisational goals and objectives, and its plans for achieving them. Figure 5.1 shows this relationship between strategy, environment and the organisation.

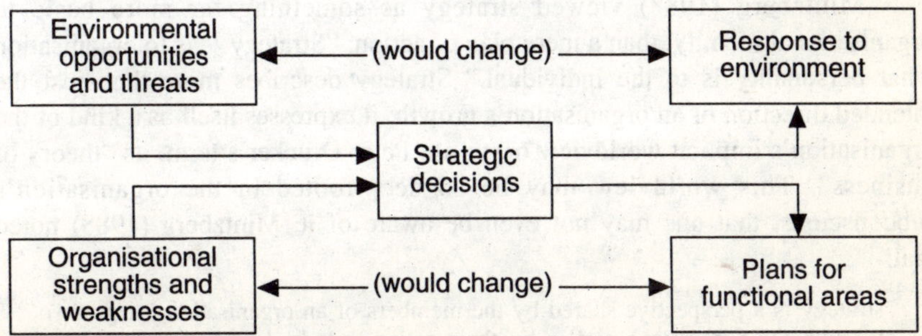

Figure 5.1 The relationship between the organisation, environment and strategic choices.

The earlier literature on strategy (Ansoff, 1965; Glueck, 1972) conceptualised it as consciously and purposefully devised plan, which is laid out and finalised well ahead of action. According to this approach, successful strategic plans must incorporate the following:

1. a systematic analysis of the organisation's internal situation and its external environment;
2. identification of relevant and viable long-range corporate goals;
3. development of systems of control, monitoring and feedback; and,
4. action planning for the implementation of the plans.

Indeed, some of the 'tools and techniques' of strategic planning of the late sixties (e.g., Portfolio Analysis, SWOT Analysis) were based on this very normative view of strategy as a plan.

Another, comparatively more recent, approach views strategy in a more descriptive manner. While the strategy of an organisation does determine its goals and choices, it is not necessary that these are always clearly spelt out. As a matter of fact, a number of organisations inspite of not having a well documented corporate plan, show a remarkable consistency in their strategic decisions. Mintzberg (1988) suggested that strategy should be understood as a pattern or perspective which emerges through the stream of significant corporate decisions. Lorsch (1986) also defined strategy similarly:

> By strategy I mean the stream of decisions taken over time by top managers, which, when understood as a whole, reveal the goals they are seeking and the means used to achieve these goals... it does not refer to an explicit plan. In fact, by my definition strategy may be implicit as well explicit.

For example, the corporate histories of many Indian organisations show a distinct pattern in the manner in which they grew and responded to environmental demands (RPG Enterprise has followed a direction of growth through acquisitions; Essar Group has grown through interlinked diversifications in the core-sector; Reliance Industries has consistently practised backward integration, and so on). Inspite of their consistency, it is not likely that these directions of growth were planned and documented at a single point of time. Strategy, thus, is not always defined and decided—rather, it evolves.

Mintzberg (1988) viewed strategy as something far more basic to organisational identity, than a mere plan of action: "Strategy… is to organisation what personality is to the individual." Strategy describes more than just the intended direction of an organisation's growth; it expresses itself as a kind of the organisation's implicit worldview or, to use Peter Drucker's term, its "theory of business". This worldview may be so deep-rooted in the organisation's subconscious, that one may not even be aware of it. Mintzberg (1988) noted that:

> strategy is a perspective shared by the members of an organisation (or group) through their intentions and/or by their action… Indeed, a perspective may become so ingrained in behaviour that the associated beliefs can become subconscious. When that happens, perspective can look more like pattern than

> like plan—in other words, it can be found more in consistency of behaviour than in articulation of intention.

Similarly, Greiner (1983) viewed strategy as an expression of organisational culture, rather than a consciously planned decision:

> Strategy evolves from inside the organisation—not from its future environment... Strategy is a deeply engrained and continuing pattern of management behaviour that gives direction to the organisation—not a manipulable and controllable mechanism that can be easily changed from one year to the next. Strategy is a non-rational concept stemming from the informal values, traditions, and norms of behaviour held by the firm's managers and employees—not a rational, formal, conscious and predetermined thought process engaged in by top executives. Strategy emerges out of the cumulative effect of many informal actions and decisions, taken daily over the years by many employees—not a "one shot" statement developed exclusively by top management for distribution to the organisation.

One would notice that these two views of strategy (as a plan and as a perspective) are actually not contradictory. A perspective can give rise to a plan, and a plan may (though not always) reflect an underlying perspective. In a way, they refer to the visible and submerged parts of the organisational iceberg, which we discussed in the first Chapter. The planning approach focuses more on the organisational response to the external environment, and refers primarily to the conscious and tangible part of the organisational strategy. The view of strategy as a perspective, on the other hand, pays greater attention to the underlying collective cultural sub-strata of the organisation, in which strategy becomes the core of organisational identity.

II. THE STRATEGY—STRUCTURE LINK

The strategic choice of an organisation not only determines its response to the environment, but also has a significant influence on the happenings within the organisation. It would seem quite natural that the organisation must develop a structure to meet its strategic goals and targets. As Drucker (1974) noted:

> Structure is a means for attaining the objectives and goals of an institution. Any work on structure must therefore start with objectives and strategy.

In his classic study, linking the strategy to structure, Chandler (1962) traced the development of nearly a hundred large American enterprises (e.g., Du Pont, General Motors, Sears) over a period of half a century. He found that as these organisation grew from single product companies to multiple product companies their structures also changed in a consistent manner. Initially, as small companies manufacturing a single product, the structures were characterised by high centralisation, coupled with low complexity and formalisation. However, as the organisations expanded their activities within the same industry, they had to be structured along functional lines, increasing the need for more complex coordination. Finally, as the organisations diversified into different products, they had to structure themselves into autonomous product-based divisional units. Based on these findings, Chandler concluded:

> A new strategy required a new or at least refashioned structure if the enlarged enterprise was to be operated efficiently.... Unless new structures are developed to meet new administrative needs, which result from an expansion of a firm's activities into new areas, functions, or product lines, the technological, financial, and personnel economies of growth and size cannot be realized.

In a certain sense, Chandler's thesis seems logical as well. If strategy is a pointer towards the ends, then structure provides the means to achieve those ends. There needs to be a synchronisation between the ends and the means. Any strategic decision (such as about product mix, customer mix, acquisition plan, diversification, etc.) would necessarily have implications for various multi-functional and functional decisions within the organisation (see Table 5.1).

Table 5.1 The Influence of Strategic Decisions on Multi-functional and Functional Decisions

Decision levels	Examples
Strategic decisions	• What domain should one operate in? • How to grow? through vertical integration, unrelated diversification, or by maintaining a niche market? • What should be one's product mix? customer mix? • What should be the organisation's competitive emphasis? etc.
Multifunctional coordinative decisions	• What should be the policy for resource allocation? financing policy? pricing policy? • How should the activities and functions be structured? what is the right organisational structure? • What kind of management information system would suit the needs of coordinating different departments/divisions? etc.
Functionally dependent decisions	• What should be the plant capacity? the production schedules? • How does one design an appropriate distribution network? • What working capital is required for departmental/divisional activities? • How much manpower is required for the departmental/ divisional activities? etc.

For example, if a company decides to become a market leader in a highly competitive market, it may (among other alternatives) choose to compete through offering a standardised product at the least price. To succeed with this strategic choice, the company must strive for tighter cost-controls, along with larger volumes of production to achieve economies of scales. These objectives, in turn, would affect many internal organisational decisions, such as financial control systems, reporting procedure and structures, plant capacities, production schedules, distribution networks, etc. To achieve the low-cost option, the company may even decide to become global in order to gain access to low-cost inputs and a wider market base to consume larger productions (thereby, increasing its complexity and need for decentralisation).

Thus to be effective, the *structure must follow the strategy.*

III. STRATEGIC CHOICES AS ADAPTATION PROCESS: A STRATEGIC TYPOLOGY OF ORGANISATIONS

It can be seen from the preceding discussion that in order to effectively execute any given strategy, organisations need to rearrange themselves, so as to align themselves with the environmental demands. Unfortunately, most researchers on strategy (e.g., Ansoff, 1965; Porter, 1980), while recognising that the internal systems and dynamics of the organisation have a direct bearing on strategy implementation, have focused primarily on the specific nature of the market environment and the required strategic response. These studies have largely neglected dealing with the specific structural requirements to support the strategic posture. On the other hand, the organisational behaviour studies which have dealt with specific structural reforms carried out by organisations to meet the environmental pressures (e.g., Burns and Stalker,1961; Lawrence and Lorsch, 1967), have analysed the market environment in a somewhat abstract and undifferentiated manner. Very few studies and conceptualisations have comprehensively integrated the marketing and behavioural aspects of strategy. In this section, we will discuss one such integrating framework (Miles and Snow, 1978).

Miles and Snow (1978) viewed successful strategy implementation as a process of establishing internal organisational mechanisms (roles, systems, structure, managerial processes, etc.) which would complement the organisation's market strategy. Thus, strategic decision-making process is essentially an adaptive process aiming at "maintaining an effective alignment with the environment while managing internal interdependencies". In other words, the organisational behaviour is not directly determined by the environmental conditions. Rather, the strategic choices made by the key members of the organisation (top management, power coalitions, etc.) mediate between the environment and the organisation. These choices are the major determinants of organisational structure and processes.

Through their studies, Miles and Snow (1978) identified three basic "problems" which the organisations must identify, confront and solve, in order to successfully adapt to the environment. These are:

1. Entrepreneurial problem. This involves the problem of specifically and concretely defining an organisation's domain; the product(s) or service(s) it chooses to offer; and its target market or market segment. The solution of this problem is essential for orienting organisational energies and resources in proper directions.

2. Engineering problem. This involves the problem of operationalising the management's solution to the entrepreneurial problem. This would involve the selection of an appropriate technology (input-transformation-output process) to ensure the proper production and distribution of the chosen products or services.

3. Administrative problem. This involves the rationalising and stabilising of the organisation's activities. This would involve (a) designing of appropriate organisational structures and systems for uncertainty reduction, and (b) creating mechanisms which would allow the organisation to continue to adapt and innovate in response to changing environmental demands.

One would notice that these three "problems" are not independent of each other, but are interrelated. The solution to the entrepreneurial problem would determine the selection of the appropriate technology (engineering problem), which in turn, would determine the required organisational structure and systems. For instance, in response to an uncertain market environment, an organisation may decide to reduce its risks by diversifying into many different sunrise industries (e.g., computer software, financial consultancy, travel and tourism, export of ready-made garments). In this manner, the management would be spreading out its investments in many domains, which though unrelated and risky, offer a fast growth-rate. Failure in one, thus, is likely to be compensated by success in others.

Having solved its entrepreneurial problem in this manner, the next step would be to operationalise this solution by selecting an appropriate technology (input-transformation-output process). In this case, the organisation must develop ways of working, which are diverse, flexible and allow the organisation to respond quickly to environmental exigencies. Thus, the solution to the engineering problem would lie in development of multiple technologies/ways of working, which rely on the skill and discretion of people down the line. In turn, the appropriate administrative solution would lie in the development of decentralised structures which emphasise those functions and activities (such as marketing), which are in direct contact with the environment.

Besides providing a model of the organisational process of adaptation (and specifying the kind of decisions which are required for effective alignment to environment), Miles and Snow (1978) also described a framework for classifying organisations according to their strategic choices. They identified three essential strategic types of organisations: **Defenders, Analysers,** and **Prospectors.** Each of these organisational types is faced with different entrepreneurial problems, and correspondingly, each attempts to adapt to the environment in a different manner. That is, each one differs from the other in the manner in which it defines and solves its engineering and administrative problems (see Table 5.2). Each of these types of organisations has a specific kind of strategy for dealing with its market environment, and is characterised by a consistent configuration of technology, structure and processes to support the chosen strategy.

A. Defenders

Defender organisations adapt a strategic posture which aims at achieving stability in their market environment. This strategic posture emerges from the way they define and solve their entrepreneurial problem which is how to seal off a portion of the total market environment to create a stable domain. The solution to this problem, as chosen by them, is through producing a narrow range of products or services, and thereby, concentrating on a narrow segment of the present or

Table 5.2 Differences in Adaptation Problems of the Three Strategic Types (based on Miles and Snow, 1978)

Adaptation problems	Strategic types		
	Defender	Analyser	Prospector
Entrepreneurial	How to seal off a portion of total market to create a stable domain.	How to locate and exploit new product/ market while simultaneously maintaining a firm base of traditional products and customers.	How to locate and exploit new product/ market opportunities.
Engineering	How to produce and distribute goods/services as efficiently as possible.	How to be efficient in stable portion of the domain and flexible in the changing domain.	How to avoid long term commitment to a single technological process.
Administrative	How to achieve strict control of the organisation in order to ensure efficiency.	How to differentiate the organisation's structure and processes to accommodate both stable and dynamic areas of operation.	How to facilitate rather than control organisational operation.

potential market. Since the entry of a competitor would create uncertainty, this domain is also aggressively defended through such economic actions as competitive pricing, high quality products, etc.

The growth pattern of the defenders also represents their strategic orientation, which is that of cautious and incremental growth through market penetration (as opposed to diversification). Since the focus of these organisations is narrow and specific, developments outside their chosen domain are not of much concern to them. Most of their product development efforts are limited to those which are closely related to their current objectives.

The solutions to the engineering problem faced by the defenders (i.e., how to produce and distribute products/services as efficiently as possible) are closely linked to their entrepreneurial solutions. If the organisation aims to produce a competitive product/service for a specific segment of the market, it must establish a reliable and cost-efficient method of doing so. Correspondingly, these organisations develop a single-core technology (or one single way of doing things), which is efficient, economical and time-tested. Major resources are also invested in technological improvement to improve efficiency. Many defender organisations attempt to achieve technological efficiency through vertical integration, that is, through successively incorporating various stages of the production process from raw material supply to the distribution of the products.

It is but natural that for the defenders, the administrative problem would be that of maintaining a strict control on the organisation so as to ensure efficiency and predictability of its operations. These organisations achieve this aim by becoming *mechanistic* (Burns and Stalker, 1961). That is, they develop structures which are characterised by high centralisation with extreme division of labour (functional structures), communication through formal and rigidly defined hierarchical channels, and an orientation to intensively plan and implement long-term schedules to control costs and maintain/improve efficiency. Production and cost-control experts mostly dominate the decision-making process in these organisations, with the result that the organisational performance is more often measured against internally set targets (e.g., against previous year's achievements) than against externally determined criteria (e.g., market-share).

It would be apparent that the defender strategy is ideally suited for a stable market environment. Examples of a defender (or near defender) strategy abound in business environment, particularly in those industries which are less prone to technological and market change. For example, the strategy followed by TISCO till the early 1990's very nearly corresponded to a defender type (see Exhibit 5.1).

Exhibit 5.1

Tata Iron & Steel Company (TISCO): The Defender Strategy

Being in the core-sector in an administered economy till early 90's, TISCO enjoyed a stable environment. Till the steel prices were decontrolled, its success depended on producing large volumes of steel in the most efficient and economical manner. This, it did by routinising its operations, developing a tall and functionally centralised organisational structure, and extreme division of labour (in 1993, it had almost a thousand job titles and 18 hierarchical levels in the managerial cadre). The emphasis in the company has traditionally been more on manufacturing and financial controls, than on marketing and product development.

To maintain the stability of its operating environment, it also integrated vertically, maintaining captive iron-ore and coal mines for its raw materials at one end, and developing a network of subsidiaries/divisions which produce value-added finished products (bearings, bars, rod, etc.) on the output end. The extensively well-administered town (Jamshedpur) has further helped in providing stability to the socio-political environment in which the organisation operates (e.g., besides providing housing and leasing out land for construction of own house on company loan, TISCO manages the medical facilities, runs schools, provides tribal and rural development services, and so on). Similarly, the personnel policies of the company also encourage total involvement of/with the employees (e.g., one member from the retired employee's family is entitled for a job in the company, local cultural festivals/sports event are organised by the company, etc.) which help in maintaining industrial peace. It is not surprising that TISCO, over the years continued to show consistent growth and, inspite of its primitive manufacturing facilities (as compared to the public sector giant SAIL), maintained high-levels of efficiency.

While the defender strategy, with its emphasis on organisational stability and technological efficiency provides sufficient strength to the organisation to cope with minor fluctuations in the environment, it becomes a major liability and even a threat to its own survival in case of a major shift in the market. The organisational efficiency, which is rooted in heavy investments in core technology and in high amount of routinisation of activities, becomes a major hurdle in technological change to meet the new market demands. Similarly, the formalised mechanistic structure creates problems for the organisation to swiftly respond to environmental changes. For instance, the very same characteristics which were the strengths of Bajaj Auto, also became its problems when it had to face a competitive and changing market (see Exhibit 5.2).

Exhibit 5.2

Bajaj Auto Ltd: Changing Strategic Orientation

Yet another organisation belonging to defender type, Bajaj Auto (which was quoted at the beginning of this Chapter) had, for years, enjoyed a stable and undifferentiated market. Till recent years, the company had operated on principles of high volumes, high quality and low costs. It had worked through tight and highly formalised controls and schedules, and the organisational activities were coordinated through 11 hierarchical levels; the company derived stability by cautiously investing profits in financial instruments; and, the marketing efforts were limited to efficient dispatch and distribution of the two-wheelers, which was achieved by maintaining a network of 900 dealers and 1400 delivery trucks. The production and engineering functions were considered dominant in the organisation. In fact, till 1987, Bajaj Auto didn't even have a well-defined marketing function, and in 1988-89, it spent barely Rs. 1.68 crores on R&D (out of a turnover of more than a thousand crore).

These same strengths, however, started becoming weaknesses once the company had to face competition from global rivals in an increasingly fragmented market. While the company enjoyed complete dominance in the 150cc scooter market, after mid-80's the two-wheeler market split into a number of segments (50cc and 80cc mopeds, 100cc and 150cc scooters, two-stroke and four-stroke motercycles). Moreover, the competitors offered better designs and more fuel efficient models. Bajaj Auto's production capacity of one million vehicles per year made it particularly vulnerable to changes in the market. While Bajaj Auto diversified its product range to enter the motercycle and moped markets, it took time to do so, and even then the basic designs of its products were obsolete by international comparisons.

In 1992, to avoid losing to its competitors, the company embarked on renovating itself by cutting down the hierarchy from eleven to six, increasing its R&D budget to Rs. 23 crores, giving greater autonomy to its four divisions, creating decentralised groups for tackling key organisational issues, e.g., cost-reduction, HRD, business planning, product development, vendor development, and encouraging cross-hierarchical problem-solving among employees.

B. Prospectors

Prospector organisations can be understood as antithesis of the defenders. They function in a perceived operating environment which is dynamic and uncertain. Correspondingly, their entrepreneurial problem is how to locate and develop new products and markets. Often these organisations develop a corporate image of innovators, entering into new, and sometimes risky, ventures. To maintain a broad and continuously developing domain, these organisations perpetually scan and monitor a wide range of environmental conditions, trends and events. They quickly respond to new opportunities, often creating new markets in their respective industries. This ability to create change (which is often in spurts, rather than gradual) also gives them a competitive advantage over their rivals.

In contrast to the defenders (whose choice of products/markets is determined by their existing technological capability), for the prospectors, the choice of technology is contingent upon the company's current *and* future product/ market strategy. Since these organisations perceive their environment as changing, any major investment in a single routine technology, will hamper with their flexibility. Correspondingly, their engineering problem is that of how to avoid long-term commitment to a single type of technological process. This is accomplished by creating multiple, prototypical technologies, which are flexible and low on mechanisation. Often these highly entrepreneurial organisations postpone investments in comprehensive production facilities till late in their market development process, relying on vendors, sub-contracting, or on sharing facilities. Such a strategy gives them flexibility to move in and out of markets without getting tied down (though, of course, it may decrease their profitability).

Given the changing domains and flexible technologies, the administrative problem of the prospector organisations can be defined as *how to facilitate rather than control organisational operations.* They accomplish this by developing *organic* (Burns and Stalker, 1961) organisational structures. The prospectors need to design organisational systems which permit flexible coordination among their diverse units. This is possible by developing structures which are highly decentralised, characterised by low division of labour and informal ways of working, and encourage lateral communication and team work. Prospectors, unlike defenders, mostly do not have a fixed long-range plan. Rather, their planning is broad, developmental and oriented towards problem-solving (it emerges through a series of market-oriented decisions). Given the nature of their strategic goals, marketing and research functions play a dominant role in organisational decision-making. However, power and influence in the organisation is likely to shift with changes in the kind of problems being tackled by the organisation.

Prospector type of organisations are more often found in nascent industries which offer a vast growth potential to entrepreneurial companies. For instance, HCL Ltd. flourished during the 80's, when computers was a sun-rise industry, and offered a fertile ground for prospectors to flourish (see Exhibit 5.3). Prospectors, however, do not always depend on favourable environmental conditions to cash on. Rather, through their entrepreneurial decisions, they also affect changes in the market. Super Cassettes Industries, for example, created a new market for music by offering products such as cheap cassettes, version recording, music bank, etc. (see Exhibit 5.4).

As in the case of the defenders, the prospectors are also likely to fall victims of their strengths. Their high risk-taking propensity can make them

Exhibit 5.3

HCL LTD.: Prospecting A New Market

The erstwhile HCL Ltd., at least till late 1980's, showed many characteristics of a prospector firm. Established by six young professionals in 1976, it grew up to be the country's number one computer company in a span of twelve years. It had many "firsts" to its credit. It was first Indian company to launch an indigenously designed minicomputer, single board desktop computer, and multiprocessor Supermini Computer System. It was also the first in India to implement Unix V.3 and the first in the Indian private sector to start an institute for information technology by setting up NIIT. It was also the first Indian computer firm to export computers to America, and so on.

Its decisions were often risky, but helped in changing the market structure. For example, in 1986 HCL slashed down the price of its PC to Rs. 20,000, causing a demand boom. Similarly, it was the first company to start using five and half inch floppy drive, even when it was not recognised as the international standard. To spread out its risks, it diversified into many other ventures, e.g., reprographics, telecommunication, softwares, peripherals, instrumentations, computer education, etc. HCL's success can be largely attributed to its quick and timely decisions, which helped it in capturing emergent markets, its strong reliance on marketing and advertising, and its formidable R&D base (it spent an unimaginable sum of Rs. 7.5 crores to develop its supermini, Magnum). On the personnel side, its functioning relied heavily on the initiative, skills and competence of its people, which it took care to nurture and develop.

Exhibit 5.4

Super Cassettes Industries: Creating a New Market

In a span of about a decade, till 1989, the Super Cassettes Industries (more widely known for its T-Series cassettes) had grown from virtual scratch to a Rs 215 crore turnover company, capturing 60 percent share of the audio cassettes market. The company has been innovative in changing and creating new domains. Through offering cheap, low-quality cassettes, it enlarged the market for a product, which till then was targeted only to the elites. When rivals cropped up in this domain, the company went for version recording (old numbers sung by new singers). When others started version recording, it started bidding for music rights for new films (sometimes even before the music was composed). It even innovated the idea of a "music bank" from which the film producers could choose best available songs to retrofit their movies. Starting from selling low-priced, substandard recorded music cassettes, over a short span, Super Cassettes diversified to a variety of businesses: manufacturing of video cassettes, televisions tapedecks; video recording; compact-disc players; film magazines; film distribution; film production and detergents.

Initially, the company had no manufacturing facility of its own. Rather, it bought cheap imported cassettes, recorded and sold them. It was only when the market had sufficiently expanded that it put up its' own cassette manufacturing plant. Even later, while Super Cassettes Industries remained the flagship of the group, its cassette business was spread over six other companies (viz., Jagdamba Electronics, Tony Electronics, Krishna International, Super Electronics, Gulshan Cassettes, and Vee Gee Electronics). Each manufacturing operation being small, it is easier to operate and manage. The corporate structure remained lean, devoid of any formalised bureaucratic setup.

particularly vulnerable to the inevitable "failure rate" associated with innovative ventures. This is likely to result in low profitability and over-extension of resources. For example, many of HCL Ltd.'s ventures turned out to be failures, and while it increased its sales and captured a large market-share for its products, it earned a bad reputation for its inability to back-up the sales with sufficient after-sales service. Similarly, Super Cassettes Industries had to move out of its diversification into VCR, VCP and colour TVs on account of low profitability. Due to such "failures", prospector organisations often find it difficult to operate at maximum levels of efficiency. Moreover, their tendency to diversify into a variety of businesses puts undue pressure on organisational systems for integration. Drucker (1974) noted that an "extreme diversity of businesses makes a company unmanageable". While such organisations try to maintain high levels of flexibility, this can lead to underutilisation/misutilisation of resources.

C. Analysers

While the defenders and prospectors represent the two ends of the strategic continuum, analysers fall somewhere in between, representing a unique blend of the two. Analyser organisations try to minimise the risks (a defender stance) while maximising the opportunities for profits (a prospector characteristic). Their entrepreneurial problem, therefore is how to locate and exploit new product and market opportunities, and at the same time simultaneously maintaining a firm core of traditional products and customers. Thus, these organisations try to achieve a balance betwen innovative diversification, while remaining close to their knitting. Their venturing into new businesses is not so much innovative as imitative. That is, they diversify into a new business only when its viability is proven and assured (often by another prospector firm). And even then, they continue to rely on their traditional products and markets for a major share of their revenues. Their environmental scanning is mostly limited to marketing (not so much to technological R&D). This results in a steady growth which is based primarily on market penetration as well as product-market development.

Correspondingly, the engineering problem of the analysers reflects the balance they try to maintain in their domain that is, how to achieve and protect an equilibrium between conflicting demands for technological flexibility and stability. Most often they achieve this by segmenting their stable core technology from the flexible component. While the core technology bears a strong resemblance to the defenders (high standardisation and routinisation, and an emphasis on cost and operational efficiency), the flexible element shows prospector-like characteristics of being low on mechanisation and formalisation, and relying heavily on the skill and initiative of personnel. These two are integrated by an applied research/engineering group which develops technological solutions and new products which can be achieved through the existing technological capabilities.

The administrative problem of the analysers again reflects this duality. The problem here is how to differentiate the organisational structure and processes to accommodate both stable and dynamic areas of operations. The solution to this problem is achieved by them through developing a loose matrix organisational structure. On the one hand, the structure represents a functional differentiation with the functional head (particularly the production and engineering groups) managing the stable domain. On the other hand, there are also product/brand managers (usually housed in the marketing departments), whose task is to pick up ideas for potential products and realise their offering to the market through coordination with applied engineering and production departments. While the functional departments are usually characterised by centralised controls and formalisation, the product groups are more decentralised (see Exhibit 5.5 for Bata India as an example of analyser organisation).

Exhibit 5.5

Bata India: Combining Continuity with Change

Towards the late 1980's, Bata India showed a perceptible change, by gradually diversifying into new, but synergistically complementary, product-markets. Conventionally known for its sturdy leather footwear, it now started branching out into sportswear, leisurewear garments and accessaries (e.g., ties, belts and briefcases). Correspondingly, the company also changed its image from one of shoe-makers to that of marketeers of lifestyle consumer items.

The change in Bata India's strategy could be seen not only in an increased range of 54 products (and in the creation of distinct brand identities, a concept unknown a decade ago), but also in the manner in which it segmented its market, and differentiated its stores (about 1400 of them) into super stores (for the upper-end high-value fashion segment), mega stores (for the middle class) and the Bata bazars (for lower-end and discounted products). The company was slowly becoming, according to senior executives, market-driven.

But inspite of these changes, it maintained a strong reliance on its core business (shoes still accounted for about 90 percent of its revenue). Even among footwears, the sports and casual segment (e.g., Adidas, Power) accounted for a small portion of sales, while more than 60 percent revenue came from leather footwear. Bata India's forays into new product-markets were not really innovative, in that its new products (e.g., North Star, Lotto,Weinbrenner, Marie Claire, Power, Adidas) had a proven record of success in the markets abroad. And while the company did put up a new plant in Bangalore (incorporating flexible integrated manufacturing process), it relied more on subcontracting its new high-value product lines (e.g, Marie Claire) to small outside manufacturers.

It may be worth noting here, that in some respects all organisations show some characteristics of analyser strategic type (or to put it the other way round, there are no pure defenders or pure prospectors). Even hard-core defenders do diversify into related fields (through vertical integration) and into new products, while maintaining a strong foothold in their traditional product-markets; and, the most staunch of prospectors continue to maintain at least one stable product/market (e.g., inspite of all its diversification, about 60 per cent of Super Cassettes Industry's revenue comes from its original business, music). Nevertheless, some organisations conform more to the analyser pattern as compared to others.

An analyser strategy is ideally suited for a moderately uncertain environment. Organisations adapting this strategy perceive the market as complex or differentiated, though relatively stable. This strategy, however, is difficult to pursue, particularly in an environment which is characterised by rapid technological and market change. The balance which the analysers are required to maintain between stability and flexibility not only makes them prone to loosing the equilibrium, but often, it also makes it almost inevitable for them to compromise with both their effectiveness as well as efficiency.

IV. STRATEGIC FAILURES

The discussion so far suggests that specific environmental influences warrant a certain kind of strategic response from the organisation, which in turn, must get translated into structural forms. Such a conclusion, however, fails to explain why structures often fail to follow the strategy. While we will be discussing the reasons for organisational failures in detail in Chapter 11, it is important to note here that most of the strategic failures are rooted in inflexibility within the organisation to meet the strategic requirements. For example, during the mid-1980's, when the liberalisation process started in the Indian economy, there were a spurt of diversifications in the industries. Even though the environment was conducive for new entrepreneurial efforts, yet most of these new ventures did not succeed. Often, the reasons underlying these failures was an inability of the organisation to mould itself to meet the strategic requirements.

Miles and Snow (1978) identified a fourth strategic pattern, which they called **Reactor** strategy, which inevitably contributes to organisational failures. They found this type of organisation subscribing to "a pattern of adjustment to its environment that is both inconsistent and unstable." According to their research, there are normally three major reasons for such strategic failures:

1. Top management may not have clearly articulated the organisation's strategy. This is often true of highly entrepreneurial companies, where the overall organisational vision and goal is in the mind of one person, whose departure may leave the organisation without any direction.

2. The management has not fully shaped the organisation's structure and processes to fit the chosen strategy. For instance, while the company may decide to embark on competitive diversification, the research, product development and marketing functions may not be sufficiently strengthened for the task.

3. The management may maintain the organisation's current strategy-structure relationship despite overwhelming changes in environmental conditions. This is often true of the highly conservative, internally-driven organisations which fail to perceive and respond to changes in the environment.

Thus, while it is true that structure must follow strategy, the actual relationship between the two is far more complex. We had noted earlier that one of the implications of viewing strategy as a pattern of decisions is the recognition of its rootedness in the endemic organisational culture and systems. If one views the organisational structure as consisting of more than the lifeless boxes in the organisational chart, and also as including the organisational processes of relating, interacting and coordinating with each other (i.e., as "process structure"), then it is easy to recognise that often *it is the strategy which is determined by the structure.* While we will discuss this aspect of organisational performance in some later Chapters, one must be cognisant of the complexity of strategy-structure link. To quote Waterman (1982):

> It is not enough to think about strategy implementation as only a matter of strategy and structure. The conventional wisdom used to be, that if you first get the strategy right, the right organisation follows... We find in practice, however, that these notions are too limiting. To think comprehensively about a new strategy and problems in carrying it out, a manager must think of his company as a unique culture and must think about the ability of the company to get anything really fundamental (i.e., not tactical) accomplished as a matter of moving the whole culture.

6 Technological Determinants of Organisational Design

Compare a large readymade garments factory with a tailoring shop. While both are in the business of making ready-to-wear garments, yet they differ significantly from each other. The readymade garments unit produces as many garments in a day, as the tailoring shop might be able to produce in a month or more. The difference is not so much due to size of the organisation, as due to the nature of technology and product. The readymade garments factory works with standard designs and sizes, while the tailoring shop must attempt each job for its particular requirements, to meet each customer's specifications and demands. One would expect that given these two different natures of jobs, the two work-places would also be organised differently. Jobs in the garment factory are more likely to be routinised to ensure maximum operating efficiency, while the work in the tailoring shop would be structured in a more informal and non-standardised manner.

This simple example highlights a somewhat obvious aspect of organisational design: technology. Besides other factors, technology is a critical determinant of the organisational structure.

I. WHAT IS TECHNOLOGY?

Technology refers to the manner in which organisational input is transformed into its output. It deals with the information, equipment, techniques and processes required to achieve this transformation. It is also important to note that while the term technology has a manufacturing/technical connotation, all organisations convert their inputs into outputs. Whether the organisation is a manufacturing firm, advertising agency, hospital, bank or a trading house, it will use some sort of technology to transform its inputs (skills, machines, material, or money) into viable products or services as it outputs. An automobile company, for example, uses technology to convert the raw material into vehicles, just like a bank uses techniques and processes to convert money, ideas, human labour and skills to provide banking services.

Studies on technology have focused on two kinds of impacts which technology has on the organisation. One line of research has concerned itself with the kind of satisfaction/alienation different technologies produce among the employees. The other line of research has explored how different characteristics of technology influence the organisational structure. These studies have used different conceptualisations to define technology. Nevertheless, certain variables (e.g., nature of work, knowledge/skill required for the job, interdependence among jobs) recur across the various frameworks, which are crucial for our understanding of technological implications for organisations. In this Chapter, we will look at three of these seminal models, which have contributed much to the understanding of how technology influences the organisational structure and control mechanisms. Moreover, while the choice of technology is often circumscribed by the organisational strategy, we will also look at the options available to managers for making the jobs more meaningful and enriching for their employees.

II. NATURE OF TECHNOLOGICAL INFLUENCES

Over the years, a number of studies (e.g., Hage and Aiken, 1967; Hunt, 1970; Mahoney and Frost, 1974; Hickson et al. 1979; Gerwin, 1979; Mills and Moberg, 1982) have attempted to identify the relationship between technology and the organisational structure. But the findings of these studies have been far from clearcut, sometimes even contradicting each other. They do, nevertheless, support the basic contention that technology does influence the structure. The apparent contradictions in the findings appear to be more indicative of the complexity of the concept and the nature of influences, rather than raising questions about the validity of the idea of "technological imperative". As Hage and Aiken (1969) observed:

> The difficulty in finding a general variable describing technology stems from the fact that the concept subsumes many different ideas. The construct is so rich that it would be better to treat it like that of the concept of social structure.

While we will look at the nature of this complexity later in this Chapter, let us start by discussing three basic models, described by Woodward (1965), Thompson (1967) and Perrow (1967), which provide broad frameworks for understanding the nature of technological influences.

A. Technological Complexity: Woodward's Study

Joan Woodward's study (1965) was a pioneering work on technological determinism of the structure. Woodward studied, approximately a hundred manufacturing organisations in the southern part of England. The focus of her study was to relate the organisational structure (e.g., extent of formalisation, hierarchical levels, span of control) with organisational effectiveness. Initially she found no such discernable relationship, however, when she grouped these firms according to their production technologies, the relationship between structure and effectiveness became apparent. She found that organisations employing different production technologies required different structures in order to be effective. That is, organisational effectiveness turned out to be a function of the technology-structure fit. Woodward classified technology in terms of levels of complexity. The three levels of technological complexity identified by her were:

1. Unit or small batch technologies. In this case the product was manufactured in small batches according to the customer's specifications and the products showed a high amount of diversity and heterogeneity. This technology was characterised by a relative lack of standardisation of products, lot size, order time, delivery requirements, and production runs. Correspondingly, it was difficult to strictly plan, schedule and monitor the production operations. Examples of this technology range from small machine shops to aircraft manufacturing units.

2. Mass production technologies. At this level products of relatively uniform specifications were manufactured in large quantities. These technologies allowed high amount of routinisation of operational activities and, thus, could be standardised, scheduled and monitored. Automobile assembly line, bottling plants, etc., would be appropriate examples of this technology.

3. Continuous process technologies. These were extremely complex production systems, using highly automated and programmed activities. Like mass production technologies, these production systems also manufactured large quantities of outputs through standardised and repetitive operations. However, the transformation was achieved through a series of interlinked activities which were carried out through machines without much human intervention. Petroleum and chemical processing plants are popular examples of these technologies.

Woodward found that among the effective companies, those which used similar production technology also had similarity in their structural characteristics (see Table 6.1). A summary of her findings is given below:

Table 6.1 Summary of Woodward's Findings (based on Woodward (1965) and Robbins (1987))

	Technological complexity Low ⟵⟶ High		
Structural characteristics	Unit production	Mass production	Continuous process
1. Number of vertical levels in production department	3	4	6
2. Supervisors span of control	24	48	14
3. Management/total employee ratio	1 : 23	1 : 16	1 : 8
4. Employment of professional workers	Moderate (mainly in line function)	Low	High (in line and staff functions)
5. Chief executives span of control	4	7	10
6. Percentage organisations having management committees	12.5	32.3	80.0
7. Complexity	Low	High	Low
8. Formalisation	Low	High	Low
9. Centralisation	Low	High	Low

1. Organisations employing unit/small batch and continuous process technologies were found to be more organic in nature as compared to mass production organisations, which tended to prefer more mechanistic methods of management.

2. The proportion of administrative and support staff increased with the increase in technological complexity. Among the mass production organisations, however, the line and staff functions were most differentiated. In the organisations using unit/small batch technologies, the staff functions were mostly carried out by the supervisors, who had developed specialist skills through experience. In continuous process companies, while there was a large proportion of staff jobs, there was also a high amount of interchangeability among the line and staff personnel.

3. The mass-production technology firms were highly differentiated, relied on extensive formalisation and did little to delegate authority. Both unit/small batch and continuous process technologies, in contrast, were loosely structured. In unit technologies, high centralisation and formalised controls were not feasible, while in the process industries, they were not necessary.

4. Organisational communication in unit and process industries was more verbal and informal, whereas mass production technologies relied on massive paperwork and documentation for communication among managers and departments.

5. Woodward also observed that mass technology organisations were the least pleasant among the three kinds of industries. Compared to unit/small batch and continuous process companies, she found that the employees in mass production firms were less trusting and open (it was difficult to get information from them).

B. Technological Interdependence: Thompson's Contribution

Thompson (1967) viewed technology as fulfilling the function of linking the organisational sub-units. Based on his work, he suggested that different technologies are characterised by different structural arrangements, which help the organisations in determining appropriate strategies for uncertainty reduction. To fully appreciate Thompson's framework, it is necessary to acquaint oneself with his concepts of *interdependence* and *coordination.*

Interdependence refers to the manner in which the organisational sub-units are arranged, so that they can effectively contribute to the organisational task. The interdependence among the sub-units can be of three types. The simplest way in which the sub-units can be interdependent is when they are *pooled,* in which case the sub-units are so arranged that they do not directly influence each other, but each makes a discrete contribution to the total organisational task. All organisations have pooled interdependencies. The somewhat more complex organisations also have *sequential* interdependence among their sub-units; that is, the output of each sub-unit also happens to be the input of the another sub-unit. Lastly, the very complex organisations, besides having pooled and sequential interdependence, are also characterised by an arrangement in which the outputs of sub-units become the inputs for each other. This interdependence is known as *reciprocal.*

Related to the fact of interdependence are the mechanisms of coordination. For a concerted organisational action, coordination is essential; and if sub-units are interdependent in different ways, it is logical to expect that they would also be characterised by different kinds of coordinating mechanisms. Thompson proposed that when the interdependence is pooled, the coordination would be achieved by *standardisation,* that is establishment of routines and rules which constrain the action of each sub-unit. Since standards are relatively fixed, they can only be appropriate for situations which are stable, simple and repetitive. The sequential interdependence, on the other hand, is a somewhat more dynamic situation, which calls for coordination through *planning,* which would involve development of schedules to govern the behaviour of the interdependent units. In a more variable and unpredictable situation, the appropriate nature of interdependence is reciprocal, which can be coordinated by *mutual adjustment,* that is, by taking into account new information during the process of action.

Thompson proposed three types of technologies, which were differentiated by the nature of organisational tasks and interdependence among its units. Since these interdependencies could be effectively managed through different kinds of coordinating mechanisms, they would give rise to different kinds of organisational arrangements. Let us look at this classification of technologies (see Table 6.2).

Table 6.2 Comparison Among Mediating, Long-Linked and Intensive Technologies (based on Thompson, 1967)

Technology formalisation	Inter-dependence	Type of coordination	Basis of department-alisation	Complexity	Formalisa-tion
Mediating	Pooled	Standards rules and procedures	Common purpose	Low	High
Long-linked	Sequential	Plans and schedules	Common process/ clientele	Moderate	Moderate
Intensive	Reciprocal	Mutual adjustment	Location	High	Low

1. Mediating technology. This technology links the input and output ends of the organisation. The examples of this kind of technology would be banks, telephone utilities, typists' pool, employment agencies, and post offices. These organisations mediate between and link the input and output units, which are otherwise independent (see Figure 6.1). To reduce the uncertainty created by the diverse and heterogenous nature of populations served by these organisations, they develop the following measures:

(a) The needs and resources of all users (e.g., of depositors and borrowers

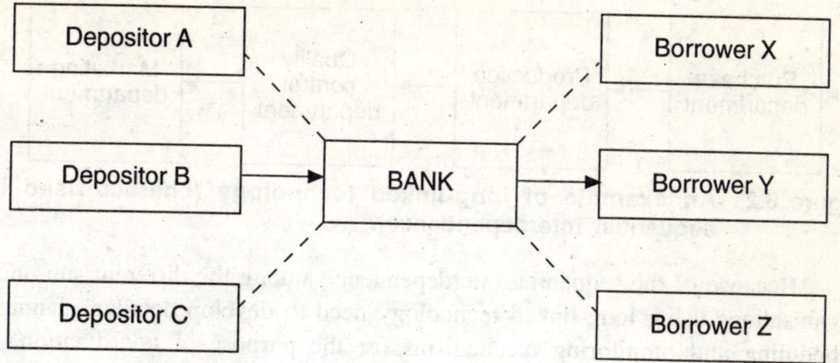

Figure 6.1 An example of mediating technology (characterised by pooled interdependence).

of a bank) are pooled in such a way, so to optimise the benefits for all. For example, in a typing pool, which provides service to a department, the total typing work may be so distributed as to optimally utilise the typing resources available, while providing an efficient service to the department.

(b) One of the sources of uncertainty for managers of mediating technology is their dependence on the client system. Correspondingly, the risks inherent in this potential dependence are reduced by increasing the population being served. The more the number of clients one has, the less one is dependent on one client or a client-segment. That is why, banks seek to increase the number of depositors and to develop a diversified loan portfolio.

(c) To deal with the diversity of demands placed on the organisation by its clients, the linking unit responds by standardising the organisation's transactions to establish conformity in the clients' behaviour, as well as to ensure efficiency of operations. Simultaneously, the organisation also segments the resources into groups/departments which share a commonality of purpose. For instance, a bank may structure itself into different departments (e.g., merchant banking, consumer finance, agricultural loans), while simultaneously segmenting its market into different kinds of clients.

It must also be noted that all organisations, in one way or the other, use mediating technology. A manufacturing firm, for example, mediates between the suppliers of raw material and the purchasers of finished products. However, they also do something more; they transform the inputs qualitatively to produce the output. And in doing so, they utilise other kinds of technology.

2. Long-linked technology. This type of technology is characterised by a fixed sequence of repetitive steps (see Figure 6.2). A typical example of this is the mass-production assembly-line. The tasks and operations in this technology are sequentially interdependent, in that the output of one sub-unit becomes the input for the next one. Thus, the arrangement of activities in each sub-unit is linked to the activities of the units which precede and follow in the chain. If one sub-unit behaves in a non-standard manner (e.g., delays its output, produces a defective output or provides incorrect information), it would affect the performance of all subsequent sub-units.

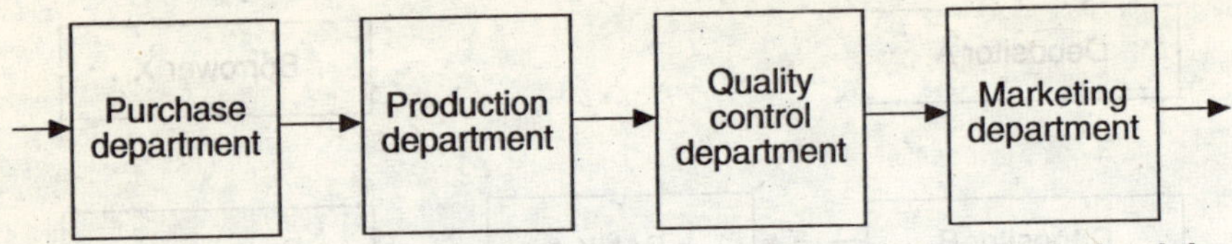

Figure 6.2 An example of long-linked technology (characterised by sequential interdependence).

Because of the sequential interdependence among the different sub-units, organisations using long-linked technology need to develop detailed planning, scheduling and monitoring mechanisms for the purpose of coordination. In comparison to rules and procedures (which are appropriate for managing pooled interdependence), plans and schedules are more appropriate for dealing with relatively dynamic circumstances. For instance, once the organisation is aware of the periodic demand fluctuations in the market (high demand for notebooks at the beginning of the academic sessions, demand for woolens during winters, and coolers and air-conditioners during summers), it can plan its purchases, requirements of manpower, production schedules, etc. to meet these demands, while also taking into account the realistic exigencies.

However, the cost of (and therefore, uncertainty in) planning would increase with the number of activities in the organisation. Organisations tend to reduce, or contain, this cost/uncertainty by putting all those activities, which share common process or clientele, together. For instance, when the number of letters and dispatches from different departments becomes too high (with every department requiring extra resources to look after this activity), the organisation may decide to open a separate dispatch department to look after this activity. Similarly, a purchase section may be set up to do all purchases, ranging from large machinery to office stationary.

Yet another step that organisations take to reduce uncertainty, is to increase their control on the input and output ends. They achieve this by integrating vertically. For instance, Reliance Industries, integrated backward into manufacturing yarn and fibres, because this was a major input for their initial business, textiles. From this, they went into further backward integration by starting to manufacture Purified Terephthalic Acid (PTA) and Monoethylene Glycol (MEG), which were basic inputs for yarn and fibres, and which till then they had to import. While such integration increases the organisation's control over its resources, it also increases its need to intensively plan and coordinate the operations among its different units, so that each unit efficiently meets the demands of the next one, while remaining financially viable.

3. Intensive technology. This technology is designed to meet the requirements of complex tasks, in which the variety of problems cannot be predicted accurately beforehand, that is, the problems arise during the process of action. Each of such problems requires a unique combination of knowledge, skills and techniques. This combination is decided by the nature of the problem. Examples of such technology are major construction projects, R&D units, hospitals, management consultancy firms and army commando teams (see Figure 6.3).

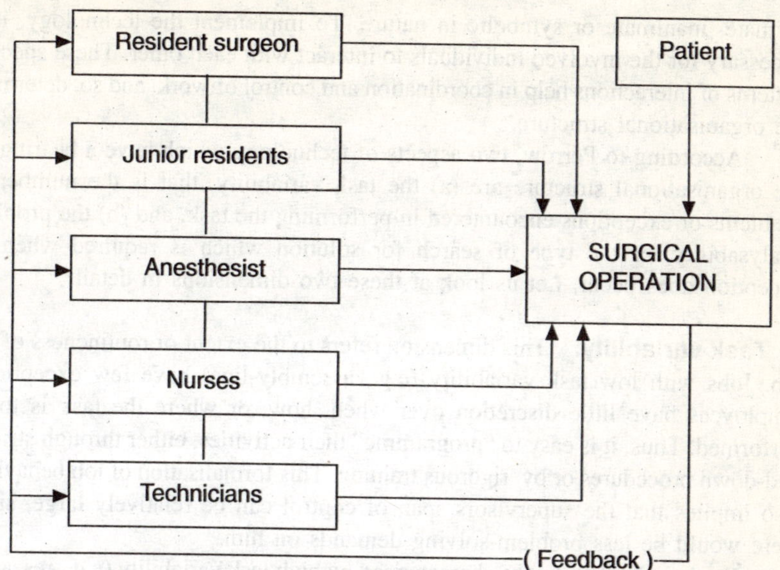

Figure 6.3 An example of intensive technology (characterised by reciprocal interdependence).

It must be noted that the problems faced and solved by this technology require interactions among specialists, whose interdependence on each other is reciprocal. The interactive and feedback needs of the intensive technology, thus, depend heavily on mutual adjustments among team members.

One of the major requirements of intensive technology is the flexibility of response. This is so, because while the organisation may have a variety of skills and resources available, but for a particular problem-situation, only a few specialised ones of these are required. The selection, combination and sequencing of these skills and resources is determined by the feedback from the problem itself: To deal with this problem-generated uncertainty, organisations ensure the availability of resources near the location of the problem itself. The locational grouping of resources also facilitates smoother coordination while meeting contingencies. Thus, organisations employing intensive technology are likely to be more differentiated and horizontally complex in nature. Moreover, the high amount of adjustment required among members also makes formalisation inappropriate.

C. Technological Uncertainty: Perrow's Framework

Perrow (1967) suggested a framework which described how technological uncertainty (or lack of it) determined organisational structure. The significance of Perrow's framework, was that his classification conceptualised technology in a more general manner, and so could apply equally well to manufacturing and service organisations. Perrow defined technology as "the actions that an individual performs upon an object, with or without the aid of tools or mechanical devices, in order to make some change in the object." He clarified that the object can be animate, inanimate or symbolic in nature. To implement the technology, it is necessary for the involved individuals to interact with each other. These specific patterns of interactions help in coordination and control of work, and so, determine the organisational structure.

According to Perrow, two aspects of technology which have a bearing on the organisational structure are (a) the task variability, that is the number of problems or exceptions encountered in performing the task, and (b) the problem analysability, or the type of search for solution which is required when an exception does occur. Let us look at these two dimensions in detail.

1. Task variability. This dimension refers to the extent of routineness of the job. Jobs with low task variability (e.g., assembly-line) have few exceptions. Employees have little discretion over when, how, or where the task is to be performed. Thus, it is easy to "programme" their activities, either through strictly laid-down procedures or by rigorous training. This formalisation of job behaviour also implies that the supervisors span of control can be relatively large, since there would be less problem-solving demands on him.

On the other hand, jobs characterised by high task variability (e.g., research, consultancy) have many exceptions, and, therefore, cannot be programmed. In such jobs, it is difficult to develop standard methods and routine procedures for performing the tasks. Rather, people who perform the tasks need to have adequate problem-solving skills and greater flexibility in their relationships (mutual adjustment) to be effective.

One may also note that the extent to which a job is routine or non-routine may also depend on the nature of environment. High environmental uncertainty would decrease the predictability of demands on the job. For example, the receptionist or the guest relations executive in a hotel has to deal with a variety of demands from the patrons. It would be almost impossible to standardise these jobs, without decreasing their effectiveness. On the other hand, the personnel managing the teller counter in a bank has to encounter relatively few exceptional problem situations, and his job can, therefore, be formalised. Organisations, however, do try to routinise their core jobs, so that control and efficiency can be optimised. Thus, they develop buffers (e.g, inventories, finished stocks, good public relations, etc.), so that the core jobs can follow a definite schedule, without being influenced by environmental uncertainties.

2. Problem analysability. If an exception or problem occurs in a job, it would require a search for a solution. This search can be systematic, logical and analytical, in that there may be an existing body of knowledge (in file, programmes or manuals) which needs to be searched for finding an appropriate solution to the problem. For example, the engineering section can search its files to look for an appropriate design for a specialised machine, or a bank may have well laid-out rules for granting loans to people. Perrow termed these jobs as analysable. Problem analysability would make it easier for the management to schedule and monitor employees' performance, and so would increase centralisation of control.

If, on the other hand, there are no pre-specified ways of dealing with task-related problems, the individual's experience, judgement, intuition and problem-solving abilities would become a critical factor in the completion of the job. Such jobs would mostly consist of problems which are ambiguous and unanalysable. They would require a creative and exploratory response. For such jobs, the management would need to assign persons with a broad general training, who can act flexibly and show diversity in their thinking about uncertain situations. Obviously, given the nature of the job, the required organisational structure should incorporate a sufficient amount of flexibility and decentralisation.

Given these two dimensions of task variability and problem analysability, Perrow identified four basic forms of technologies: (a) Routine, (b) Engineering (or Planned Contingencies), (c) Craft (or *ad hoc*), and (d) Non-routine (see Figure 6.4). These are now briefly discussed.

Problem Analysability	Few exceptions	Many exceptions
Unanalysable	**Craft or ad hoc technology** (e.g., craft industries, health clinic) **Formalisation:** Moderate **Centralisation:** Low	**Non-routine technology** (e.g., R & D, software firms) **Formalisation:** Low **Centralisation:** Low
Analysable	**Routine technology** (e.g., assembly line, paper mill) **Formalisation:** High **Centralisation:** High	**Engineering or planned contingency technology** (e.g., civil construction) **Formalisation:** Low **Centralisation:** High

TASK VARIABILITY

Figure 6.4 Perrow's classification of technologies.

(a) *Routine technologies*: These have few exceptions and are characterised by easy-to-analyse problems. The mass-production processes used for making automobiles or refining petroleum crude belong to this category. This technology is similar to Woodward's Mass Production technology and Thompson's Long-Linked technology. Routine technologies give rise to formal, centralised and mechanistic structures. The control and coordination is achieved through planning and application of rigid rules, allowing little discretion to employees in managing their jobs.

(b) *Engineering or planned contingencies technologies*: There are a large number of exceptions to these, but they can be handled in a structured and systematic manner. Activities of maintenance crew, tax consultants, or civil construction firms would fall in this category. The corresponding structures are flexible but centralised. These structures provide high discretion to the technical specialists, who coordinate their activities through reports and meetings (mutual adjustments). However, down the line, the operators have less discretion, because their activities are managed by the plans developed by the specialists.

(c) *Craft or ad hoc technologies*: These deal with relatively difficult problems, but with a limited set of exceptions. Such technologies would include schools, shoe-making, work of performing artists, etc. These technologies create decentralised structures, which use training and meetings as means of coordination and control.

(d) *Non-routine technologies*: These are characterised by many exceptions and difficult-to-analyse problems. Typical examples of these technologies would be basic research activities, software development firms, think tanks, etc. These technologies require highly flexible, decentralised and organic structures. They are similar to Thompson's Intensive technology, in that the coordination and control of activities in these organisations is achieved through informal interactions and adjustments.

D. Integration and Implications

The preceding discussion focused on three useful frameworks, which managers can use for identifying specific technological contingencies of their work-situations, and accordingly planning the structural arrangements. Let us briefly look at the conclusions one can draw from these models. To summarise:

- Woodward's investigations showed that there is no single best structure. Rather, the differences in technologies may make it necessary for different organisations/departments to develop different structures.
- Thompson's model clarified the reasons for developing technology-specific structures. Since each technology is based on different patterns of interdependence, different mechanisms are required for coordination and control, which necessitate the development of corresponding structural arrangements.
- And finally, Perrow provided a framework for understanding technology in terms of the kind of problems it requires the employees to solve. According to this framework, the effectiveness of a particular organisational structure will depend on the nature of the problem-solving process and the kind of solutions (e.g., routine or creative) required for doing work in the organisation.

One would also notice that, while these three conceptualisations focused on different aspects of technology, the degree of routineness appeared to be a common theme cutting across them (Robbins, 1987). Woodward's mass production and continuous process technologies, Thompson's mediating and long-linked technologies, and Perrow's routine and engineering technologies described characteristics of technology which are relatively more routine in nature. On the other hand, unit/small batch technology, craft and non-routine technologies, and intensive technology share the common attribute of dealing with relatively non-routine tasks.

Studies exploring the technology-structure relationship also support the hypotheses proposed by these frameworks. For example, Gerwin (1979) found that routine technologies are positively related to formalisation. Similarly, Hage and Aiken (1969) found that routineness of work was normally accompanied by presence of rule manual and specific job descriptions. In another study, Van de Ven, Delbecq and Koenig, Jr. (1976) found that routine technologies were more often accompanied by centralised structures, while non-routine technologies were characterised by decentralisation of authority.

It would, however, be naive and simplistic to treat the technology-structure relationship in isolation. While it is amply clear that such a relationship exists, studies also indicate that this relationship is moderated by a number of other factors. For instance, one of the Aston group studies (Hickson, Pugh and Pheysey, 1979) found relationships consistent with the findings of Woodward. However, when they also took organisational size into account, these relationships vanished. They proposed that technology influences the structure only when the organisations are small. In large organisations, technology plays a much minor role, influencing the structure only at the operational core level.

The nature of the business in which an organisation is, also has a decisive influence on the choice of technology and the organisational structure. Mills and Moberg (1982), for example, compared the technology-structure relationship in manufacturing and service industries, and found that the dominant technologies used by the two types of organisations are qualitatively so different, as to make any cross-sector generalisations superfluous. Thus, whether the organisation is a bank, hotel, or is manufacturing bearings and cars, it is likely to make a difference in the kind of influence its technology will have on its structure.

Lastly, it is necessary to appreciate that the nature of relationship between technology and structure is not immutable. For instance, as we mentioned earlier, routine jobs are often accompanied by centralisation. However, centralisation is only a method of coordinating and controlling employees' behaviour. The same aim can be achieved by formalising the work-contents (in which case, the controls can be decentralised). Thus, organisations do have options, even if limited, in changing the nature of the technology-structure relationship. In the following section, we will look at some of these options.

III. JOB DESIGN: MANAGERIAL OPTIONS FOR TECHNOLOGICAL CHANGE

An organisation can have at least two reasons for considering changes in its technology. We saw in the earlier section how technology influences the organisational structure. However, structural changes in organisations are not always brought about to meet the technological requirements. An organisation may also decide to change its structure to meet the strategic requirements of dealing with the environment. In such cases, structural changes would necessitate changes in technology, i.e., redesigning of jobs to suit the structure.

An even more potent reason for changing technology or redesigning jobs is the fact that often most "efficiently" designed jobs prove to have quite ineffective consequences. For example, while assembly-line may be the most efficient method of mass production, it has also been found to result in increased turnover, absenteeism, alcoholism, etc. (Blauner, 1964; Kornhauser, 1965), thereby, possibly actually increasing the inefficiencies and costs. In the previous discussion on the technology-structure relationship, one would have noted that the nature of managerial practices (i.e, degree of formalisation and centralisation, span of control, etc.) were proposed to be exclusively determined by the nature of job, neglecting the human component altogether. A comprehensive and realistic view of the organisational functioning (and, correspondingly, the selection/ designing of appropriate technology), however, would be incomplete without taking this human component into account.

One of the first approaches to integrate the human and technological demands in the job was the socio-technical systems perspective (Trist, 1981). This approach argued that the accomplishment of a task depended on not only a technology but also on a social system (i.e., the personality and attitudes of employees, their patterns of interaction, their relationships with supervisors, etc.). Thus, designing work is more than mere designing of a job; it incorporates designing of the underlying social relationships. Correspondingly, this approach proposed the following basic guidelines for designing socio-technical systems:

1. The unit for work-design should be the work system rather than separate jobs, to which a work system can be reduced.

2. The focus of design should be on the work group, rather than on the individual job holder.

3. A viable work system should be internally controlled by the work group, rather than relying on external control of individuals by the supervisors.

4. The individual must be viewed as complementary to the machine and not as an extension of it.

5. A viable work system would tend to increase the variety in the nature of work for the individual and the organisation, rather than decreasing it.

Studies and field experiments have shown the validity of the socio-technical perspective in designing work systems. De (1979), described a number of Indian examples of diverse nature, in which jobs were redesigned to form semi-autonomous, integrated work teams with beneficial results. For instance, in the condenser manufacturing unit at BHEL, Haridwar, a new form of work system was introduced in 1975, in which each shift consisted of an integrated team, responsible for a complete job. De reported:

> With the introduction of a new form of work organisation there was an improvement in productivity... Progressively the old pattern of one-man, one-function was superseded by the acquisition of multiple skills and the development of a group system of working, with internal monitoring of group norms, internal control of work flow and work allocation, and identification with the product and its quality. Particularly significant from the management's point of view was the gradual drop in the personal idle time (e.g., time spent loitering at the workplace, or spent outside the workplace without justifiable reasons).

In a review of socio-technical programmes, Trist (1981) also found that these work systems resulted in providing more variety and challenge in jobs, decreased external controls and supervision, increased a sense of ownership and personal responsibility, and also made provisions for transmitting performance feedback.

Clearly, for any manager to design new forms of work systems, it is necessary to understand what a job consists of, and what can be done to change the characteristics of that job. One of the major contributions in this direction came from the Job-Characteristic Model (Hackman and Oldham, 1975; Oldham and Hackman, 1980). This model identified five core characteristics by which a job can be described and which would have an impact on the productivity, motivation and satisfaction of the employees. These characteristics were:

(a) *Skill variety*: This refers to the variety of activities (and, therefore, the variety of skills and talents) required by a job.

(b) *Task identity*: This refers to the degree to which a job allows the conduction of a complete and identifiable piece of work.

(c) *Task significance*: It is the degree to which the job has any significant impact on the work and lives of others.

(d) *Autonomy*: It is the degree of discretion which the person has in planning, scheduling and making decisions about his work.

(e) *Feedback*: It refers to how much and how often the person receives direct and clearcut information about the effectiveness of his performance.

Oldham and Hackman (1980) proposed that these characteristics can be modified by redesigning the jobs (see Table 6.3). This can be done through five "implementation concepts" or job enrichment strategies. Once the manager, or

Table 6.3 How Implementing Concepts Influence Core Job Characteristics (based on Oldham and Hackman, 1980)

Implementing concepts (Job enrichment strategies)	Core job characteristics
1. Combining tasks	• Skill variety • Task identity
2. Forming natural work units	• Task identity • Task significance
3. Establishing client relationships	• Skill variety • Autonomy • Feedback from the job
4. Expanding job vertically	• Autonomy
5. Opening feedback channels	• Feedback from the job

change agent, has analysed the job in terms of its characteristics, he can use these strategies for improving the problematic aspects of the job. These strategies are described below:

A. Combining Tasks

Often jobs are fractionalised, with each task segment being completed by one person. While this may be an efficient division of labour, it contributes to monotony and loss of task identity. Managers can put these tasks together to form larger and more meaningful modules of work. For example, a product can be assembled, with each person repetitively doing a small part of the total job, or the whole assembly can be entrusted to one person or to a team. Combining tasks increases skills and brings in variety and task identity.

B. Forming Natural Work Units

The underlying principle of this strategy is to enhance a person's sense of continuing responsibility for an identifiable piece of work. To create a natural work unit, one must identify the activities which constitute the job, and then group them together in natural categories. For example, a typist in a typing pool can be given jobs randomly, or can be assigned continuing responsibility for all jobs requested by a specific department or executive. This would help creating a sense of "ownership", and increase task identity and task significance.

C. Establishing Client Relationships

Often persons working on a job have no contact with the ultimate users of their output or service. Encouraging and enabling the employees to develop a relationship with the client, not only creates the opportunity for them to receive a direct feedback, it also helps in increasing the skill variety and autonomy in the job, since the employees have to use their interpersonal skills to manage and decide about this relationship. For instance, the shopfloor operators may be encouraged to regularly interact with the marketing executives to understand the problems they face in selling the products made by the production department.

D. Expanding Jobs Veritically

Most jobs are so designed that those who conduct the jobs are not the ones who plan and control them. Vertical expansion of jobs, or vertical loading, involves giving employees responsibilities of planning, scheduling and controlling their jobs (in addition, of course, to doing them). This can be done, for example, by giving greater discretion to the workers in setting schedules, deciding on work methods, checking on quality, training new workers, managing time and priorities, trouble shooting and taking crisis decisions, financial decisions, etc.

E. Opening Feedback Channels

Though almost all jobs have provision for getting a feedback, the more immediate and direct the feedback, the more effective it would be. Moreover, people learn better if they receive the feedback as soon as the job is done. Feedback provided while the job is being done is more immediate, and increases the worker's sense of personal control over his work. Apart from establishing client relationships, this can be achieved in many other ways, e.g., making workers responsible for quality, encouraging more frequent performance feedback meetings between superiors and subordinates, developing systems for regular communication of performance records, etc.

7 Types of Organisational Structures

If we consider different organisations, each appears to be unique and distinct from the others. They differ from each other in terms of their sizes, aims, sectors, type of employees, management styles and systems, and so on. The range is wide and diverse: from a bureaucratic government department to a small road-side restaurant; from a diversified conglomerate to a product development team; from an efficient heavy engineering unit to an academic institution, and so on. In fact, one may even be tempted to assume that there are as many kinds of organisational structures as there are organisations.

Even theoretically (i.e., at some level of abstraction), it is conceivable that there can be a very large number of structural forms. For instance, based on our previous discussion in Chapter 3, we can assume that organisational structures are made up of only six basic components (viz., horizontal complexity, vertical complexity, spatial complexity, professional formalisation, organisational formalisation, and centralisation), and each of these can vary in three ways (low, moderate and high). Based on these apparently valid assumptions, one can make a simple calculation to get as many as 729 ($3 \times 3 \times 3 \times 3 \times 3 \times 3$) different types of organisational structure.

Such a situation, however, would make the study and designing of organisations a near impossibility. Fortunately, the reality is somewhat simpler. Even in their diversity, organisations exercise relatively limited, and manageable, number of options in structuring themselves. Miller and Mintzberg (1984) argued that in designing themselves, organisations do not select separate components or attributes to fit them together in a linear manner. Rather, they tend to structure (or configure) themselves around a handful of themes or gestalts. Instead of trying to do everything well, organisations (at least the effective ones) seem to consciously or unconsciously select a theme, and then try to bring all the elements in line with this theme. Miller and Mintzberg termed these themes or gestalts as configurations and defined them as "commonly occurring clusters of attributes or relationships...that are internally cohesive...".

There are also understandable reasons why organisational structures should occur in a limited number of configurations. While theoretically, a large number of organisational forms are possible, only a few of them would be able to meet the internal and external demands efficiently and competitively. Most of the combinations in the above calculation, for example, would be internally inconsistent, and so, would perish by themselves. As Miller and Mintzberg (1984) noted:

> the organisation may be driven toward configuration in order to achieve consistency in its internal characteristics, synergy (or mutual complementarity) in its processes, and fit with its situation.

Apart from the necessity of survival, the fact is that organisations do not change on a continuous day-to-day basis to achieve a fit with their environment (it would also be uneconomical for them to do so). Rather, they tend to maintain internal consistencies by continuing for long with a configuration even when it has become out of tune with the external demands. It is easier and economical, for organisations to put up with growing maladaptation with a changing environment for some period, than to disrupt their internal consistencies on a continuous and regular basis. The restructuring comes through a sudden strategic leap, changing the organisations from one configuration to another.

Finally, the decision-makers in the organisations, after all, are not researchers and innovators. They are mostly practical businessmen who prefer the tried and tested methods, doing what they perceive the other successful people, specially those in the same industry, are doing. Thus, configurations get replicated, and remain limited in number.

An understanding of these configurations is essential for any manager to identify the options he has for designing organisations. In this Chapter, we will look at one major scheme for classifying organisations into different, identifiable and realistic structural configurations.

I. BASES OF STRUCTURAL CONFIGURATIONS

If organisational structures occur in a limited number of configurations, the next question which needs consideration is the bases on which these structures are formed. Child (1972) defined structure as "the formal allocation of work roles and the administrative mechanisms to control and integrate work activities, including those which cross formal organisational boundaries." One would notice that this definition involves both division of work as well as means of integrating this differentiation. Thus, any structural configuration must include criteria by which various roles, activities and coordination mechanisms can be differentiated as well as grouped together in the organisation.

One of the most comprehensive and rational approach for classifying structures was proposed by Mintzberg (1980, 1981, 1983). According to him, an organisation can be seen as composed of five basic parts (see Figure 7.1). These are:

A. The Strategic Apex

This consists of the top-level management, in-charge of the overall organisation. This may consist of a top-management team or a single individual.

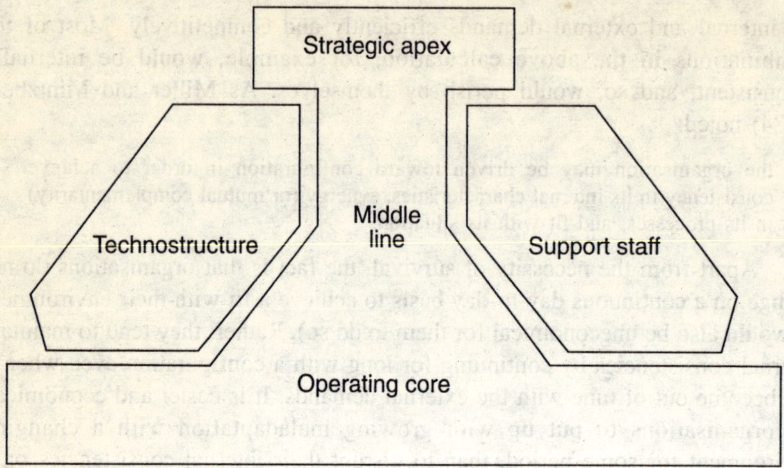

Figure 7.1 The five basic parts of organisations (Mintzberg, 1983).

B. The Operating Core

This consists of employees who perform the basic work related to the production of goods or service, for which the organisation is meant.

C. The Middle Line

This consists of people who connect the strategic apex to the operating core. These are intermediate managers who transmit, control and help in implementing the decisions taken by the strategic apex.

D. The Technostructure

This consists of staff functionaries and analysts, who design systems for regulating and standardising the formal planning and control of the work. In most organisations, this function is looked after by departments such as finance, production planning, personnel, etc.

E. The Support Staff

This consists of people who, though not directly involved in the work-process, provide indirect support to it. Services like cafeteria, mailing, transport, etc. are considered to be part of the support staff.

By putting these parts together, one can get the whole organisation. But not all organisations are identical; they differ in terms of the part which exercises greater control, and the manner in which the activities of the operating core are coordinated. Mintzberg identified five basic mechanisms by which organisational activities are coordinated, giving rise to five distinct forms of organisational configurations (see Table 7.1). He proposed that the activities within the organisation can be coordinated through:

Table 7.1 Relationship between Coordinating Mechanisms, Key Parts of Organisation, and Corresponding Organisational Configurations (based on Mintzberg 1981, 1983)

Coordinating mechanisms	Key parts of organisation	Configurations
Direct supervision	Strategic apex	Simple structure
Standardisation of activities	Technostructure	Machine bureaucracy
Standardisation of skills	Operating core	Professional bureaucracy
Standardisation of output	Middle line	Divisional form
Mutual adjustment	Support staff	Adhocracy

1. Direct supervision. When the strategic apex is dominant, controlling organisational activities through direct interventions, this would lead to the development of a *simple structure*.

2. Standardisation of activities. When coordination is achieved through development of rules and procedures relating to work activities, the technostructure, which formulates these rules and standards, will be more dominant. The corresponding organisational structure will be a *machine bureaucracy*.

3. Standardisation of skills. To achieve this, the organisation would require highly trained professionals to manage its operating core, where they would wield considerable influence. This arrangement would be a *professional bureaucracy*.

4. Standardisation of output. When coordination is achieved through making people accountable only for their output and performance, it would require a highly differentiated and empowered middle line to oversee that the organisation's purpose is met. This would result in a *divisional form* of structure.

5. Mutual adjustment. In most complex organisations, the rules and standards cannot be fixed, and different parts of the organisation need to interact on a continuous basis for coordination. The support staff, plays a key role in coordinating activities, and the corresponding organisational configuration will be *adhocracy*.

Each of these configurations is distinctive, and is characterised by a set of internally consistent design parameters (e.g., nature and extent of specialisation, formalisation, bases of grouping roles and activities, extent of centralisation). Moreover, they also differ from each other in terms of their strengths and weaknesses and appropriateness for different situational factors (e.g., size, age, technology, environment). In the following sections we will discuss each of these structural configurations in some details.

II. SIMPLE STRUCTURES

Consider an automobile service station, a young and small entrepreneurial company, a nation run by a dominant autocratic/charismatic leader, or the state of management in an organisation facing a major strike. These are all examples of simple structures, which actually are more of "non-structures".

These structures are loosely formed, but tightly run, where the power is centralised in the hands of one or few managers in the strategic apex, to whom everyone reports directly. These are typically flat and organic structures, with hardly any specialisation or formalisation of activities. As can be seen from Figure 7.2, they employ very few middle managers, since the coordination is achieved through direct supervision. Lack of standardisation and formalisation

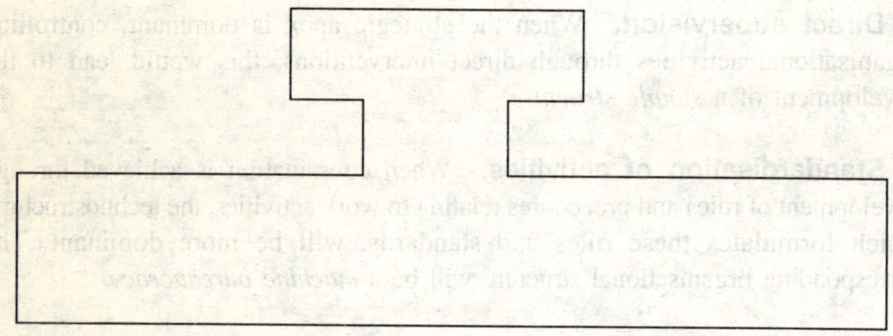

Figure 7.2 The configuration of simple structure (Mintzberg, 1983).

makes techno-structure (i.e., role of staff analysts) redundant. Even the support staff is minimum to keep the organisation lean and flexible (e.g., instead of having a cafeteria, there may be an understanding with the nearby *dhaba* to supply tea, or major typing work may be contracted outside).

Most often these organisations are an extension of the chief executive's personality, moulded by his vision (or lack of it). The centralised control, coupled with informal channels of communication makes it easier for the decision-maker(s) to receive information quickly through informal means (see Exhibit 7.1 for a real life example). This gives these organisations the advantage of swiftness in taking strategic decisions. It is not uncommon in such organisations, to find the chief executive engaged in conversation with a shopfloor operator or one of the clients, bypassing whatever little chain of commands there may be. These organisations are capable of innovating and rapidly adapting to changed demands, which can help them much in out-maneuvering their more established but bureaucratic competitors (one would recall how in the recent past, a small organisation like Nirma managed to compete and win against the giant Hindustan Lever, or how Super Cassettes Industries was able to overthrow the dominance of its more established competitors, HMV and Music India Ltd.).

Exhibit 7.1

FNF Strips Company: A Simple Structure

FNF Strips Company is a small family-owned organisation in the business of manufacturing ferrous and non-ferrous strips, and is situated in Andhra Pradesh. The owner was also the chairman and managing director of the company, and below him there were six functional directors who were related to him (one son, one son-in-law, wife, two nephews and the son of a family friend) and also owned shares in the company.

The total strength of FNF Strips was about 150 and most of the employees were employed as "temporary" workers (although they had been with the company for the last eight years or so) in the manufacturing unit. These people had been handpicked by the owner in the earlier days of the company, when the owner used to look after the factory. The structure in the factory was the only part of the organisation which was somewhat elaborated, and in recent years an "outsider" was appointed as the Vice-President to manage it (the Factory Manager and two of the shop managers were also the owner's relatives). The owner, however, had continued to maintain control on the factory operations; he would visit the factory every day, give instructions to supervisors and workers, sometimes even overruling the directions given by factory executives. The technical investment decisions were mostly based on the owner's subjective judgement, than on any objective process of planing and market survey. Once, for instance, he ordered a costly high capacity plant from West Germany, which was too sophisticated for the volumes required by the company. Its operations became viable only after three years, during which the company built up a large inventory of unsold stocks and huge debt.

The main office of the organisation was a rented flat next to the owner's residence. Apart from the owner, and the functional directors, there were just about five or six other employees housed in this office. These included two typists (one of whom also worked in the owner's residence after office hours) and a "marketing officer" (whose tasks also included errands like receiving guests, arranging for taxis, purchase of raw materials and stationary, etc.). This lack of role boundaries could also be seen among the functional directors, who would often look after each others jobs, though in all cases, the final consent had to come from the owner.

The author was involved with this organisation as a consultant during the late 1980's; the above description is based on the notes taken during that period. For ethical reasons, the name of the company is disguised.

Simple structures are mostly suited to a simple and dynamic environment. In fact, very often these organisations remain in such an environment by choice (of the strategic apex, naturally). Having to deal with only a few environmental elements, not only makes it easier for the chief executive to comprehend the environment and to take right decisions, but also helps in maintaining his control over the organisation. The instability in the environment, on the other hand, provides scope for greater maneuverability and risk-taking. This is also the reason why organisations, when suddenly confronted with a hostile threat, tend to revert to a simple structure, temporarily centralising the power and flattening the structure.

However, the same characteristics which are strengths of simple structures, can also become their major weaknesses (see Table 7.2 for the strengths and

Table 7.2 The Advantages and Disadvantages of Simple Structures

Strengths	Weaknesses
• It facilitates control of all business activities.	• It is very demanding on the owner-manager.
• It facilitates rapid decision-making and the ability to change with market demands.	• It becomes increasingly inadequate as volumes increase.
• It has the capability to innovate.	• It does not facilitate development of future managers.
• Its informality and flexibility can be quite conducive for satisfaction.	• It can make the CEO focus on day-to-day operations and neglecting strategy.

weaknesses of this structural configuration). These organisations are mostly young and small, and therefore, are highly vulnerable to any major change, both in the internal and external environment. A week long economic blockade or *bandh* can very seriously jeopardise their cash-flow and stocks situation, just as a heart attack suffered by the chief executive, or a single bad strategic decision taken by him can totally wipe the organisation out. Those organisations which survive and grow, on the other hand, do so only by becoming more bureaucratised. In fact, most successful organisations begin as simple structures, in which the founding owner-managers exercise considerable direct and personalised control and direction. But they grow only when they manage to develop a more formal and differentiated structure.

III. MACHINE BUREAUCRACY

Machine bureaucracies are probably the most popular, and yet most criticised of all organisational structures. Indeed, the most popular connotation of bureaucracy is that of a giant, monolithic, impersonal and inefficient system. And yet, without such bureaucracies, there would be no railways to transport more than one crore people everyday from one place to another (see Exhibit 7.2), no postal department to deliver crores of letters, no large integrated steel plants or mass manufactured consumer goods industries or public utilities, and so on. As Mintzberg (1989) remarked:

> ...you won't find me working in one (bureaucratic organisation)... but I do not hesitate to fly one of them to conferences, have them print my books or deliver my mail, even provide me and the kids with an occasional hamburger. Like many other people, I can't live without them even though I choose not to live within them.

This may be true for most of us. Probably that is why bureaucracies have continued to flourish and grow, even though their imminent "death" was predicted more than 25 years back (Bennis, 1966). The fact is, that even in this present era of change, bureaucracies work—sometimes even efficiently.

Machine bureaucracies are characterised by coordination of work through a high degree of standardisation of work, which results in low-skilled, highly specialised jobs. This standardisation is maintained by laying down extensive formalised rules and procedures for regulating the organisational activities and work-flow. The division of labour is sharp, and activities and roles are divided into functional groups.

Since the whole organisation depends on standardisation of behaviour, technostructure is the key element in this configuration (see Figure 7.3). It is

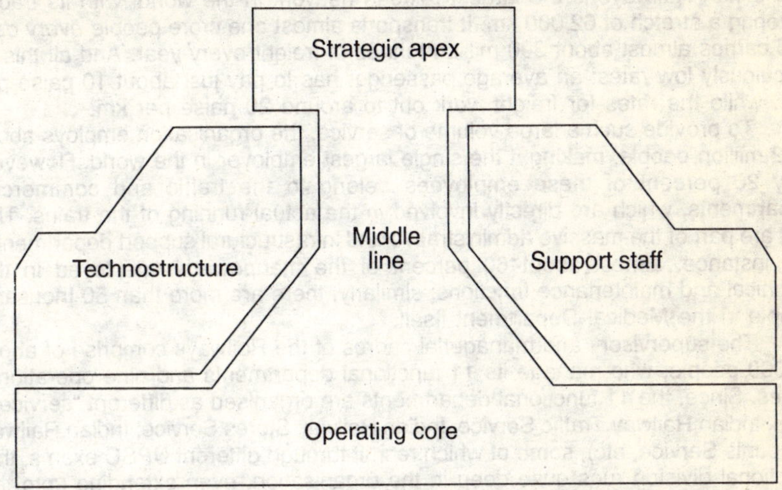

Figure 7.3 The configuration of machine bureaucracy (Mintzberg, 1983).

highly elaborated and differentiated, housing an army of staff analysts (e.g., industrial engineers, process and control engineers, quality control engineers, planners, financial analysts, cost and works accountants, operation researchers, and so on) whose sole task is to develop norms of work behaviour and activities, to ensure greater efficiency and reliability in others' work. Despite their lack of formal authority, these staff analysts wield considerable informal influence (hence, the reason for the almost inevitable staff-line conflicts in machine bureaucracies).

To ensure implementation of rules, procedures, and systems, these organisations also develop a very large and elaborate middle management cadre. Besides working with staff analysts to incorporate their standards in the operating units, the middle managers also perform two other important functions: they handle the conflicts which inevitably arise between the segmented but sequentially-linked operating units (e.g., between maintenance and production, production and marketing) through direct intervention and supervision; and, they elaborate the action plans flowing down the hierarchy and pass on the feedback upward to the decision-makers in the strategic apex. The middle-level management is also functionally grouped, so that the formal power and control is centralised at the top.

Since the smooth functioning of machine bureaucracies is always threatened by changes, they tend to seek stable environments to function, as well as to stabilise the environments in which they operate (one would notice the similarity of machine bureaucracies with our description of TISCO; refer Exhibit 5.1).

Exhibit 7.2

The Indian Railways: World's Largest Machine Bureaucracy

The Indian Railways is the largest railroad network in the world, with its tracks covering a stretch of 62,000 km. It transports almost one crore people *every day,* and carries almost about 300 million tonnes of freight every year. And all this at ridiculously low rates: an average passenger has to pay just about 10 paise per km., while the rates for freight work out to around 20 paise per km.

To provide such a large volume of service, the organisation employs about 1.62 million people, making it the single largest employer in the world. However, only 20 percent of these employees belong to the traffic and commercial departments, which are directly involved in the actual running of the trains. The rest are part of the massive administrative and infrastructural support departments. For instance, almost about 60 percent of the manpower is deployed in the technical and maintenance functions; similarly, there are more than 50 thousand people in the Medical Department itself.

The supervisory and managerial cadres of the Railways comprise of about 27,000 people, who manage its 11 functional departments and nine operational zones. Since, the 11 functional departments are organised as different "services" (e.g., Indian Railway Traffic Service, Indian Railway Stores Service, Indian Railway Accounts Service, etc), some of which recruit through different UPSC exams, this functional division runs quite deep in the organisation, even extending upto the level of Member, Railway Board. Over the years, while some operational decentralisation has taken place, the functional hierarchy of commands and centralisation is maintained. For instance, the Railways does its own collection and accountals of cash received, brings it to a central organisation before depositing it in the bank. Similarly, the disbursement of salaries is still predominantly done through cash, with the cashier going to the outlying stations and handing over the salaries to the employees in their hand.

The complexity of the structure can be gauged from the fact that there are about 700 job categories in the organisation, which are spread over its 58 divisions. Apart from the thousands of railway stations across the country the Railways has about 60 technical maintenance workshops, five central training institutes, about 150 odd training centres and schools, and a centralised R&D facility. In addition to all these, there are also many miscellaneous departments such as stationary and printing, rubber technology, mining, engineering, chemical and metallurgical, etc.

In a bid to achieve self-sufficiency, over the years, the organisation also integrated backward by putting up its own production units (e.g., Chittaranjan Locomotive Works, Diesel Locomotive Works, Wheel and Axle Plant, Integral Coach Factory, Railway Coach Factory, etc.). It also floated five public section organisations (RITES, IRCON, Indian Railways Finance Corporation, Container Corporation of India, and CRIS) to help it manage its environment better. Besides these major ventures, the organisation manages its own printing press for printing tickets, runs its own schools for railway employees, operated a power house for years, has established base-kitchens and guest houses (Yatri Niwas) for catering to passengers needs, and even runs a Soda Bottling Plant (in SE Railways)!

That is why, one often finds them maintaining a large support staff—cafeteria, transport, townships, hospitals, legal council, etc.—which helps them in influencing and stabilising their environment. It is for this reason also, that these organisations tend to integrate vertically. They acquire the sources of their raw material (or enter into stringent legal contracts with their suppliers), open their own show rooms, put up industries for value-addition, or enter into long-term agreements with their major customers/clients.

It is not surprising that these organisations tend to grow very large. In a way, their size is an asset for them, since it gives them sufficient resources not to get influenced by minor fluctuations in the environment. On the other hand, this stability also encourages them to further bureaucratise (i.e., segment and routinise) themselves in order to control their work activities. It is these characteristics, which make these organisational configurations ideal for producing goods and services on a mass scale in a reliable manner.

As long as the environmental demands remain simple and predictable, machine bureaucracies are probably the best instruments of doing things economically and efficiently. By substituting rules and procedures for decisions, they work on low requirements of operational and managerial skills, thereby saving costs. Their large sizes and volumes help them in achieving economies of scale. On the other hand, by fractionalising and segmenting the jobs, they also create monotony, alienation, and inter-functional conflicts. Table 7.3 summarises their strengths and weaknesses.

Table 7.3 Strengths and Weaknesses of Machine Bureaucracies

Strengths	Weaknesses
• Achieve efficiency through specialisation.	• Promote narrow functional specialisation and potential functional rivalry.
• Encourage development of functional expertise.	• Experience difficulties in inter-functional coordination and decision-making.
• Low cost of operational and managerial expertise.	• High costs of coordination and support.
• Centralise strategic decisions giving a focus to organisation.	• Limit internal development of general managers.
• Large size and standardisation promotes stability.	• Find difficult to innovate and adequately respond to environmental changes.

IV. PROFESSIONAL BUREAUCRACY

Inspite of its apparent monotony, society does require people to perform routine activities in a reliable and standardised manner. In fact, many of these activities may not even be as simple and meaningless as the ergonomic operations of an assembly-line operator. Consider, for example, the need of the hospitals to perform similar operations on patients day after day, with same precision and reliability, or the need of the universities to teach the same course/syllabus year after year to the students with same effectiveness. These are complex tasks, requiring sophisticated skills, yet they have to be performed on a routine basis and on a mass scale. To achieve this end, organisations develop a structural configuration, which Mintzberg termed as Professional Bureaucracy.

These configurations are similar to machine bureaucracies in that their work processes and activities are highly standardised and routinised. But this is where the similarity ends. While the machine bureaucracy coordinates through standardisation of work, the professional bureaucracy achieves the same aim by standardising skills. That is, instead of exercising control and coordination through enforcing rules and procedures, these organisations achieve reliability of performance by employing trained professionals to manage their operating core. This is largely also because the core activities of these organisations require complex expertise and skills, and cannot be broken down into smaller, low-skilled tasks. Nevertheless, the professional training and indoctrination received by the employees, over a period of time, ensures standardised performance and efficiency of work processes and activities in the organisation. Hospitals, universities and institutions of higher learning (IITs, IIMs, etc.), consultancy agencies, chartered accountancy firms, research organisations, etc., are typical examples of professional bureaucracies.

Since skilled and trained professionals need considerable control over their own work, these organisations give them sufficient autonomy and freedom to decide and manage their own activities. As a result, a highly decentralised structure emerges, in which the operating core exercises considerable power and influence over both operational and strategic decisions. In most professional institutes, for instance, the academic, and even many administrative decisions (e.g., decisions regarding course structure, areas of research and consultancy, utilisation/sharing of facilities) are taken by various internal committees and councils formed by the professionals.

The professional formalisation of work procedures influences the structure of these organisations in many ways. It gives considerable independence to professionals to work together, without any need for administrative coordination and control mechanisms (e.g., the surgeon, anesthesist and the nurses may perform a complex operation, without any need to even exchange a single word, or a group of faculty may teach the different courses to complete the syllabus for the year, without anyone to oversee that they are doing their work). Therefore, these organisations have little need for developing tall hierarchies with middle level managers. In a professional institute, for instance, some fifty odd professors may require just one dean for administrative coordination. Even the few administrative posts in these organisations do little controlling; their main task is to interlink the efforts of different work units, to ensure funds and resources, and to manage the boundaries.

Since the standardisation of skills takes place outside the organisation, there is little need to have an elaborate technostructure (see Figure 7.4). In fact, in these organisations, even those few administrative norms (e.g., for hiring, promoting, distribution of resources) which are required for intra-organisational coordination, are often decided by the professionals at the operating core level. It may also be worth mentioning here, that these decisions emerge more through

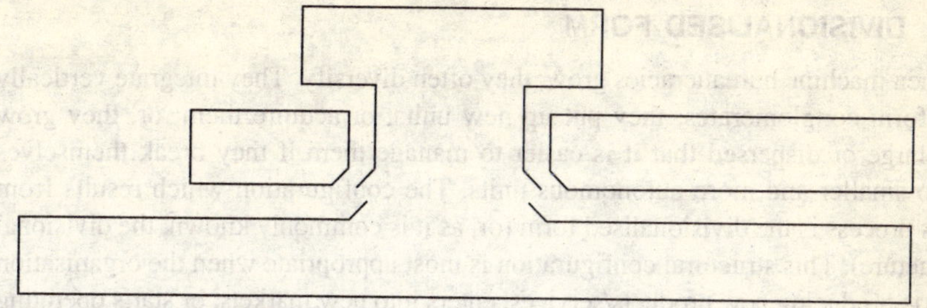

Figure 7.4 The configuration of professional bureaucracy (Mintzberg, 1983).

an interactive process than through conformity to any external, objective criteria. That is, they represent an outcome of diverse influences (motivated partly by common interest and partly by self-interest) from a group of independent professionals, often holding highly individualised viewpoints about the problem and the required solutions.

An organisation manned by highly professional experts cannot afford to use them uneconomically for low-skilled routine jobs. To do these simple jobs (e.g., typing, housekeeping, mailing, keeping a periodic check on the patient's temperature), they require a large support staff. The support staff, however, is organised on more bureaucratic lines to ensure efficiency. Thus, most professional bureaucracies have two parallel hierarchies—one which is democratic, with a bottom-up power structure for the professionals, and the other, which is organised in a more centralised top-down manner for the support staff.

Professional bureaucracies have their own strengths and weaknesses (see Table 7.4). They are ideal configurations to deal efficiently with a stable (requiring

Table 7.4 Strengths and Weaknesses of Professional Bureaucracies

Strengths	Weaknesses
• Can accomplish complex, but known, tasks efficiently, on a large scale.	• Would find it difficult to innovate; depends on "pigeonholing" of solutions.
• Provides conducive work environment for professionals.	• Norms of profession supersede internal authority in organisational functioning.
• Is a democratic structure which can successfully tap specialised expertise for organised purpose.	• Internal politics and rivalry among professionals may lead to loosing synergy and focus.

standardisation) but complex (requiring decentralisation) environment. They also provide an autonomous, yet organised, environment for professionals to work in. They are, however, not the perfect instruments for innovation; they can only do those complex tasks on a regular basis, which are already known. The democratisation of decision-making, and lack of internal control mechanisms make the professional bureaucracies particularly vulnerable to conflicts and politics among the work units, and consequently result in loss of focus in their efforts.

V. DIVISIONALISED FORM

When machine bureaucracies grow, they often diversify. They integrate vertically or form conglomerates; they put up new units, or acquire them; or, they grow so large or dispersed that it is easier to manage them if they break themselves into smaller and more autonomous units. The configuration which results from this process is the divisionalised form (or, as it is commonly known, the divisional structure). This structural configuration is most appropriate when the organisation starts producing new products/services, enters into new markets, or starts operating from different locations.

While the origins of divisional structure are quite old (when Alfred P. Sloan reorganised General Motors by "decentralising operations while centralising planning"), and it has been quite popular in the US since 1960s, it is only within the last decade or so that it has "arrived" in our country. One finds a large number of successful companies which have adapted this structural form. ITC, Voltas, Crompton Greaves, Blue Star, BHEL, Shaw Wallace and HMT, are some of the well-known examples of this trend. Even many of the conglomerates such as RPG Enterprises, UB Group, Tata Sons, etc., follow the pattern of divisionalised form of organisations.

Divisional structures are similar to professional bureaucracies in that they are also a collection of independent entities, which are stringed together by a rather loose administrative order. The difference is that, while in the professional bureaucracies these entities are individuals, in the divisionalised form they are operating units in the middle line, known as divisions.

Each of these units is actually an organisation by itself (most often fashioned along the lines of a machine bureaucracy), which is developed around a particular market, product or location (see Figure 7.5). The divisions enjoy

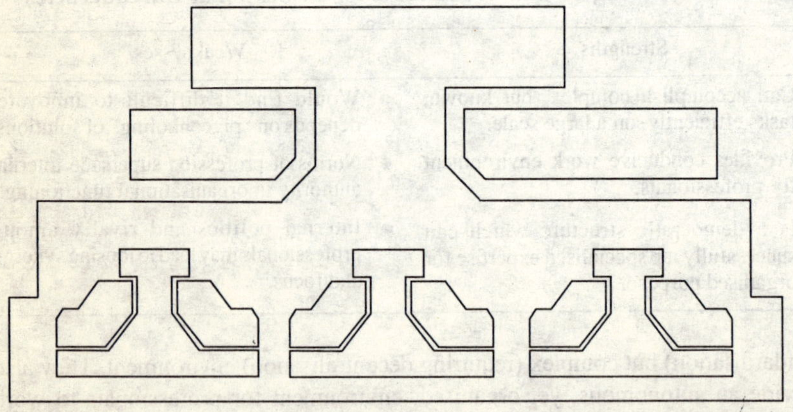

Figure 7.5 The configuration of divisionalised form (Mintzberg, 1983).

relative autonomy in the manner in which they may decide to function. This is so because each division deals with different environmental constraints and opportunities, making it difficult to control them through either direct supervision or by uniform rules and policies. But some form of control and coordination by the strategic apex (the headquarters) is required. This is achieved by standardisation of outputs, i.e., by making each division accountable for its performance.

One implication of establishing a performance control system is that each unit's performance should be measurable (e.g., return on investment). This is one reason why the divisions are often structured as machine bureaucracies. Since each division is considered to be an integrated unit, its goals tend to get fractionalised, thus encouraging bureaucratisation. Besides, the other structural options—simple structures and adhocracies (to be discussed in the next section)—perform in a manner where it is difficult to set standards of performance; and the performance of professional bureaucracies often cannot be measured. Moreover, the fact that the divisional managers are made responsible for the performance of their respective divisions, also encourages centralisation of controls by them.

With the autonomy given to the divisions to decide their own ways of operating (though the overall corporate strategy is still decided by the strategic apex), the need to have an elaborated technostructure at the headquarters is minimal. The technostructural activities attached to the strategic apex are mainly concerned with exercising budgetary controls on the divisions, deciding on transfer pricing policies (in case one division is a supplier of inputs for another division), fixing norms of sharing common resources, etc. The support staff at the headquarters, however, is comparatively larger, consisting of certain common facilities, e.g., legal, public relations and HRD. The administrative infrastructure at the headquarters also serves the function of integrative devices to maintain consistency of efforts and identity in the organisation.

There are numerous advantages, as well as disadvantages, of divisionalised form (see Table 7.5). One of the most important advantage is that it encourages

Table 7.5 The Strengths and Weaknesses of Divisionalised Forms

Strengths	Weaknesses
• Decentralises coordination and appropriate authority for rapid response.	• Fosters potentially dysfunctional competition for corporate resources.
• Allows divisions to develop and implement appropriate strategy for their particular environment.	• Creates ambiguity about the extent of sharing of power between the divisions and the headquarters.
• Ensures performance by making divisions accountable for it.	• Can lead to neglect of corporate social responsibilities.
• Frees the CEO for broader strategic decision-making.	• Can lead to inconsistencies in policies and practices across divisions.
• Provides a good training ground for strategic managers.	

efficient allocation and utilisation of capital, because it allows the organisation to put its money in its strongest markets. It also helps the organisation to spread out its risks, depending on different markets and products for its survival and growth (instead of being dependent on a single market and product, as is the case with machine bureaucracy). This potential for maneuverability in and out of markets, also makes the divisionalised organisation strategically more responsive. And finally, the diversified field of activity, as well as the autonomy it gives to its divisional managers, makes it an excellent ground for developing general managers.

Looking at the disadvantages, the limited decentralisation of powers at the divisional level invariably brings in an ambiguity about power sharing between the division and the headquarters. This can become a major source of conflict. Moreover, the accountability for outputs, which are mostly measured on a short-term (annual) basis, often makes the divisions averse to taking initiatives in long-term innovative ventures. In fact, since the accountability of divisions is limited to quantifiable and measurable outputs, it may encourage them to totally ignore their non-quantifiable social and ethical responsibilities. Also, the autonomy given to the divisions can often result in inconsistency in policies and practices across divisions, which can upset many parties within the organisation.

VI. ADHOCRACY

Let us consider a designing riddle. An organisation, by its very definition, is organised to achieve outputs which can be planned and foreseen. The planning for targets, and their achievement, is the basis of all efficiency. But then, how do organisations achieve innovative outputs which cannot be planned for in advance? A creative advertising firm, after all, is not fully aware of the nature of the likely advertisements when it takes up an account. Neither does a consultancy team know the recommendations it is going to make (in fact, not even the actual nature of the client's problems) when it takes up a consultancy assignment. So how do they organise themselves to achieve their goals?

In the latter half of this century, the need for collective, organised efforts to achieve complex and innovative goals has become more and more common. While simple entrepreneurial structures, as we saw earlier, can be innovative, the complexity of these goals is beyond the limited innovative capabilities of simple structural configurations. This has given rise to, what Mintzberg termed as, the Adhocratic Structures. Adhocracies describe the structural configuration of a variety of organisations, such as the film-making units, task forces, think tanks, consultancy teams, advertising agencies, manufacturers of engineering prototypes, etc. In many way, these structures are the most difficult configurations to describe. This is also partly so, because they violate the very basic tenet of a structure—that a structure is structured. These are, in a manner of speaking, unstructured structures (see Figure 7.6).

Adhocracies are characterised by a high amount of complexity, non-standardisation and fluidity of processes. Given the innovative nature of work, any kind of standardisation is difficult. To manage the complexity of job requirements, these organisations employ highly specialised and trained experts, and work with low levels of formalisation in a highly organic manner. However, unlike professional bureaucracies, they cannot simply rely on standardised skills

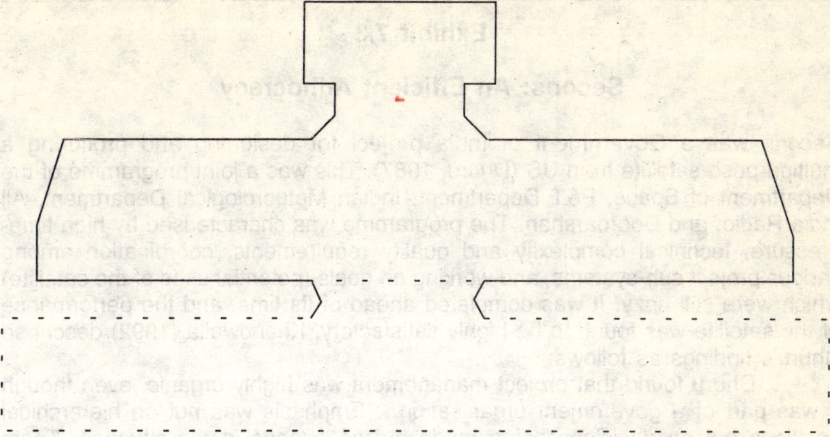

Figure 7.6 The configuration of adhocracy (Mintzberg, 1983).

for achieving coordination. This would discourage innovation. To innovate, the experts must work together and combine their skills, rather than working independently (as happens in professional bureaucracies). Thus, in these organisations, the existing skills merely become the bases for interaction among multi-disciplinary experts. The boundaries of conventional specialisations are done away with, by assigning the jobs (or projects), not to individuals, but to multi-disciplinary teams (e.g., through matrix structures, task forces, self managing teams).

Lack of standardisation, as well the requirements of professional interactions, encourage a coordination process through mutual adjustment. There is much reliance on informal communication, and agreements among experts to get the work done. This gives rise to two major consequences for these structures: one, there is virtually no technostructure; and, secondly, since the influence process is informal, the power within the system keeps on shifting according to the nature of the problem being tackled. Thus, unlike other configurations, the power in adhocracies is selectively decentralised, or dispersed (see Exhibit 7.3 for an example of adhocratic structure).

Such a distribution of power also blurs the distinction between the strategic apex and the rest of the structure. The strategy is not developed at the top and then implemented lower down (it is also not always possible to do so, when the innovative outcome of one's efforts cannot be predicted). Rather, it develops out of the numerous decisions taken while working on the project. The strategy in adhocracies is continually developing, as the project proceeds, and all those who get involved in the project become, in a sense, the strategy makers.

Mintzberg (1981) distinguished between two kinds of adhocracies: the operating adhocracy and the administrative adhocracy. The *operating adhocracies* take up projects on behalf of clients. They treat each client's problem as unique, requiring a creative solution (unlike professional bureaucracies which tend to provide standardised solutions to different problems). In such a situation it is difficult to separate the process of arriving at the solution (planning and designing)

Exhibit 7.3

Secons: An Efficient Adhocracy

Secons was a Government of India project for designing and procuring a multipurpose satellite from US (Dhuru, 1987). This was a joint programme of the Department of Space, P&T Department, Indian Meteorological Department, All India Radio, and Doordarshan. The programme was characterised by high time-pressure, technical complexity and quality requirements, coordination among various project sub-systems, and working on goals (potential uses of the satellite) which were still hazy. It was completed ahead of its time, and the performance of the satellite was found to be highly satisfactory. Khandwalla (1992) described Dhuru's findings as follows:

...Dhuru found that project management was highly organic, even though it was part of a government organisation... Emphasis was not on hierarchical positions but on decisions being made by the experts in the situation. Team functioning and team-building were emphasised... Space Lab used a matrix structure for Secons, with specialists drawn from different departments and put into various temporary project teams. There was extensive delegation of authority and a strong emphasis on lateral and horizontal coordination.... The project management board, the project maintenance office, the various project managers and project coordinators, the review council, task-forces and various other sub-committees functioned as multiple coordinative mechanisms. This is not to say that there was no hierarchy, no rules and procedures, and no sophisticated planning, monitoring and control systems. These were there. But the overriding priority in this organisation of specialists, however, was getting the job done with minimal time and cost overruns, and a great deal of flexibility had to be exercised, given the uncertainties experienced by the project management.

The members of the project team observed that the most important traits needed in an effective project manager were innovative ability, initiative, resourcefulness, and human relations and communication skills. Innumerable formal and informal meetings were a feature of the management process, with Space Lab employees spending 50 percent of their time in meetings. Personal influence was widely used within the organisation and in dealing with sub-contractors etc. for getting the jobs done. The work climate was achievement-oriented rather than authoritarian control or dependency oriented, and was also marked by norms of experts power and 'extension' (that is commitment to collective achievement, altruism, good of the organisation etc.).

---

from its actual execution. Thus, in these organisations the distinction between the problem-solving team and the operating team disappears, creating an organic whole, in which the managers, staff and the operating experts work together as a project team in highly fluid relationships (this form of adhocracy is represented in Figure 7.6 as the portion above the dotted lines).

The *administrative adhocracy,* on the other hand, takes up projects on its own behalf. In such cases, the distinction between the administrative and the operating work is maintained (the latter is shown by the dotted lines in Figure 7.6). This results in a two-part structure: the innovative work is carried out by a project team comprising of managers and staff experts, while the operating component, which executes the ideas, works separately in a standardised manner.

For instance, in a magazine publishing house, while the editorial and marketing staff may form a project team for bringing out a special issue, the printing function may continue to work independently in a standardised manner.

In spite of being very appropriate for innovative tasks, adhocracies also have their limitations (see Table 7.6). They are quite effective as small and temporary systems to deal with complex and dynamic environments. But their effectiveness also bears the cost of inefficiencies. To survive and maintain the same levels of effectiveness, they need to invest large resources and skills for integrating their activities and liaisoning among the various sub-units. This can be quite a drain on the organisation over a period of time. The inherent ambiguity of these structures, besides being a source of stress for the members, also encourages political motives. Therefore, with growth in size and age, they are likely to succumb to the pressures for bureaucratisation (in fact, often organisations which start as adhocracies, grow into and stabilise as professional bureaucracies).

Table 7.6 The Strengths and Weaknesses of Adhocratic Structures

Strengths	Weaknesses
• Encourage innovation and initiative.	• Are inefficient in utilisation of resources.
• Are flexible and responsive to changing environments.	• Increase stress through inherent role ambiguity.
• Discourage empire-building through cutting across functional/role boundaries.	• Encourage people to use political means for achieving their ends.
• Provide a good training ground for strategic managers.	• Weak control structure; low personal accountability.

VII. IMPLICATIONS

But does the preceding discussion mean that there are actually only five kinds of organisations?

Actually, no. Organisations are quite varied and distinct from each other. In fact, Mintzberg (1989) himself reported a study in which out of 123 organisations only about half could be neatly fitted into these five categories. The others were hybrids, conforming to two or more configurations. This is likely, since organisations are complex entities, with different parts facing different environmental demands, and, therefore, developing along the lines of different configurations. In the same organisation, for example, it is quite logical to expect that the structural configuration of the assembly-line shopfloor would be quite different from that of the training department.

Moreover, these configurations describe the ideal organisational prototypes. They describe certain consistent patterns, in which various elements of the organisation neatly fit together to form a gestalt. Real life organisations may not necessarily conform to these ideals. Some organisations show this consistency, others don't. This may also be the critical difference between the effective and the ineffective organisations.

What these configurations, however, do provide us with, are useful models to think rationally about the design options. They point out to the basic fact that different kinds of organisations have different aims. What matters in achieving effectiveness is not so much the kind of organisational structure one adapts, but how consistent this structure is both internally as well as externally (with the goals and environment of the organisation).

8 Organisational Power, Conflict, and Politics

As already discussed, organisations are self-consistent systems. The effective organisational structures, it was suggested, somehow follow a logic, in which the nature of environment, strategy, technology and structure match the demands and requirements of each other. We also saw that this consistency in the pattern, is achieved through the coordination and control mechanisms, which appropriately and rationally distribute the power and positions across the organisational roles.

Thus, the rational approach assumes that people occupying equal hierarchical positions or similar roles will be vested with equal power, while people in subordinate positions will exercise less power than their superiors (with a few exceptions, as in professional bureaucracies and adhocracies). Such an understanding of the organisation, however, only presents a part of the picture. While environment, strategy, size and technology do determine the structure, they are not the only determinants. Studies (Child, 1972; Pugh, 1973) have shown that these tangible variables, at best, only explain about 50 to 60 per cent of variance in the structure (Robbins, 1987).

Such studies suggest that there are also other somewhat non-tangible, and even non-rational factors, which influence what happens to/within the organisations. This seems realistic also. Organisations do not always function in a rational manner. For example, it is not uncommon to find, that among colleagues having similar seniority and functional responsibilities, some exert more influence on organisational affairs than the others. Similarly, even among departments, there exists an implicit hierarchy, which makes certain departments more powerful than others. Among the equals in the corporate animal farm, it seems, some are invariably more equal than others !

What these realities also point to, is the fact that the authority (i.e., the right to influence) of a position, is not necessarily equal to the power (i.e., the ability to influence) of that position. While the authority may be rationally delegated in the organisation, the power of a position depends on a number of "extraneous" (personal and situational) factors. These differences in the extraneous factors result in inequities and imbalances in the power structure within the organisation, opening up opportunities for many apparently non-rational factors (e.g., conflicts, politicking, etc.) to creep in the organisational functioning. In this Chapter, we will focus on the role and dynamics of power and politics in organisations.

I. SIGNIFICANCE OF POWER AND POLITICS IN ORGANISATIONS

In Chapter 1, we had noted the inevitability of power inequity and the political struggle and conflicts surfacing in an organisation. The hierarchical and authority-based nature of the organisations, the differences in the need for power, the organisation's need to optimise, leading to struggle for resources, etc. makes them ideal grounds for exercising legitimate and illegitimate influences (see Exhibit 1.4). Moreover, these inherent anachronisms, which characterise the power relationships among the organisational members, further encourage them to adapt political means for achieving personal and organisational goals.

The popular connotation of terms like politics and political skills is rather negative, implying that their use in the organisation is bound to have dysfunctional consequences. However, the fact that exercise of political skills (or exercise of power through political skills) is so inherently interwoven in the fabrics of organisational life, suggests that their use may not always be dysfunctional for the organisation. Power, after all, refers to one's ability to influence flows of available energy and resources towards certain goals as opposed to other goals (see Exhibit 8.1). In this sense, both power and political skills serve similar

---

Exhibit 8.1

Symbols of Organisational Power

Executives can use power and political skills in many different, concrete and symbolic, ways. Acquiring status symbols (e.g., size of the office, number of telephones, perks, etc.) is one of the most common ways in which an executives power in the organisation gets manifested. Effective, and *really* powerful executives, however, tend to use power in a manner which contributes to their effectiveness. Some of the indicators of effective utilisation of one's power are (Kanter, 1979):

- The executive has early access to crucial organisational information about major decisions and changes.
- The executive can favourably intercede on behalf of someone who is in trouble with the authorities.
- The executive can get a desirable placement, promotion or above-average salary for subordinate(s).
- The executive can get approval for expenditure which is beyond budget.
- The executive can influence the agenda for meetings.
- The executive has fast, easy and regular access to top decision-makers.

(It is worth noting that, in contrast to authority, which refers only to downward influence, the above manifestations of power, describe power as predominantly referring to horizontal and upward influence.)

---

functions. Both refer to the ability to influence, and both can be equally used to achieve legitimate or illegitimate goals. The difference, probably, lies in the means of influence: exercising power would involve the use of legitimate means (one's position, expertise, reward and punishment, etc.), whatever be the ends, while political skills refer to the use of illegitimate means (withholding information, ingratiating, game-playing, etc.) to achieve ends, which may be quite legitimate.

These arguments are not intended to convey, that playing politics is a necessarily desirable form of organisational behaviour. Undoubtedly, politics in organisations has dysfunctional consequences: it wastes organisational energies, is used to resist necessary changes (or to bring about those changes which are not required), creates unnecessary stress, hampers with goal achievement, and so on. But it would be equally unrealistic to ignore the positive contributions which power-politics makes to the organisations. Mintzberg (1989) argued that politics has at least four functional uses in organisations:

1. Politics ensures that the stronger members of the organisation are brought into positions of leadership (specially, since bureaucratic structures and autocratic superiors tend to suppress strong subordinates). It allows those with more initiative and competence to prove their worth by getting ahead and to start taking organisational responsibilities matching with their potential.

2. In organisational decision-making, the tendency of those in authority is to present a one-sided case on any issue. Politics ensures that all sides of the issue come to surface and can be debated. Thus, politics can provide an alternative way to a more democratic functioning.

3. Most organisational changes are resisted by the established systems of authority (the "vested interests"), for whom the change is threatening. Politics turns out to be necessary for removing these blocks to the required changes.

4. Political skills of the executive are also necessary to make it easier to arrive at and implement decisions. Effective executives do need to rely much on their skills of persuation, negotiations, making trade-offs, building networks, etc., to achieve perfectly legitimate organisational goals.

II. STRUCTURAL DETERMINANTS OF ORGANISATIONAL POWER

Power has often been understood as a personal characteristic—some people, because of their personality, expertise, or skills, have it, while others don't. However, if one takes a broader view of power, viz. the "ability to influence", this ability derives not only from the personality and interpersonal skills of the individual, but also from the particular structural situation, in which he or she is placed. After all, the personal secretary of the CEO is always likely to wield more power over others as compared to other secretaries. Similarly, if a particular job is more important to achieve organisational goals (or the job-holder is able to convince others that it is so), its occupant will enjoy greater power. Many studies (e.g., Hickson et al., 1971; Kanter, 1979; Astley and Sachdeva, 1984; Brass, 1984; Hackman, 1985) have supported the contention that the peculiar characteristics of a job contribute much to the person's organisational power. The following discussion on such job/structural characteristics is based on these findings.

A. Hierarchical Position

Obviously, the most common base of power is the position which the individual occupies in the formal hierarchy of the organisation. This position gives him formal authority to influence subordinates' behaviour, by legitimately demanding compliance, and by sanctioning rewards and punishments for performance. By virtue of position, one can even make organisationally legitimate demands on one's colleagues (e.g., the production in-charge can legitimately ask the purchase manager to plan purchases for spare parts). The higher the position, the more power one is likely to exercise.

Of course, hierarchical position is not the only basis of power. There are also individual differences in the manner in which people exercise their authority, some of which can be more effective than others. Bachman et al. (1968), for instance found that use of power based on ones position, and the ability to reward and punish appears to be negatively or inconsistently related to organisational performance. Shetty (1978), reviewing the research literature, also found that use of such power is more likely to have dysfunctional consequences, whereas power stemming from expertise and relationship with subordinates may be more functional. These findings suggest that the formal, position-related power may not be the most effective basis for influencing others.

B. Non-Routineness

As we discussed earlier (refer Chapter 3), if a job is of routine nature, it is more likely to be controlled through standardisation of work procedures. This would decrease the degree of freedom which the occupant can exercise. A non-routine job, on the other hand, allows the person performing the job a high degree of autonomy and flexibility. In an organisation, if the nature of the job is non-routine, it justifies a variety of behaviours, which the person can indulge in. Moreover, since there are no standards to decide the legitimacy of his demands or behaviours, it also allows him to make a variety of demands on the organisational infrastructure. As one would notice on studying Exhibit 8.2, the underlying commonality among the non-routine jobs is low formalisation. One can conclude, therefore, that less formalised and standardised jobs are more likely to make the occupant experience power in the organisation.

C. Centrality to Workflow

Centrality refers to how critical a job is, for the organisation to achieve its strategic goals. Often a job can be quite a non-routine one, without wielding any power, because it does not contribute very significantly to the process of organisational goal achievement. On the other hand, jobs, which are central to the workflow of the organisation, even the routinised ones, are likely to have more influence on organisational decision-making.

Exhibit 8.2
Which are the Powerful Jobs?

- if the job involves dealing with environmental uncertainties, e.g., marketing jobs in a competitive industry;
- if the job has innovative and creative goals, for which a standard cannot be predicted;
- if the job is new in the organisation (new department or function, few predecessors) so that the process of standardisation is not yet complete;
- if the job has high interpersonal component (dealing with clients and customers, liaisoning, etc.), making it difficult to formalise its contents;
- if the job is central to the strategic intent of the organisation, e.g., finance and accounts jobs, if the organisational strategy emphasises cost-control;
- if the job is critical to organisational performance, and cannot be substituted, e.g., a specialist's job which is central to the workflow;
- if the job allows one to have control over critical resources, e.g., finance jobs in a capital-intensive industry;
- if the job involves access to sought-after information, e.g., job of the secretary to the CEO; and so on.

In fact all jobs contribute in some way or the other to the achievement of organisational goals. So how can one identify which jobs are more central to work-flow as compared to others?

In our discussion on strategy (refer Chapter 5), we had seen that each strategic stance of the organisation, emphasises different priorities, and therefore, gives varying importance to different functions. That is, the centrality (or importance) of any particular job or function would depend on how directly it is related to organisational strategy. If the strategy focuses on product-market diversification, the marketing and product-development functions would be more central to organisational workflow. On the other hand, in a mass-manufacturing firm, with an assured market, marketing would be a peripheral function, while the production, quality control and finance functions would become more important.

This would also explain why in many mass-production companies, till recently, the personnel, training and HRD functions were treated as inconsequential departments (often used as "dumping ground" for those out of favour). However, with the new strategic emphasis on achieving ISO 9000 certification and TQM, training and HRD have become more central functions (e.g., many organisations, such as Indian Aluminium, Usha Martin, and Modi Xerox have combined the HRD and TQM functions into one post), and therefore, are now more important in the organisation.

D. Control Over Inputs

If a job, by virtue of its position in the structure, has control over resources, which are required for others' functioning, it will have power over others, more so, if these resources are scarce and critical to others' functioning. For instance, the power which trade unions exert on the management is mostly based on this demand and supply equation. The unions control the workers, who are a critical input for effective organisational functioning. This control gives the unions an advantage in the exercise of power and in getting their demands met by the management.

Often, many support functions (e.g., industrial engineering, maintenance and finance) exert power over line-functions because of their control over critical inputs. Unless the industrial engineers recommend the work norms or manpower requirements, or until the finance people sanction the money, the activities of the line department would remain affected. One important input, which is often used for power maximisation is the information. The lowly clerk who knows the complicated rules of the bureaucracy, the expert who possesses specialised knowledge for solving critical problems, or the secretary who is privy to the board room gossips, all carry power, because they are in the possession of information, which is vital to others.

It is interesting to note in this respect, that till a few years back, the tax consultants and lawyers used to command a lot of respect (and fee) from their clients. This was so, because only they possessed the information to understand and manipulate the complex taxation laws and rules. However, during the late 80's and early 90's, as these rules were simplified, these professionals seem to have gradually lost their power in the eyes of the society. It may not be unreasonable to assume, therefore, that many specialists, within the organisations, will resist changes which aim to simplify their areas of activity (and so, rob them of their power). For instance, if the rules governing land registration are simplified, numerous government clerks and officials will certainly loose their power.

E. Uniqueness

Related to control over inputs is the insubstitutability of the resources. If a machine breaks down, and the maintenance support is not forthcoming, it is likely that some experienced shopfloor operator may devise a makeshift arrangement to continue with the work uninterrupted. But if the problem to be solved is complex, such as a sudden fire on the Bombay High (or in the oil wells of Kuwait), only a person with highly specialised competence, like Red Adair, can solve it. Such jobs are unique and cannot be substituted, which makes them quite powerful in the system.

In the organisations, jobs which require specialised skills invariably carry greater power. Actually, almost all jobs require a certain level of specialised competence and skills. However, many of them can be substituted. For instance, even the job of a car-driver in the transport section of an organisation requires special skills. But these skills can be substituted by those of taxi-operators. That is why car-drivers do not influence organisational matters (unless, of course, they force the management to enter into an agreement barring it from hiring taxis, thereby, making their own skills in the organisation insubstitutable). But the skills of doctors in the hospitals, professors in academic institutions, cost accountant in an industry, executive chefs of five-star hotels, etc., cannot be easily replaced by another operator. This explains why these job-occupants enjoy a considerable say in the organisational matters.

F. Proximity to Power

Finally, if the job allows one to be in the proximity of the place where crucial organisational decisions are taken, it gives one greater opportunities to influence these decisions. Of course, this influence is more often informal in nature than formal. Young and junior subordinates are sometimes invited to make presentations (e.g., the marketing executive looking after a new territory may be asked to make a presentation in the annual sales conference), but such occasions are rare. Mostly, the influence is informal, as the subordinates may be interacting with their senior officers on an informal level only while sharing a table in the executive cafeteria, or commuting in the company bus.

It is important to understand that this proximity to power can be both in terms of chain of command, as well as physical in nature. For example, members of certain task forces,—even though consisting of lower rank executives—report directly to the top management. This gives them greater access to strategic information, as well chances to express their views (even on matters not directly related to the project entrusted to them). If one is discussing proposals of a technology plan, it is not difficult to also put forth one's views about how the training department should be restructured to shift its emphasis from management training to focus more on skill training for workers.

Even physical proximity opens up new and informal channels of communication. Executives from units located near the corporate office have greater opportunity for meeting the top management. Similarly, members of corporate staff, irrespective of their ranks and seniority, are more likely to enjoy more power from hob-nobing with decision-makers (at least, their colleagues in the field are more likely to look at them as carriers of reliable information, and therefore, accept their words at face value).

III. POWER IMBALANCES: SOURCES OF ORGANISATIONAL CONFLICTS

People like to be powerful, to have control and mastery over their life and work. Adler (1927), in fact, proposed power as a basic human motive. An ideal condition of organisational life would be, if every job-occupant feels equally and adequately empowered to manage his work. However, it is generally accepted that organisations do not (and probably cannot) distribute power equally across different hierarchical levels. In addition, as we saw in the previous section, power is also not distributed rationally in the organisations. The structural arrangements in organisations, inadvertently end up by giving some departments or jobs more power than they rationally require, while leaving others with lesser influence than they deserve.

These power imbalances stimulate the less powerful to put in efforts to enhance their power, leading to organisational conflicts. Like organisational power, organisational conflicts also have their roots in organisational structure. Many studies (e.g., Seiler, 1963; Strauss, 1964; Walton and Dutton, 1969 and Walton, Dutton and Cafferty, 1969) have identified a number of structural factors, which contribute to organisational or interdepartmental conflicts. In this section, we will briefly review these findings under four broad categories—horizontal differentiation, interdependence among subunits, performance and reward criteria, and incongruent relationships.

A. Horizontal Differentiation

The very fact that organisations put people in different groups and functions, creates potential for conflicts. This peculiar aspect of human nature was reported by Bennis and Slater (1968), when in an experiment the students were randomly divided into 'red' and 'green' groups. These groups did not compete, or even interact; they just sat in the same room and completed a questionnaire. It was found that "only 10 minutes are needed to activate defensiveness and fear, reflected in the hostile and irrational perceptions of both "reds" and "greens"." Similar findings were reported by Blake, Shephard and Mouton (1964) with a group of executives. These executives were divided into two groups, where they automatically developed their own group structure, norms and cohesiveness. When they were given identical problems, for which they had to find the "best" solution, there was a marked tendency to enter into a win-lose power struggle, to perceive the other group members as adversaries, and to down-grade their solution.

Similar dynamics is likely to occur in organisational settings. Lawrence and Lorsch (1967) noted that as organisations become more differentiated, the different sub-units (departments, groups, divisions, etc.) develop significant task-based internal differences. These differences are in terms of (a) the degree of structure, (b) the orientation among members towards the environment, (c) their planning time perspectives, and (d) their interpersonal orientations. Shapiro (1977), for instance, noted that marketing and manufacturing executives typically differ from each other in their assessment of and problems related to planning, quality assurance, cost control, customer service, product development, etc. It is important to note, however, that horizontal differentiation only creates a potential for conflicts, but does not necessarily lead to conflicts (much would depend on the integrating mechanisms in the organisation).

B. Interdependence among Sub-units

Obviously, if two units are mutually independent of each other, and have no opportunity to interact, there would be no reason for any conflict to develop between them. Conflicts occur only when there is some extent of interaction and interdependence among units. This interdependence can be in three ways:

1. The units may be **mutually dependent** on each other to accomplish their goals. This dependence can be for receiving and giving assistance, information,

compliance or doing other coordinative acts, which help each unit to achieve their specific goals. For instance, consultants in a team, or executives in a task force are mutually dependent on each other. The problem they often experience, is related to overlapping of issues, such as task overload, sharing of common resources, dealing with common clients, etc.

2. The units may be **asymmetrically dependent** on each other. That is, while unit A may be dependent on unit B for assistance, coordination, information, or inputs, etc., this dependence is only one-way. In such an arrangement, unit B would have little incentive to coordinate. Moreover, since the units are arranged in a sequential long-linked chain, it also encourages a unit to get away by blaming the preceding unit for its own failure. For instance, the marketing department may blame the production for low quality, while the production department may pass off the blame to the purchase department for low-grade materials, and so on.

3. The dependence among the units can also be because of their dependence on common resources. For instance, in most organisations different sub-units depend on a common pool of organisational resources, such as physical space, equipment, personnel, operating or capital funds, and centralised services, etc. In situations when these resources are scarce in an organisation, and where their allocation is not mediated effectively, the chances of competition and conflict among the sub-units are high.

One would notice that such interdependencies are quite common in any organisation. Organisations are, after all, composites of interdependent units, which are bound together by common goals. It follows, therefore, that the potential for conflicts is always inherent in any organisation.

C. Performance and Reward Criteria

The interdependence among horizontally differentiated units has some noteworthy consequences for the organisations. As organisations grow in complexity, often the goals of their sub-units become more and more independent and compartmentalised from each other—even to the extent that the goals of one unit may interfere with the goals of other units. For example, one of the goals of the stores and purchase function is to keep the inventory low to avoid the blocking of capital. But achievement of this aim can sometimes seriously hamper the smooth functioning of the production department.

Organisations, of course, evolve coordinating mechanisms to integrate such separate goals. The fact, however, remains that organisations expect their different wings to perform in manners which may not be very consistent. This often results in conflicts among the sub-units. Work in most organisations stipulates the units working as a team. The performance, however, is appraised and rewarded for each units achievements. We can consider, for instance, the following case: In a construction company, different projects in the region were expected to share the common plant and equipment facilities. In practice, however, some projects would hoard certain critical equipments (even when not required immediately) which would hamper with the other projects' progress. The conflict situation arose because those who violated the norm of sharing, were able to finish their projects without time and cost overruns (and correspondingly, their executives received more recognition, bonus and promotions).

The inconsistencies in the performance and reward criteria among different sub-units also arise on account of the differences in the nature of their activities. Shukla (1986), for instance, noted that organisations are often divided between the innovating functions (e.g., R&D, value engineering, product development, HRD, etc.) who are responsible to bring about change, and operating functions (e.g., production, finance, etc.) whose task-efficiency depends on maintaining the status quo. Similarly, in his discussion on the marketing-manufacturing conflict, Shapiro (1977) noted:

> Because the costs of a broader (product) line are primarily in the manufacturing area, the manufacturing manager emphasises the advantages of a narrower line. The reverse is true of marketer. Thus the situation literally forces each manager into an adversary position. Each creates pressure for the policy that minimises his costs, maximises his benefits, and leads to positive evaluation and an appropriate reward.

Differences in performance and evaluation criteria also arise because of the variety of goal characteristics among the sub-units. Some have more long-term goals (e.g., R&D, HRD), while others have short-term targets (e.g., production, marketing); certain goals can be measured (e.g., rejection rate, machine down time, etc.), while others are immeasurable (e.g., industrial harmony); some are based on "hard" data (e.g., capacity utilisation, inventory levels), while others rely on "soft" data (e.g., customer satisfaction), and so on. Naturally, such different goals cannot be measured on a common criterion, even though use of differential criteria paves way for conflicts to occur.

D. Incongruent Relationships

Through their control and coordinating mechanisms, organisations aim at structuring and regulating the relationships among their members and sub-units. This, unfortunately (or fortunately?), is not completely possible. Certain areas of ambiguities are invariably left unattended. In fact, as we saw in some of the earlier Chapters, certain environmental, strategic or structural considerations encourage deliberately ambiguous definitions of roles and relationships. Some of the common sources for these incongruences in inter-role/functional relationships are:

1. The organisational definition of a relationship contradicts the cultural norms. For instance, many old workers resent complying to young professionals, since culturally age is related to authority.

2. Certain roles and functions, particularly the creative ones, need to be characterised by low formalisations, which encourages ambiguities in expectations from/by the incumbents. Since the perceived legitimate expectations may not be met, conflicts can result.

3. Organisations, which consist of heterogenous and specialist groups, are more likely to experience conflicts. This is so because diversity of expertise and

orientations makes it difficult for the organisation to perfectly coordinate their activities.

4. The more complex (horizontally, vertically and geographically) an organisation is, the greater are the chances for communication distortions to occur. This, in turn, would create potentials for conflicts.

IV. MANAGING ORGANISATIONAL CONFLICTS: A CONTINGENCY PERSPECTIVE

Like power and politics, conflict is also a largely negatively understood term. Most often, it is interpreted as a hinderance in the teamwork, which is supposed to be essential for achieving a common organisational goal. Correspondingly, management of conflicts is often equated with elimination or avoidance of conflicts. Responsible managers, it is assumed, must ensure that conflicts do not arise and harmony prevails. This popular view (shared by many managers) was further strengthened in a study by Singh and Parthasarthy (1985). Based on the responses of 242 executives, they concluded that avoidance of conflicts and compromising when a conflict situation arises, appeared to be the most prevalent styles of conflict management among Indian executives.

Conflicts, however, are not always dysfunctional (even if they are uncomfortable). Boulding (1964) demonstrated that groups which contained deviant members who would challenge the established order, produced better ideas and more elegant solutions, than the perfectly harmonious groups (ironically, when asked to drop one group member, the groups ousted their deviant members, inspite of their positive value). Similarly, Pareek (1982) concluded that conflicts give impetus to richer exploration, more extensive debate and better solutions.

There are, admittedly, conflicts which can lead to disruption of organisational activities. However, as Robbins (1987) noted:

> An organisation totally devoid of conflict is probably also static, apathetic, and nonresponsive to change. Conflict is functional when it initiates the search for new and better ways of doing things and undermines complacency within the organisation.... The manager's job is to create an environment in which conflict is healthy but not allowed to run to pathological extremes.

Rclated to this negative connotation attached to conflict is also the assumption that the best way of managing conflicts is through **collaboration** (this view is even shared by many management experts, e.g., Blake, Shepard and Mouton, 1964). Practising managers do realise that while collaboration may be an ideal wotth striving for, it is often not the most feasible one in reality. In this section, we will propose that, besides collaboration, there are also other strategies which can be effective and useful to manage conflicts in organisational situations. Derr (1978) proposed that besides collaboration, two other methods, **bargaining** and **power-play**, can be equally useful in managing conflicts, depending on the nature and context of conflicts (see Table 8.1). Moreover, organisations also use **structural and procedural strategies** to contain and resolve conflicts. We will discuss these in this section.

Table 8.1 A Comparison among the Three Modes of Resolving Inter-group/ Departmental Conflicts

	Collaborative	Bargaining	Power play
Objectives	Win/Win	Win/Lose	Win/Lose to Lose/ Lose
Focus	Organisational/Inter-group solution	Intra-group solution	Personal gain
Assumptions about people	Open, honest trusting, collaborative	Unite when faced with common threat	Act only for self-interest
Information	Openly shared	Strategically shared	Secrecy and distortion
Problem-solving mechanism	Joint problem solving	Trade-offs	Unilateral, mutual, manipulation
Power sharing	Equality	Struggle for parity	Power inequalities accepted
Type of solution	Internal, psychological contract	External, legal contract	Unclear, unstated contract

A. Collaboration

Collaboration is one of the most popularly recommended approach for managing conflicts. Most of the OD intervention techniques, in some way or the other, rely on establishing a collaborative climate among conflicting parties. It stands to reason also, that if people have problems with each other, the most rational and civilised way to deal with them is to understand each other's point of view and to arrive at a mutually acceptable solution.

There are numerous advantages of using a collaborative approach (Thomas, 1976; Derr, 1978) to manage conflicts. Some of the most significant ones are listed below.

- Collaboration creates a climate of authentic and open interpersonal relationships among organisational members and sub-units. Such a climate is conducive to long-term smooth functioning of the organisation.

- Collaboration is a problem-solving approach, and therefore, encourages more creative and innovative activities in the organisation.

- Collaboration facilitates information flow and feedback processes in the organisation. In doing so, it also lays the foundations for the emergence of self-correcting mechanisms in the organisation.

- Collaboration ensures long-term commitment of the organisational members to problem-solving, and thus, it also reduces the need for the introduction of more formal coordinating mechanisms.

Organisations can achieve collaboration among sub-units as also among member's roles in a number of ways. OD techniques describe both structural as well as process-oriented interventions for collaboration. Three of the most common methods for managing conflicts through encouraging collaboration are described below.

1. Creating superordinate goals. Intergroup conflicts often develop because people get so involved in the achievement of their compartmentalised objectives, that they neglect the common goals for which they are working. These priorities, often perceived at the level of the group heads, also get pushed down the hierarchy, and become a major contributor to interdepartmental conflicts.

Many researchers (e.g., Sherif, 1966) suggest that a common understanding of shared goals can greatly facilitate a climate of collaboration. The current popularity of promoting a corporate vision (quality of product, customer service, increasing exports, etc.) also highlights this process of creating superordinate goals, which help in unifying conflicting organisational energies. Research findings of Sherif and Sherif (1969) suggested that introduction of a "common enemy" helps in reducing hostility between groups. Thus, when organisations face stiff competition in the market, it provides an opportunity of pitting the organisational team against the market forces (it is interesting to note the extent to which the popular managerial terminology reflects this metaphor of battle, e.g., winning and losing, capturing the market, beating the competition, flagship company).

2. Joint problem solving. This is one of the most frequently used techniques for increasing collaboration. It requires the conflicting parties to come together, analyse and define the problem, understand each other's viewpoints, and arrive at a rational and objective solution through mutual interactions (see Exhibit 8.3).

Exhibit 8.3

Intervention Format for Building Collaboration

A number of formats have been described by management theorists and practitioners (e.g., Blake, Shepard and Mouton, 1964; Beckhard, 1969; Hornstein et al., 1971; Burke and Hornstein, 1972; Harrison, 1972; Likert and Likert, 1976, etc.) for effectively facilitating collaboration-building processes between conflicting groups. The underlying commonality among these interventions is in terms of the process which they commonly follow. The typical format for conducting these interventions:

- encourages conflicting parties to define and articulate their problems and perceptions separately;
- provides them opportunity for sharing these perceptions;
- once sharing is done, is to discuss and arrive at a common understanding of the problem;
- jointly explores alternatives for solving this problem, and arrives at a mutually acceptable solution;
- builds an action plan for implementation of this solution; and
- follows up and reviews the implementation at a future date.

The aim is to solve a problem, which is experienced by all parties, not to win or lose against each other. The usefulness of bringing people, face to face, lies in helping them to identify not only the differences, but also the similarities in their perceptions.

3. Increasing interactions. Often many interdepartmental conflicts are rooted in misperceptions and lack of understanding between different units. As we saw earlier, the functional segmentation is further augmented by each sub-unit developing its own norms of working and interacting. In the process of doing so, they also becomes insensitive to problems and requirements of other sub-units.

These demarcations can be broken down, if organisations provide more opportunities to the employees in these sub-units to interact with each other. If people interact with each other, not only would they develop better understanding of each other's way of functioning, but also may discover common interests, problems, and priorities. For instance, the annual sales conferences, besides dealing with substantive organisational issues, also create a sense of comeraderie and understanding among executives looking after different territories. In many organisations, the same purpose is achieved through more formalised means: they create a system of inter-unit, inter-divisional, and even inter-functional transfers (e.g., Hindustan Lever).

Inspite of the popularity of collaboration as a conflict management strategy (at least in the management literature), it is often not the most feasible one. Derr (1978) pointed out that success of collaborative efforts depends on four basic preconditions:

(a) conflicting units must be interdependent, i.e., should have long-term stakes in solving the problem;

(b) they must be equal in terms of their power in the organisation;

(c) there should be potential for mutual benefit as a result of solving the common problem; and,

(d) there should be organisational support (in terms of time, money and energy) available for the collaborative efforts.

It needs no great emphasis to point out that these conditions are not always present in the organisations. Sub-units lack power parity (in fact, that itself may be the reason for conflict); for most departments, the stakes in solving a problem are short-term (meeting the annual targets); and only a few organisations are willing to invest resources in real team-building efforts (except as a cosmetic training programme). Most of the time, divisions and departments are left with no other alternative, than to adopt other strategies for managing conflicts.

It is also worth noting that the primary goal of any organisation is not achieving harmony and collaboration, but achievement of its strategic objectives. In many complex organisations, collaboration may not be a realistic, or even desirable, goal to strive for. Too much emphasis on collaboration ("we must live like a happy family") can increase the chances of "group think" (Janis, 1982).

Or, it can even become a tool in the hands of the political forces. As Rico (1964) remarked:

> The individuals or groups who are most vocal in advocating 'harmony and happiness' in an environment devoid of conflict, may only be protecting their vested interest in *status quo*.

B. Power-Play

Power-play or power-politics is the archetypal antithesis of collaborative strategy. Whereas collaboration is a win/win strategy, which aims at establishing acceptable rules of interaction, power-play aims at a win/lose situation by circumventing or distorting the established rules. Derr (1978) defined power-play as "a secretive mode that could work in the best interest of those, whose covert objective is autonomy and whose desired impression is that of being committed." He also noted that this method of conflict management has often been condemned because it unleashes aggressive and hostile feelings, distorts or suppresses valid organisational information, displaces energies to unproductive purposes, and at times, even subverts organisational goals.

Nonetheless, power-play is an organisational reality, which often fulfils useful aims. There are a number of situations in which power-play and politicking may be an appropriate (or at least, an efficient) means of dealing with conflicts. Some such situations are:

- when people need to work for their rational self-interest (which may not necessarily be contrary to organisational interests). For instance, experts in the organisation may like to maintain their autonomy, use their specialisation for organisational purposes, but without wanting to invest too much of their energies in building collaborative relations.

- when the organisational environment is competitive, in which a collaborative stance may make one more vulnerable. For instance, if different divisions have to compete for budget allocation, then the sharing of critical information with others would make them aware of one's weaknesses, and give them a strategic advantage.

- when preconditions for collaboration are not met, but coexistence is necessary for achievement of personal goals. Such a situation would result in a sort of dynamic equilibrium between the conflicting parties. For instancc, the relations between management and union often endeavour to maintain a balance between compatible self-interests (also note that inspite of their power-play, both often benefit. While the management is able to save through redeployment of labour, the workers manage to get better salaries or amenities).

- when the dispute is ideological in nature. For instance, the conflicting parties may be unwilling to look at the dispute as a problem to be solved or negotiated over. The only course open in such a situation is to achieve one's ends at the cost of others.

What behaviours constitute power-play? Often the political behaviours in organisations have been described as "games". Mintzberg (1983a) listed out a number of political games, which are often played by people in the organisation with the intent of optimising their power. For instance, experts in the organisation may seek to safe-guard their power, by keeping their skills from becoming common to all, or privileged information may be used by a less powerful member to "blow the whistle" to an influential outsider on questionable/illegal behaviour by the organisation. Similarly, Wofford, Gerloff and Cummins (1977) identified a list of power tactics used by executives and sub-units in the organisations. Let us look at some of the commonly used political behaviours.

1. Withholding information. This is the most common power tactic. Information is a source of power. If one retains control over this source, it would ensure others' dependence, and give one an advantage. For instance, if the copies of personnel policies manual are not made available to all line managers, it leads to their dependence on the personnel department.

2. Blocking-off incoming information. If one can manage to block or delay the information from reaching oneself, it not only allows one to avoid or delay making commitments, but also ensures that the other party is forced to make a "personal request". Departments often build complicated (and vague) procedures, nurture inefficiencies, or create internal bottlenecks to ensure that they can seal off requests and demands from other departments. For instance, the stores section may develop a complex system for indenting spare parts (with the legitimate excuse of avoiding pilferage) to emphasise its power over the shopfloor sections.

3. Delaying agreements and decisions. The longer one can delay an agreement which would make one accountable, the greater maneuverability one would have. Often this tactics is used in the form of appointing a committee to look into the problem. The trick involved is in making a vague commitment (e.g., "we need to discuss it in detail"), which ostensibly indicates one's sincerity, but in reality keeps the problem hanging.

4. Emphasising perfectionism. Being perfectionists, quality-conscious and uncompromising on solutions is a legitimate behaviour in most organisations. But it can also be used as a tool to obstruct the work processes of other organisations. It is often used both ways—one may demand perfectionism from others (e.g., the maintenance crew will not be released till the machine runs noiselessly), or one may practice perfectionism oneself (e.g., the finance department will not pass a bill till all related documents, even the trivial ones, are enclosed). In either case, it puts pressure on the other party.

5. Protecting one's territory. Organisations are horizontally differentiated along functional specialities. The more one can maintain the uniqueness of one's job activities, the greater would be one's value. This is true of not only highly skilled specialists, but even of the unskilled job categories (e.g., the cleaning staff may get unionised and protest against their jobs being made a part of the helpers' jobs on the shopfloor).

C. Bargaining

Bargaining is a middle-ground between the collaborative and political strategies of conflict management. It incorporates elements from both strategies—the problem-solving stance of the collaborative approach, as well as the tactical moves and counter moves of the power-play. It is also one of the most commonly practised conflict management strategy. Bacharach and Lawler (1981) noted:

> Bargaining is a central element in a mixed-motive setting. Given simultaneous incentives to cooperate and compete, mixed-motive relationships are inherently unstable and inevitably involve some distrust. In this context, bargaining is the primary means for keeping the conflict within acceptable bounds and avoiding a complete bifurcation of the relationship.

Bargaining may not be the ideal approach, but it is definitely a practical one. It has its limitations: the win/lose stance can create new interpersonal or organisational confiicts; it can only help arriving at less than perfect compromise solution; and, it involves commitments which are more legal and formal than intrinsic in nature. Inspite of these imperfections, it is useful in a number of ways:

- It ensures that the conflicting parties openly share their concern for, and also arrive at, some immediate solution.

- It provides an opportunity to the conflicting parties to interact with each other, implicitly or explicitly acknowledge mutual interdependence, and thus, build grounds for better understanding.

- It is an efficient way of establishing power parity, paving way for future collaboration. Not only can the two parties recognise the value of what each can give or withhold, they also enlarge their areas of agreement by arriving at some common solution.

- It is probably the most efficient way in which scarce resources can be distributed.

While bargaining is a rather complex and dynamic process, it does invite certain predictable forms of behaviour from the involved parties. Based on studies on bargaining behaviour (Thomas, 1976; Derr, 1978; Bacharach and Lawler, 1981; Walton, 1987), one can identify the following four critical features of this approach:

1. Selective sharing of information. In the bargaining process, parties use information selectively and strategically. While much information may eventually be exchanged by the parties during the process, this sharing is done in stages, to enable one to maintain some strategic advantage. On certain issues, complete information may not even be shared altogether. For instance, the management may reveal its budget for welfare activities only after it has gauged the nature of demands the union is likely to insist upon.

2. Continuous revaluation of one's position. Since the picture of the problem as construed/presented by the other, emerges gradually during the process, it becomes necessary for each party to re-evaluate their position during the process. This is often because each may realise that their insistence on some preferred alternative can have undesirable consequences for some other important concerns. For instance, the marketing wing may stop insisting on a new product-line, when it realises that this may affect its other important orders.

3. Variations in pressure tactics. Corresponding to revaluation of one's position, the process is characterised by what Thomas (1976) described as the "escalation/de-escalation" dynamics. Thus, during the bargaining process, the conflicting parties may increase or decrease the amount of pressure during various phases. For instance, one may increase or decrease the number of disputed issues, adopt flexibility on extreme demands, switch from an environment of agreement to that of hostility, and so on.

4. Trade-offs. The solutions in bargaining are achieved through periodic trade-offs during the bargaining process. Each party successively gives some concessions to the other, in exchange to certain items of perceived importance. The net result is that most of the solutions arrived through bargaining are compromise solutions.

D. Structural and Procedural Strategies

Organisational conflicts, as we discussed earlier, often originate from the specific organisational conditions. It would be a reasonable contention, that manipulation of organisational elements would also help in resolving these conflicts. In fact, one of the purposes of coordinating and integrating mechanisms is basically to ensure avoidance of conflicts among the various sub-units. In this section, we will discuss some of the conflict management strategies, which involve rearrangement of organisational elements.

1. Reducing interdependence among units. Since one of the main reasons for conflicts to occur is the interdependence of the sub-units, to reduce the conflicts these sub-units could be made more autonomous and independent. For instance, if one unit is dependent on the outputs of another, the conflict can be reduced by creating a buffer stock in the first unit. Alternatively, the first unit may be given freedom to obtain its inputs from other sources. Organisations, when they rearrange themselves by creating profit centres, also reduce the interdependence among the sub-units.

2. Top-down interventions. If two parties fail to resolve their disagreements, it can be handled at the level of their mutual superior. The superior, in this case, takes up the role of an arbitrator and integrator. In certain cases, this role can also be played by a formal organisational system. For instance, the grievance redressal system in an organisation, often helps in resolving conflicts which cannot be ordinarily resolved by the parties involved.

3. Enlarging resources. Since conflicts often arise because of scarce resources, expanding the resource base can be a successful strategy for eliminating conflicts. This, however, is easier said than done. Organisations work on the principle of optimising output even with limited resources, and increasing resources would definitely involve greater investments, which the organisation may not be willing to make. The ultimate decision would depend upon considerations such as the relative costs of resources and the adverse impact of conflicts. Even within these limitations, however, it is often possible for the organisations to increase their resource utilisation. Manpower, equipments, and other resources can often be creatively and flexibly redeployed to overcome periods of scarcity.

4. Combining conflicting units. This strategy is sometimes used in the organisations by restructuring the conflicting units in a manner so that one incorporates the other. For instance, in many manufacturing companies the quality control function is a part of the production department. It ensures that conflict between the two functions can be resolved at a local level. Similarly, in one of the academic institutes, the conflict between the Personnel & IR Department and Organisational Behaviour Department arose due to the overlapping nature of these disciplines. The strategy used was to combine the two and form a new department of HRD.

V. IMPLICATIONS FOR MANAGERS

A focus on the role of power in organisations is important for one to understand and to cope with the reality of organisational life. For the practising managers, the preceding discussion offers numerous insights for effective functioning:

- It is important to recognise that organisations are not merely rational entities, designed by tangible situational contingencies. Rather, many intangible human and structural factors also conspire to create what an organisation would ultimately be. In fact, as we saw, many rationally structured activities also carry an underlying implication for power distribution and sharing among the members. An awareness of these implications is essential for managers to function effectively.

- Ideologically, a collaborative stance is necessary for the organisations to become more humane systems to work in. It is equally important, however, to recognise that collaboration may not always be a successful strategy to deal with the conflicts and power-issues. The ability and skills for using other strategies for conflict-resolutions (i.e., bargaining and power-play) are perhaps equally important for managers to be effective in achieving results.

- Lastly, a fuller appreciation of the role of power in organisations would be incomplete, without focusing on how it influences the decision-making and leadership processes in the organisation. This we will do in the next Chapter.

9 Organisational Decision-Making and Strategy Formulation

1. In the early 1980's, Tata Industries developed a strategic plan for the Tata group of companies. The plan categorised the existing Tata companies into six primary business groups (metals and allied industries, engineering, chemicals and agro-chemicals, consumer products and services, trading and utilities) and identified two more areas of activities (hi-tech and international business). The whole exercise was based on certain forecasts about the changes in business environment within the next decade or so, e.g., rate of growth of economy, opening up of economy, growth of service and joint sectors and availability of skills. The plan made sense, and the forecasts turned out to be prophetic, but it was not implemented because of internal opposition and indifference.
2. In an interview with Business Today (June 22–July 6, 1992), RP Goenka described how he takes decisions about takeovers and acquisitions: "I have never looked at the balance-sheet of any company that I took over. It was pure gut-feel and I never went wrong. The moment I ignored the gut reaction, I made a mistake."
3. In 1974, BHEL did a formal analysis of the power requirements of the country within the next decade. The anticipated threefold growth in the power generation requirements, also meant an increase in the transmitting capacities and industrial electrical equipments (e.g., motors, compressors, process boilers and traction equipments). Based on these projections, a plan was developed, which led to BHEL's diversification into turnkey erection projects and alternative energy sources, greater focus on internal R&D activities for indigenisation of technology, divisionalisation of production facilities, and so on.

One implication of our discussion in the previous Chapter, is that the influences on organisational decisions (e.g., decisions regarding strategies, investments, budget allocations and inter-functional systems) are not always rational, objective and based on tangible contingencies. The role and dynamics of power and politics in organisational functioning raises new questions about how organisations take and implement decisions. Specifically, if power is distributed in a non-rational (even if understandable) manner in the organisation, who takes the decisions? Are appropriate decisions taken unilaterally and then implemented in a systematic manner, or do they emerge through a series of small tactical and political readjustments? How do different political forces influence the ultimate shape of an organisational strategy? What is the role of leadership? In what manner can a manager think that he can be an effective decision-maker? Is there a perfect way to take best decisions? and so on.

The above examples also highlight that there are more than one ways in which significant and right decisions are taken in the organisations. The same process of arriving at a decision, which saw its smooth implementation in BHEL, for example, was resisted in the Tata Sons. One can assume, therefore, that not only are there different approaches to decision-making but also that each approach may be appropriate only for a given situation. But before we discuss the dynamics of organisational decision-making, let us focus on what are the organisational decisions.

I. WHAT ARE ORGANISATIONAL DECISIONS?

All executives take decisions, they plan their activities, decide whether or not to sanction a leave, appraise the performance of their subordinates, plan for reducing costs and overheads, decide on steps to be taken for streamlining their department's functioning, select among options for improving efficiency, and so on. In doing so, they aim at optimising the returns on their efforts. In fact, taking decisions is one of the most crucial function of the managerial role.

The same applies to the organisations. Organisations are social units with a purpose and goal, which they seek to optimise through the decisions they take. According to Ansoff (1965), the main purpose of organisational decisions is "to configure and direct the resource conversion process in such a way, as to optimise the attainment of the objectives." Since there are various kinds of resources which need to be optimised (e.g., plants and inventory, money, human resources), correspondingly, there are a variety of decisions, which need to be taken in the organisation. Very broadly, one can classify organisational decisions into three broad types (Ansoff, 1965, see also Table 9.1).

A. Operating Decisions

Operating decisions are the day-to-day decisions, which aim at maximising the efficiency and profitability levels of the organisation's current operations. The necessity of these decisions, arises due to the complexities and uncertainties which are inherent in the routine functioning of the organisations. Mostly these decisions deal with internal organisational issues such as pricing, production schedules, inventory levels, operational monitoring and control, marketing policies and strategies, etc. The responsibility for taking these decisions is generally decentralised at the operating levels.

B. Strategic Decisions

In contrast to the operating decisions, the strategic decisions focus on issues external to the organisation. These decisions, deal with problems such as the goals and objectives of the organisation, selection of a product-market mix, strategies for diversification, investment and expansion, etc. The ultimate objective of such decisions is commitment of the total resources of the organisations, so

Table 9.1 Distinctive Characteristics of Operating, Strategic, and Administrative Decisions (based on Ansoff, 1965)

	Operating	Strategic	Administrative
Key issue	Maintain operating efficiency.	Commit organisational resources.	Create linkages between the operational and strategic decisions.
Focus	Internal environment.	External environment.	Coupling of the internal and external.
Key characteristics	Decentralised; routine; self-regenerative.	Centralised; non-routine; non-self-regenerative.	Balancing; ongoing; triggered by the operating or strategic decisions.
Examples	Production plan; pricing; inventory level; monitoring and control, etc.	Goals/mission; investments; expansions; growth strategy, etc.	Structure; rules and procedures; MIS; reward system; acquisition/development of resources and facilities, etc.

as to maximise the returns. Mostly these decisions are centralised, though the decision-maker may solicit views and information, or try to gain consensus around the decision.

It is important to note that, unlike the operating decisions, the need to take strategic decisions is not so obvious. In normal course of working, one generally cannot do without taking decision about, say, how to tackle the increasing costs; however, one has to be strategically sensitive to perceive the need (and opportunity) to diversify (or invest in a particular project). Thus, there is always a danger that the organisations may invest more energies on taking operating decisions, while neglecting the strategic ones.

C. Administrative Decisions

A balance as well as integration between the operating and the strategic decisions, is essential for organisation's success and effectiveness. If the strategic decisions over-commit the existing resources to new ventures, there may not be any resources left for the existing routine functions within the organisation. On the other hand, if all resources remain blocked in the routine operations, the organisation may suffer strategically. Also, the strategic decisions can be successful only if they get translated into the organisation's operating reality.

Administrative decisions serve this linking function. These are decisions which aim at structuring the organisation's resources for optimum performance. The aim of these decisions is to provide a coupling between the economic and social factors affecting the organisational performance. They deal with issues such as designing the structure and information-flow, formulating the systems and procedures and acquiring and developing resources, etc.

II. INFLUENCES ON ORGANISATIONAL DECISIONS

One way to build up a framework for understanding the organisational decision-making process, can be by starting with the question: Who has the power to influence organisational decisions? Following this line of enquiry, one can identify four influencing forces, and correspondingly, the following four ways in which decisions are taken in the organisation:

1. Influence lies with the environment/market. Correspondingly, within the organisation, power would lie with those who can rationally interpret and define the environment, and suggest rational approaches for dealing with it, viz., the analysts. The resulting decision-making process would be characterised by a normative/rational approach.

2. Influence lies with the top management. The decisions are shaped by the visions of the top decision-makers, who broadly and intuitively assess the environmental opportunities. The corresponding decision-making process can be described as entrepreneurial approach.

3. Influence is distributed among "pockets of power". The decisions would emerge in disjointed steps, through a power struggle among the stake holders. This process would describe the political approach to decision-making.

4. Influence is shared by everybody in the organisation. The decisions emerge through proportionate contributions of all concerned. This is a consensus building approach, in which the decision-making process seeks commitment of all, to rationally arrive at decisions which conform to a broad vision.

In the following sections, we will discuss each of these approaches in detail.

III. THE NORMATIVE/RATIONAL APPROACH

The systems perspective views organisations as consisting of rationally interrelated sub-systems (e.g., market environment, strategy, technology and structure). This interrelatedness implies that the activities and changes in one sub-system would influence the activities in other sub-systems. The rationality of the system also means that it is possible to identify the relationships among the sub-systems, and to predict how changes in one are likely to affect the others. This interrelatedness may, at times, give rise to apparent conflicts among the sub-systems' goals (e.g., whether the investments should be made in modernisation of existing technology, or the funds should be allocated for new product development). However, since organisations are driven by a common set of goals, it is possible to rationally optimise the solutions for different sub-systems. This essentially, is the basic premise of the normative/rational approach to decision-making.

A. The Nature of Rational Decisions

Consider, for instance, the problem of inventory levels in an organisation. The manufacturing department may favour long uninterrupted runs to minimise its per unit cost, resulting in large inventories of similar finished products. The sales department, on the other hand, would like large inventories of varied products, so as to meet the customer requirements. And, the finance department, would naturally like to minimise the capital tied up in inventory, and therefore, prefer a high rate of inventory turnover (leading to low inventory levels). How should the organisation solve such a problem?

Obviously, the solution would depend on what is required for the company's benefit, the opportunities and constraints it is facing in the market, its own resources, and so on. The organisation must address itself to questions such as the nature of the market, the demand potential for its products, the financial viability of maintaining large inventories, comparative contributions of production cost savings and sales turnover to the profits, etc. The analysis of the situation, would help the company in fixing an overall strategy, and in deciding the manner and direction in which its resources should be aligned. That is, having decided on the strategy, the company can rationally fix its priorities in a manner, which allows optimum utilisation of its resources.

Thus, the normative/rational approach deals with decision situations in an objective and scientific manner, in which the vagaries created by human motives do not feature. One would notice that the objectivity of the approach, also allows the reality to be modelled and the decisions to be made in advance (e.g., the phasing out of investments over the next five years). Organisations achieve this foresight and planning in decision-making, through using management tools and techniques, such as decision models, operations research, technology assessment studies, MBO, experience curve, product-market matrix, etc.

The strategy formulation process in normative/rational approach also follows similar lines. In Chapter 5, we had discussed the interpretation of strategy as a plan. Strategy is seen as emerging from the classical process of long-range corporate planning. Ackoff (1970) described planning as "something we do in advance of taking action, it is anticipatory decision-making...". There are three characteristics of this approach (Mintzberg, 1973):

1. In the planning mode, the analysts (the corporate planners, the financial analysts, the market researchers) play a dominant role;

2. The focus is on systematic and comparative analysis of proposals for their feasibility, identification of their relative cost-benefits and risks, and evaluations of their efficiency (or economic value);

3. It aims at achieving an integration of various decisions and strategies. Mintzberg noted that: "...this interrelatedness (of decisions) is the key element of planning. An organisation plans in the belief that decisions made together in one systematic process are less likely to conflict and more likely to complement each other than if they were made independently."

B. The Payoffs of Rationality

A formal corporate planning process, helps the organisations to focus on the future implications of present decisions, as well on the present implications of future events (Loasby, 1967). It helps the organisations to monitor the course and direction of their progress by developing long-term indicators of success.

But does it give the desired results? The findings are far from clearcut. Gray (1986) found that a large number of American organisations use formal corporate planning systems, with relatively favourable results. Similarly, Chaudhury (1979) and Chopra (1989) noted, that formal planning systems are also prevalent in many, though not all, successful Indian organisations. While in the recent years, long-range planning has been criticised for its rigidity, the research findings (e.g., Thune and House, 1970; Vancil, 1970; Rue and Fulmer, 1973; Schoeffler et al., 1974, etc.) present a mixed picture of its success.

Thune and House (1970), for instance, in a study of 36 companies found that those which had formalised long-range planning system were more successful, as measured on five criteria of financial performance. However, whether planning actually led to better performance was not so certain, since in many industries (e.g., petroleum, food-processing), they found, it was the improved performance which led to implementation of formal planning procedures. Some organisations, it seems, first shoot accurately, and then learn how to aim at targets. Moreover, the success of planning systems in improving performance was not found to be universal across industries. Thune and House's findings appeared to be generally applicable to certain industries (e.g., drug, chemicals, machinery) but not to others (e.g., steel, oil, food-processing).

In another study, Rue and Fulmer (1973) also noted this industry-specific success of planning systems. They studied 386 organisations for the impact of planning activities on performance (as measured by sales growth, growth in earnings, earning to sales ratio, and rate of return on investment). They found that in durable goods industries the planners outperformed the non-planners, while in service industries, it was the non-planners who performed better than the planners. Thus, the viability of long-range planning depends on the industry-specific environment. As Mintzberg (1976) noted:

> When an organisation is in a stable environment and has no use of very creative strategy... then the development of formal, systematic strategic plans (and main-line strategies) may be in order. But when the environment is unstable or the organisation needs a creative strategy, then strategic planning may not be the best approach to strategy formulation...

This seems logical also. Organisations operating in a stable environment can more accurately predict the demands, fix their targets, decide on strategies for achieving them, and successfully implement these strategies. This simple picture, however, becomes complicated when one considers another study (Vancil, 1970), which found that while organisations project their future targets, the actual performance, though improved, does not really conform to these projections. That is, the process of fixing the targets appeared to influence the performance more than the targets themselves.

Vancil's findings can be understood, if one appreciates that besides fine-tuning the decision process, the planning practices are also likely to encourage new and functional processes in the organisation (Quinn, 1978). They would, for instance, encourage managers to increase their time horizons in decision-making; promote more rigorous communication systems about organisational goals, its strategic issues, and resource allocation; protect long-term investments in developmental activities such as R&D; create a basis for evaluating and integrating short-term plans, and so on.

It is also possible that the relationship between planning and performance is actually due to some third underlying factor, which influences both. For instance, changes in the top management may simultaneously improve the performance, as well as institute a formal planning system. Firms employing formal planning procedures are also likely to be more professionally managed, employing more competent managerial resources. Thus, a planning or normative/rational approach may be a characteristic of a well-managed organisation, rather than its single cause of good performance.

C. Limits to Rationality

While, as we saw, the normative/rational approach has numerous payoffs (both planned and unplanned), it has its potential costs as well. Besides its limitations, it can even be dysfunctional to the organisation in many ways. Firstly, it can make the organisation quite rigid and bureaucratic in its decisions orientation. Since future problems are assumed to be predictable, it promotes a tendency among the organisations, to develop ready-made solutions for every problem (elaborate rules, procedures, excessive reliance on techniques, and so on). Thus, the organisation can become more prone to being lethargic, unprepared and insensitive to changes in the market.

Secondly, the realities of management are more holistic and dynamic in nature, than static and analytical (Mintzberg, 1975, 1976). For instance, the fact that one's major customer attended the competitor's son's wedding is sometimes a more meaningful information than an extensive report on the competitor's strengths and weaknesses. To quote Simon (1987):

> Over the past 40 years, the technique of decision-making has been greatly advanced by the development of a wide range of tools—in particular, the tools of operations research and management science, and the technology of expert systems.... They have had greatest impact on decision-making, that is well-structured, deliberative, and quantitative; they have had less impact on decision-making that is loosely structured, intuitive and qualitative; and they have had least impact on face-to-face interactions between a manager and his or her workers—the give and take of everyday work.

Related to the above point is the third drawback of this approach, namely, it totally ignores the human component in decision-making. As Madsen and Polesie (1981) concluded after their analysis of five cases on designing of a budgeting system:

> The designing process... has two interacting frontiers; one is conceptual, the other is social. The former can be mastered by logical thinking and skill in the

handicraft of system design. The latter must be negotiated with and accepted by members of the organisation.

It is this top-down approach of the normative/rational decision-making, which makes it quite susceptible to dysfunctional political forces. Since in this approach, the analysts wield considerable power over the line functions, this situation can create sufficient impetus for the latter to politically resist the decisions.

Lastly, if in an organisation everything is planned for, there is not much scope left for the unplanned efforts; for innovative ventures aim not at performing well in an environment, but at creating new environments to work in. Very often, it is the unplanned intuitive decisions, which have often contributed much more to an organisation's success and effectiveness than could have been achieved by a planned and targeted approach. On the contrary, a formalised decision-making system may even lead to false conclusions. When Carlson, for instance, approached IBM to sell his patent for electrography, a formally conducted market survey showed that the invention had no market potential, and so IBM refused to buy the patent (it was later bought by Haloid corporation, later renamed Xerox, and they revolutionised the market).

IV. THE ENTREPRENEURIAL APPROACH

While the normative/rational approach may appeal to the sense of order and precision of the management scientists, theorists and planners, it may not be the most accurate description of how effective organisations always function. The analysts and planners may provide the solutions, but the actual decisions, most often, are in the hands of the top management, who are more of doers than analytical thinkers. Thus, organisational decisions very often reflect the goals and visions of the leader(s) at the strategic apex. Many studies (e.g., Tichy and Devanna, 1986; Ohmae, 1987; Bower and Winberg, 1988; Singh and Bhandarkar, 1990, etc.) have highlighted the dominant role corporate leaders play in organisational success.

A. The Power of the CEO

There are some very obvious (and some not so obvious) reasons to believe that the top management group, and particularly the CEO, exerts a major influence on the decision-making process. Mintzberg (1983a) stated that "the CEO is inevitably the single most powerful individual in the whole system of power, in and around the organisation." While this may not be true in all cases (e.g., in many of the public sectors, family-owned concerns and professional bureaucracies) but being the CEO does give one the maximum opportunity for becoming "the single most powerful individual" in the organisation.

The CEO is likely to be most powerful, of course, by virtue of occupying the highest position in the institution. He has the legitimate authority to control, command, reward, and even coerce people to his wishes. He can decide the organisation's course of action, allocate resources, change the structure, etc., simply because he is entitled to do so. But, besides these, there are also some other, more potent, reasons for his power.

Firstly, the CEO "embodies" the organisation and its purpose. His actions and utterances symbolise the philosophy by which the organisation is supposed to be functioning, and tend to get translated into its operating policies and practices. This opportunity to "manage the meaning" (Smircich and Morgan, 1982) for the organisational members is one of the most powerful influences, which the CEOs exert on the decision-making process.

Secondly, the CEOs attain their positions because of their personal characteristics which, among others, also include their ability to exercise informal (or political) control over others. Mintzberg (1983a) noted that:

> ...leaders typically exhibit well-honed political skills, those of persuasion, negotiation, and so on. They could not have made it to the top without these skills. And so, ironically, the CEO is probably the most adept at using that system of influence, which those who wish to counter his power must rely on...

And lastly, the CEOs are possibly the most well-informed persons in their organisations. Because of their position, they have access to information, both within and outside the organisation, which nobody else can have. Often, they are the only ones who have the "complete picture". Wrapp (1967) in his article on the 'good managers' commented that an effective manager:

> ...has a special talent for keeping himself informed about a variety of operating decisions, being made at different levels in the company. As he moves up the ladder, he develops a network of information sources in many different departments. He cultivates these sources and keeps them open no matter how high he climbs in the organisation.

While all chief executives may not do so, but, undoubtedly, they have the maximum opportunity to practice this networking and gain power through information. What makes their position even stronger, is the fact, that much of this information is soft in nature, and therefore, cannot be documented. This makes them unique in terms of their information resources.

Many researchers have explored and attempted to establish a link between the chief executive's power and the nature of organisational decision-making. Mintzberg (1973), proposed that when power is concentrated in the hands of the chief executive (or strategic apex), organisations are likely to behave in an entrepreneurial manner. He contended that the decision-making process in such organisations would be characterised by following qualities:

1. The decisions would aim at achieving quantum jumps in the face of uncertainty;

2. The decision process would involve active search for new and risky ventures; and

3. The dominant goal of the organisation would be growth, as compared to profits.

To understand why this should be necessarily so, one must appreciate, that in organisations dominated by the leaders at the strategic apex, the decisions are likely to become an extension of their thinking patterns and motives. Thus, to understand how decisions are made in these organisations, one must comprehend the peculiarities of the thought processes and motives, which characterise the top managers.

B. How Do Top Managers Think?

Studies conducted on senior managers indicate that their ways of comprehending situations and solving problems are very different from what one normally assumes. In his study, for instance, Isenberg (1984) found that the senior executives rarely think "rationally"; the projected general image, that they systematically formulate goals, focus on tangible probabilities, logically select alternatives for maximising returns, and so on, is merely a product of some popular and faulty stereotype. Rather, their comprehension of situations and issues is mostly broad and general in nature, and they are more often preoccupied with only a few basic concerns, with which they deal in a non-rational and intuitive manner. Similarly, Mintzberg (1975) reported that senior managers typically prefer non-quantifiable soft information, broadly scan through situations, plan their activities in an ad hoc manner, and seem to work with an implicit, probably unconscious, framework, which they keep locked up in their mind. In yet another study on 200 top executives from various organisations, Agor (1986) found that they primarily used 'intuition' for taking many significant and strategic organisational decisions (e.g., investments, launching a product or restructuring the organisation). Even more significantly, the use of intuitive ability is directly related to managerial levels; managers at the top of the hierarchy rely more on intuition than the middle and lower-level executives.

These studies suggest that the top managers' thinking style is more often broad-based, general and intuitive, rather than focused, systematic and analytical. Their strategic decisions would naturally portray these characteristics. Ohmae (1982) in his description of the top manager as a strategist, suggested that their effective strategies do not result from analysis. Rather, they emerge from a mental state in which:

> ...insight and consequent drive for achievement, often amounting to a sense of mission, fuel a thought process, which is basically creative and intuitive rather than analytical. Strategists... use (analytical processes) only to stimulate their creative process, to test the ideas that emerge, to work out their strategic implications, or to ensure the successful execution of high-potential 'wild' ideas that might otherwise never be implemented. Great strategies, like great works of art or great scientific discoveries, call for a technical mastery in working out, but originate in insights that are beyond conscious analysis.

C. Uses of Intuition

Intuitive abilities are particularly suited for coping with uncertain situations. In his study, Agor (1986) also found that the senior managers typically use their intuitive abilities to deal with situations, which were far from clear-cut and tangible (see Exhibit 9.1). As one would notice, these are also the kind of situations which are likely to be faced more often by the senior managers. The evidence also points to the fact that intuitive ways of handling a situation may be more effective for dealing with uncertainties. In a study of 50 CEOs, Daft et al. (1988) noted that, under conditions of environmental uncertainty, those who conformed to the thinking pattern described above (relying on soft personal information resources, engaging in more frequent and broad environmental scanning for threats and opportunities, etc.) were found to be more successful than those who didn't. Thus, the intuitive thinking style of the top managers makes them better equipped for dealing with environmental uncertainty.

Exhibit 9.1

Intuition in Decision-Making

In his study of 200 senior executives, Agor (1986) found high popularity of "intuition" in decision-making. The executives reported that they use intuitive decision-making in the following situations:

- when a high level of uncertainty exists.
- when little previous precedent exists.
- when variables are less scientifically predictable.
- when "facts" are limited.
- when the facts don't clearly point the way to go.
- when analytical data are of little use.
- when several plausible alternative solutions exist with good argument for each.
- when time is limited and there is pressure to come up with the right decision.

Being adept in intuitive thinking, these executives are also more likely to seek out the uncertain situations where they can use these abilities successfully. For instance, a decision to enter a new and emerging market would better utilise their skills than remaining in traditional markets. As Porter (1980) noted:

> Formulation of strategy in emerging industries, must cope with the uncertainties and risk of this period of an industry's development. The rules of competitive games are largely undefined, the structure of the industry unsettled and probably changing, and competitors hard to diagnose.

Naturally, the decision-making energies of powerful top managers (i.e., when they are less accountable to others for their actions) are more likely to focus on those entrepreneurial and innovative ventures, which provide them with new risks and opportunities for successfully using their intuitive capacities. Drucker (1986) also noted that the entrepreneurial strategies are driven by an ambitious aim of gaining dominance through high risk-taking. He found that these strategies rely on creating new markets through such high risk actions such as:

1. concentration of efforts and resources on a new opportunity;

2. acting on the unexpected failures or successes;
3. taking advantage of new and emerging technologies; and
4. cashing on rapid changes in market or industry structure.

It is also worth noting here, that this drive towards market dominance and growth also satisfies the personal needs for power and achievement of the corporate leaders (after all, what other organisational avenues for need fulfilment are left once the person reaches the top levels!).

There is, incidentally, also a political reason why powerful CEOs may drive their organisations towards uncertain environments. An organisation which is in perpetual uncertainty, provides good justifications for centralisation of power, therefore, further strengthening the CEOs control. Mintzberg (1983a) noted:

> A crisis is no time for debate or politics, or, for that matter, standard procedures. The organisation must act quickly, decisively, and in a tightly integrated fashion. And so the tendency is to suspend whatever distribution of power is normal in the organisation and instead grant unusual power to the chief executive.

In fact, this ability to successfully deal with the uncertainties (which are mostly created by their own strategic decisions) further enhances the CEOs power, by giving him a charismatic image. In a survey (Singh, 1985), the responses from more than 500 Indian executives showed that the "ideal" successful chief executives had a typically entrepreneurial image: the ability to plan and see ahead, produce and create new ideas and a willingness to take risks (in comparison, specialised in-depth competence, experience and consistency of past performance were viewed as least important characteristics for success as CEO!). Corporate leaders who conform to this popular image, are likely to command greater respect and exercise more power over their subordinates.

D. Limitations of Entrepreneurial Decisions

Like the normative/rational approach, the entrepreneurial approach also has its limitations and drawbacks. In their study, Covin and Slevin (1988) found that the entrepreneurial top management style helped in improving an organisation's financial performance in organic organisational forms, but not in mechanistic organisations. In fact, the financial performance of the mechanistic organisations suffered when the top management was entrepreneurial. It seems, therefore, that the entrepreneurial approach may be more suited to young, small and informally structured organisations. As we discussed earlier, this approach would be appropriate when the market environment is uncertain, and when the organisation is manageable in size. However, as the organisation grows and the environment stabilises, it may become much too demanding for the top managers, to carry the entire burden of decision-making by themselves.

Secondly, since such organisational actions become synonymous with the self-interests of the decision-maker(s), the top managers are likely to develop personal or financial vested interests in maintaining a status quo (Miller and Friesen, 1980). Thus, in the long run, an entrepreneurial approach may actually make the organisation resistant to change.

Lastly, as Pfeffer (1981) noted, strategists are likely to get bound by their previous decisions, even in the face of evidence that the decision should be changed. In fact, when their decisions fail, they tend to increase their commitment to them, constrained by the belief that effective leaders should behave in a consistent manner. Thus, ironically, the same stance, which is supposed to make the decision-making more innovative and risk-taking, often ultimately leads to a conservative and rigid strategic orientation.

V. THE POLITICAL APPROACH

Two of the underlying assumptions in the rational/normative and entrepreneurial approaches are:

1. organisations are capable of operating as a unified entity with a single goal, which is acceptable to all; and,

2. the process of implementing a decision, starts only after it is made; thus, the commitment to organisational decisions is required only after the finalisation of the decision, and not during the process of making it.

The reality of organisational life, however, is somewhat different. As we discussed in the previous Chapter, organisations are characterised by a multiplicity of goals and motives. What may be considered by some as a rational optimisation of outcomes, or as an entrepreneurially insightful decision, may not be equally satisfying to all constituencies in the organisation. And so, it is likely to be supported by some, and resisted by the others.

Recognising this aspect of organisational decision-making, many theorists (e.g., Cyert and March, 1963; Thompson, 1967; Hickson et al., 1971; MacMillan, 1978; Pfeffer, 1981; Narayanan and Fahey, 1982; Stevenson, Pearce and Porter, 1985) have proposed that organisational decisions are an outcome of the power struggle among the constituent sub-units and coalitions of interests. It would be reasonable to assume that, since the decisions emerge through the interactions among the parties involved, the contents of the decisions would also be influenced by the processes of decision-making. Thus, any attempt to understand and manage organisational decisions must focus as much on the context and processes, which circumscribe the decision outcomes, as on the decisions themselves.

A. Organisational Politics and Coalitions

Many researchers (e.g., Wrapp, 1967; Mintzberg, 1975) have highlighted that, given the organisational realities, managers have to necessarily operate beyond their prescribed role-boundaries to be effective in their job. A managers' task is to influence the nature and course of organisational processes, and politics is one way of doing so. According to Farrell and Petersen (1982):

> Political behaviour in organisations may be defined as those activities that are not required as a part of one's organisational role, but that influence, or attempt to influence, the distribution of advantages and disadvantages within the organisation.

Similarly, Quinn (1980) noted:

> Political behaviour consists of activities undertaken primarily to increase an individual's or a group's referent or legitimate power. Achieving increased political power... does give the executive greater capacity to influence events.

These political attempts to influence the decisions by various organisational sub-units are also inevitable in the organisations due to limitations of resources, interdependence of tasks, limited availability of information, differences in powers enjoyed by the organisational sub-units, differences in interests and goals, etc. It is common to find that organisational managers and departments, who share a commonality of interests, create informal alliances or coalitions with the expressed intentions of forcing or resisting certain changes. These alliances are of a temporary nature, in the context of a particular decision (Cyert and March, 1963). Moreover, different coalitions may pursue conflicting goals, which make the goal-setting and problem-solving processes in the organisations less stable and rational. Since these coalitions play a major role in the politics of organisational decision-making, it is essential to understand their nature and structure.

Stevenson, Pearce and Porter (1985) reviewed the various definitions of coalitions in the management literature. Summarising their conclusions, they identified eight characteristics of coalitions, which distinguish them from other informal social and reference groups:

1. Coalitions consist of interacting group of individuals. Mere commonality of interests is not a sufficient condition for formation of a coalition. The members of coalitions must be in regular contact with each other. Departments and roles which are interdependent, therefore, are more likely to become part of a coalition.

2. Coalitions are deliberately formed. That is, unlike most other informal groups, members of a coalition share an explicit understanding of the purpose for which they have come together.

3. Coalitions are independent of the formal organisational structure. While the membership in a coalition may overlap with the formal organisational groupings (e.g., all staff departments may form a coalition), it is not necessarily always so. Even when such an overlapping occurs, the goals and interests of the coalition may be very different than its formally stated goals.

4. Coalitions lack a formal internal structure. That is, the internal structure and roles in a coalition are less stable and person-dependent. Often the informal structure of the coalition itself represents an outcome of a political process. This aspect of coalitions has critical implications for the nature of its influence on organisational decision-making.

5. Membership in a coalition is based on mutual perceptions. Who is, or is not, a part of the coalition, is determined by the informal acknowledgement of each other's membership among the members. While, by their nature, coalitions have fuzzy boundaries, in which certain members may be more "in" as compared to others (Boissevain, 1974), a reasonable consensus does exist about who are members, and whose membership and commitment is open to question.

6. Coalitions are formed around specific issues. They come into existence to advance the collective interests of the members. Once the purpose is achieved, they may also cease to exist (though, they may continue purely for social purpose). It is also necessary to appreciate that while members perceive a common objective for the coalition, their reasons and motives for joining it may be quite divergent.

7. Coalitions focus on issues external to themselves. This is so because the very reason for forming a coalition is to allow the members to exert more influence on an external agent than they can do individually. The nature of these influences can be proactive (e.g., they can propose new agendas for the organisation) or reactive (e.g., they may oppose emerging proposals in the organisation).

8. Coalitions require concerted action from the members. Taking deliberate and orchestrated group action is a basic requirement for coalitions. In fact, this is the primary difference they have with other social or reference groups, which get formed around common problems.

B. The Politics of Decision-Making

Coalitions, thus, play a significant role in influencing not only the specific decision outcomes, but also the extent of organisational support a certain decision will enjoy. Since they evolve and get formed around specific issues, they highlight a crucial aspect of organisational decision-making, which is totally neglected in the rational-normative and entrepreneurial approaches; in other words, the development of commitment to a decision evolves simultaneously with the process of its formulation. The evolution of a decision is, therefore, intricately tied to the evolution of the coalition around it.

It is also important to note that according to the political perspective, an organisational decision evolves and emerges over a duration, and is not "made" at one particular point of time. Narayanan and Fahey (1982) described this process as comprising of six stages (activation, mobilisation, coalescence, encounter, gambits and decision), starting from a vague notion shared by individuals separately and ultimately culminating in a tangible decision outcome sponsored and supported by the dominant coalition.

The first stage of coalition formation/decision evolution is *activation*, which is characterised by people individually becoming aware of certain salient issues and concerns. Normally, such awareness is an outcome of major changes in the external or internal organisational environment (e.g., major fluctuations in organisational performance, environmental opportunities, mass resignations, systems failures, sudden changes in manpower profile due to mass recruitment, etc.). The recognition of issues at this stage is still fuzzy, vague and intuitive. Individuals put together diverse pieces of data (bits of conversations, articles, performance reports, etc.) to see some pattern emerging. Once they have developed sufficient clarity about these issues and concerns, and are able to articulate them in a manner intelligible to other organisational members, the process moves over to the next stage of *mobilisation.*

Organisational actions are a result of collective efforts, and so, to become a part of the organisational agenda, the individual perceptions and understanding must reach the level of collective awareness, discourse and discussion (Wrong, 1980). At the mobilisation stage, information exchange still occurs at informal levels; however, some nascent alliances and networks of interrelationships begin to take shape. Narayanan and Fahey (1982) noted two major implications of this stage:

> First, the broad contours of potential strategic change begin to emerge. Second, public articulation of issues tends to reshape social reality which individuals often internalise as public facts...Thus, political commitment to decision or potential decision outcomes builds up during this stage.

The next stage, *coalescence*, is marked by the gradual formation of transitory alliances or coalitions, consisting of individuals who have common stakes in a desired outcome, and who are willing to invest their resources for the cause. Since there is an inequitable distribution of power and influence resources among the coalition members (due to personal or organisational reasons), the coalitions themselves have a political structure (MacMillan, 1978). This asymmetry of power and roles within the coalitions, is an important structural determinant of its processes (Hickson et al., 1971). Correspondingly, the specific decision alternative, which is sponsored by the coalition, is itself a product of the political processes of intra-coalition bargaining and negotiation.

One must note that when the organisation is grappling with decision on an issue, there are likely to be more than one coalitions existing around the same issue (e.g., issues such as, which areas the organisation should invest in; whether the performance appraisal system should be made open; which budgetary heads should be cut to reduce costs; who the next CEO should be, etc.) Stevenson, Pearce and Porter (1985) suggested that if a coalition is strong and visible, and if the issues raised/forced by it are salient for the organisation, it is likely to stimulate the emergence of competing coalitions. Thus, when the coalition begins to espouse a preferred option, it has to *encounter*, and actively interact and negotiate with other organisational entities (sub-units, individuals, coalitions).

This process of negotiating and bargaining is characterised by extensive deployment of *gambits* by the coalitions to achieve their goals. For instance, coalitions may selectively advocate decision criteria, which favour their own position (e.g., budget allocation among divisions should be directly proportional to the profits earned by them); they may manage the symbolic functions (e.g., beliefs, attitudes, symbols, myths to create a climate conducive to the achievement of their goals) or, they may highlight selective pieces of information to shape and manipulate the definition of the issues (e.g., showing intra-unit sales as a part of the gross sales turnover). Such gambits are aimed at strengthening the coalition's own position, and discrediting the opponents' claims. These maneuvers also help in greater information sharing among the opponents, leading to the emergence of zones of consensus, even inspite of the disagreements.

The final *decision*, reached through these maneuvers and counter-maneuvers, is one which is politically feasible. Of course, none of the political actors would admit the political nature of their efforts and stance (that would be a political folly); the decision-making process is overtly enacted as a rational activity, which supposedly culminates in a consensus among the opponents. The process may even end with a symbolic show of solidarity (handshakes, joint inaugurations, parties, etc.) among the competing coalitions, in an attempt to give a semblance of rationality and objectivity to what was otherwise a political struggle. The actual decision outcomes, however, are quasi-resolutions of the conflicts, characterised by compromises and accommodations. Since residual conflicts continue to remain beneath the surface, they may trigger off issues in future, and lead to the formation of different coalitions, and a new round of political activity in the organisation.

C. The Nature of Political Decision-Making

Mintzberg (1973) described the political decision-making process as "adaptive", since the resulting decisions adapt to an existing internal situation, rather than being driven by any external goal or vision. He suggested that such decisions will be characterised by the following qualities:

1. They will be taken when clear goals do not exist in the organisation, and will reflect a division of power among the coalitions.

2. They are more likely to yield "reactive" solutions to existing problems, rather than being characterised by a "proactive" search for new opportunities.

3. They will lead to decision outcomes which are incremental and disjointed in nature.

Studies also suggest, that a political approach to decision-making may be more prevalent during certain organisational situations than during others. Gray and Ariss (1985) proposed that political struggles in decision-making are more likely to occur in mature and/or declining organisations, than in young entrepreneurial firms. In the early periods of growth, the impact of the founder's personality and ideology is quite dominant and acts as an integrating force for the various constituents; the decisions during this stage, are more entrepreneurial than political. However, as the organisations become mature and new leadership takes over, this influence becomes less dominant. The processes of formalisation, consolidation and achieving stability, which characterise a maturing organisation, also tend to throw up issues of control of resources among the departments and sub-units. Similarly, when organisations are in the stage of decline and renewal, the concerns for change versus maintaining status quo become salient decision-seeking issues. Gray and Ariss (1985) contended that the political activity is most intense and overt at this stage.

It seems, thus, that the absence of a dominant leadership creates ideal conditions for organisations to indulge in political activity. A leadership vacuum at the top, not only deprives the organisation of a binding force, it also invites many contenders to occupy it (Kets de Vries and Miller, 1984, 1987).

VI. THE CONSENSUS BUILDING APPROACH

The discussion in the preceding sections highlights some very crucial implications for effective decision-making in the organisations. We saw that the different decision-making approaches, while having their specific advantages, also have their own limitations, which become more apparent in certain contexts. An effective decision-making approach, therefore, would be one which is able to overcome, or at least, largely minimise the influence of these inherent constraints of the approaches. That is, an effective decision-making approach must:

1. allow the maximum possible information to reach the decision-maker.
2. incorporate mechanisms, which help the decision-maker to sift through this information and arrive at a set of optimum decision alternatives, and
3. increase chances of arriving at a decision, which is politically acceptable to different coalitions and constituencies, without compromising on its quality.

The consensus building approach offers such an alternative. In the following discussion, we will aim at developing an understanding of the organisational processes which constitute consensus, and the mechanisms which consensus seeking executives use for arriving at decisions.

A. The Meaning of Consensus

Consensus is more than mere acceptance of a decision by everyone. Strong charismatic leaders often manage to receive a high level of acceptance and commitment to their decisions from their followers. This may, however, only show a high level of trust in the leader, and not a common and shared understanding of the issues involved. Consensus, on the other hand, has as much to do with personal commitment to a course of action, as with a shared intellectual agreement about the rationale, as to why such a course of action has to be followed. Floyd and Wooldridge (1992) defined consensus as follows:

> We define strategic consensus as agreement among top, middle, and operating-level managers on fundamental priorities of the organisation. This agreement shows itself in the actual decisions taken by managers…

It is important to note, that consensus results not only in people following certain decisions in unison but, more importantly, also in their taking actions and decisions, which are congruent to the mutually agreed upon priorities. To accomplish the latter, it is essential that people share a more or less similar understanding of the basic priorities for which the decisions need to be taken. Floyd and Wooldridge (1992) suggested that consensus about decisions can be understood as involving two dimensions: (a) the common cognitive understanding and perception about the decision priorities, and (b) the shared emotional commitment to act and decide in an agreed upon direction. Unless the decision-making process (and the decision-maker) takes care to ensure a high degree of understanding and commitment, the consensus would be weak (see Figure 9.1).

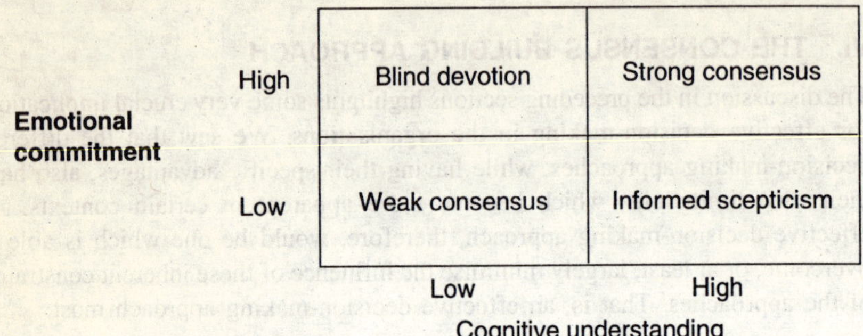

Figure 9.1 Illustration of the interaction of emotional commitment and cognitive understanding for achieving consensus.

For instance, if organisational members are committed to the decision, but do not share a common perception and understanding, their stance would be one of blind devotion. They may follow a decision because it is personally satisfying or emotionally fulfilling, but the lack of grasp of the total picture would severely handicap their efforts in the face of contingencies and exceptions. On the other hand, in many organisations, circulars, corporate communications, meetings, etc., ensure that middle and lower-level managers are kept aware of corporate decisions. Inspite of this shared knowledge, the top management often finds that the middle and lower-level managers do not "cooperate" and drag their feet in implementing the decisions. The reason, obviously, lies in the informed scepticism shared among people, which does not enthuse them about the decision, and which is often rooted in the perception of conflict between the corporate priorities and personal or professional aspirations. True consensus is achieved only when, both commitment to and understanding of the decisions are high.

B. Mechanisms for Developing Consensus

For any manager, the "how" of developing a consensus, is a critical determinant of his effectiveness as a decision-maker. The need to involve others and to gain their commitment in decision-making, becomes even more critical with increase in uncertainty, the need for improved quality of decisions, and a larger span of control/group size (Heller and Wilpert, 1981). There are also indications, that the current emphasis on "participation" does not always lead to consensus building. In his study of 12 Indian organisations, Maheshwari (1980) observed that a participative approach by the top management mostly tended to stop at the senior managers' level. The departmental heads, he found, were not keen to continue the process of participation downwards. Building consensus, thus, would involve more than use of formal forums of involvement and consultation. As Floyd and Wooldridge (1992) noted:

> Regular workshops are useful, but shared understanding relies on continuous discussions of strategy. This occurs as middle and lower-level managers make

proposals, probe into the top management's criteria, and challenge the status quo. The emphasis is on a daily, two-way communication, involving a wide range of managers.

Many management researchers (e.g., Wrapp, 1967; Quinn, 1978, 1980; Lorsch, 1986; Kotter, 1990; Floyd and Wooldridge, 1992) have explored the somewhat intangible ways, in which successful managers succeed in achieving organisation-wide consensus on crucial corporate and strategic decisions. Based on these studies, one can identify the following mechanisms which are involved in building consensus.

1. Receptivity to signals. The effective decision-makers recognise the uncertainty (the information and cognitive limits) in which they function, and so, make conscious efforts to reduce it by remaining open to multiple channels of information. They show an awareness of the fact that organisations, as systems, normally tend to overlook early signals of crisis as well as opportunities. Correspondingly, their receptivity to information is marked by two distinctive features. Firstly, they develop and nurture a large informal network, which enables them to receive objective information in the shortest possible time. This networking extends to not only within the organisation (the staff and line executives, trade union executives, workers, etc.), but also outside the organisation (suppliers, customers, politicians, technologists, etc.).

Secondly, they attribute a high value to the "soft" information, which may be non-quantifiable, sometimes even non-verifiable (a rumour, chance remark, or an inconsequential detail). In fact, for them, such informally communicated pieces of information have as much, if not more, credibility and relevance, as the contents of a well-researched and documented report. They recognise, as Starbuck, Greve and Hedberg (1978) put it, that much "of the content in every report is ritualised irrelevance". It tends to miss out on the richness and nuances of relevant information, which can only be grasped and communicated through interpersonal interactions.

Such sensitivity to a varied amount and nature of information, helps the decision-makers in identifying broad patterns and issues, which may be relevant to the organisation. While there may be numerous decision areas requiring attention, effective executives select and focus on only a few key thrust areas. Being aware of their own cognitive limitations and also the uncertainty of the terrain they are charting, the initial decisions are often vaguely worded as broad visions and questions (e.g., "our objective is goals with profits"; "we aim to give the customer value for money", or "we must become competitive at the international standards", etc.). Such broad visions permit the decision-makers, to provide the organisation with a sense of direction without their actually committing themselves or the organisation to any specific set of objectives, prematurely (Wrapp, 1967). Moreover, being vague and broad, these vision statements do not create a threat for people to coalesce against, thus, avoiding political oppositions.

2. Building awareness. Having identified the broad directions in which the organisation is likely to move, the next task for the decision-maker, is to create an awareness of the forthcoming changes. This is essential both for creating preparedness for change within the organisation, as well as for stimulating and channelising the problem-solving energies within the organisation. Most often this is achieved through highly visible actions by the decision-maker, which symbolically communicate and build credibility behind the new decisions and strategy. For instance, a decision for cost cutting in an organisation, may be preceded by (and communicated through) the gesture of top executives offering to share their vehicles for commuting to the office with other employees.

3. Allowing "Gestation" period. Consensus-seeking decision-makers realise that bringing change overnight can generate resistance and reactions. It is essential for the organisational members to become comfortable with the idea of introducing changes, before actually implementing them. They must talk through the threat issues, become more aware of the implications of anticipated changes, and acquire more comprehensive and accurate information, to judge the new decisions against the existing and more familiar options. To achieve this, managers seeking change often create forums, committees, task-forces, etc., or commission studies and researches, so that the change issues become more familiar and comfortable to people.

4. Tentative partial solutions. The initial decisions, may often appear to be merely tentative and experimental moves. They may look more like minor "tactical adjustments", involving such actions as a few transfers and promotions, creation of new sub-departments, making minor adjustments in the existing budgeting structure, and so on. The advantages of such a method are that (a) it is easier to get agreements from people on minor adjustments than on a major shift, (b) it does not unnecessarily jeopardise the existing strengths of the enterprise, for a decision whose viability is still uncertain, and (c) even if these experimental moves fail, they do not destroy the decision-maker's credibility.

It is only when the consequences of these small, apparently uneventful decisions start emerging, can one see the new synthesis getting formed. Thus, the change is felt as gradual, and appears to build on the existing strengths of the organisation, rather than heralding a complete break from the past.

5. Gaining political support. Effective executives, even under pressure, are conscious of the political nature of most organisational decisions, and try to integrate the power needs of the key constituencies. Formation of committees, task-forces and teams allows them to co-opt those prominent members in the decision-making process, who are most likely to feel alienated with the change. Quinn (1980) observed that this aspect of decision-making calls for a high degree of political acumen from the decision-maker:

> By selecting the committee's chairman, membership, timing and agends, guiding executives can largely influence and predict the desired outcome, and force other executives toward a consensus. Such groups can be balanced to educate, evaluate, neutralise, or overwhelm opponents...

Besides the manipulation implied in such actions, they benefit the decision-maker in two other ways: one, they often make the potential opponents, supporters, even champions, for the new decision; and, secondly, the interactive consensus building process also improves the quality of decisions.

6. Crystallising and gaining commitment. Crystallising the decisions into a broad plan, and ensuring commitment to it, is in itself a skill. Consensus-seeking executives tend to be sensitive to the timing and context, which dictate when to converge to a viewpoint, and when to keep the options open. As we discussed earlier, they avoid premature crystallisation of decisions, which would inadvertently provide a focus for opposition to emerge, or would act to suppress the creative energies in the organisation. On the other hand, they also realise the danger of keeping the options indefinitely open, which can result in losing the focus of decision-making process. In any case, a decision has to converge to a point where consensus can be crystallised and the implementation procedures can be formalised.

Formalisation and institutionalisation of the decision is an essential activity for ensuring its effective implementation. The plans, procedures, control and reward systems must communicate and reflect the intended emphasis of the decision, and must aim at aligning the decision implementation with the interests of the organisational members. For instance, a decision to diversify into new areas, would be successful only when the new venture is structurally and systemically integrated with the existing organisation, and provides sufficient incentive to people to feel attracted towards it.

VII. IMPLICATIONS FOR MANAGERS

The preceding discussion helps us in appreciating the complexity of decision-making process and the constraints within which it unfolds. Probably, one of the most crucial implication it has for the practising manager is the recognition of the three "limits" within which much of the organisational decision-making takes place:

1. Information limits. Given the complexity of the decision-making situation, most managers are constrained to take decisions in the absence of complete information. In fact, it is even difficult to identify what would constitute relevant information, till after receiving the feedback on implementation of the decision. Thus, a purely rational and analytical method of decision-making may not always yield the ideal solution.

2. Cognitive limits. Even if all information is available with the decision-maker, the total quantum of information would be too large to be processed by one person. With the increase in environmental uncertainty and organisational size, it becomes more and more difficult for one person (or a group of persons) to "figure it out" from the top, however entrepreneurial and visionary the strategic apex may be.

3. Process limits. The ultimate test of the effectiveness of decision-making is not in the intellectual quality of the decision, but in the form in which it finally gets implemented. Thus, any decision will be equally influenced by the acceptance it generates, and the extent to which it influences (and is influenced by) the existing political equilibrium in the organisation. Integration of the political processes in the decision-making process is, therefore, essential for effective implementation.

We also saw how a consensus building approach combines the strengths of the other three approaches and creates conditions in which it is possible to overcome these limits to a large extent. In a way, these different approaches also highlight the basic difference in being a manager and being a leader (Zaleznick, 1977; Harari and Mukai, 1990; Kotter, 1990; Nadler and Tushman, 1986). The focus of the managerial role is on coping with complexity and aims at bringing about order and stability. To accomplish this, managers rely primarily on formal mechanisms of target setting, planning, budgeting, organising and controlling. Leaders, in contrast, focus more on bringing about change, which they achieve through setting directions through symbolic actions, empowering people through involving them in the decision-making process, and aligning and motivating organisational efforts towards the desired ends. Thus, the rational-normative approach corresponds more to the managerial aspect of the decision-maker's role, whereas the true leaders would rely more on a consensus building approach.

Lastly, it is important for the decision-maker to appreciate that an effective decision-making process, is actually a balance between the rational and irrational, tangible and intangible, and the organisational goals and an individuals' self interests. Effective decisions, emerge neither from a completely analytical-computational method, nor from a manipulative process of game-playing. Rather, they are achieved by blending the two, and arriving at a synthesis.

10 Organisational Culture

1. In the Reliance Group, one of the much talked about and practised principles is the value of time. There are also countless stories of how people (ranging from departmental managers to Dhirubhai Ambani himself) took quick decisions to meet a crisis, how people show their concern about doing things, and doing them in shortest possible time. Not surprisingly, the Reliance Group completed their Patalganga project in a record time of 15 months. Even their collaborators, El Du Pont de Nemours found this achievement unbelievable and unparalleled.
2. Sundaram Fasteners Limited, the first Indian company to get ISO 9000 certification, has another unique distinction of not having lost a single day due to labour trouble over last almost three decades. Insiders (including the union leaders) attribute this to the "family approach" practised by the top management. The chief executive, Suresh Krishna, is very emphatic about the need to communicate with the workers on a regular basis. Among a number of things which are done in the company, is an interesting practice of inviting the workers' families to visit the factory, and to interact with the senior managers.
3. S.K. Bhattacharya in his book *Achieving Managerial Excellence* writes: "In refreshing contrast to most other financial institutions, ICICI's (Industrial Credit and Investment Corporation of India's) culture actively discourages note writing at all levels and encourages discussion... so that things, can be done methodically but expeditiously. It is this anxiety to do things, which inculcates in all ICICI managers the understanding that analyzing and validating a recommendation by way of written notes... is less important than thinking through the assumptions in the proposal, in business terms..."

Given above, are a few examples of how organisational cultures operate, are sustained and even changed. The culture of an organisation has a decisive influence on what happens in its day-to-day functioning. As one can see from the above examples, these cultural influences are as, if not more, critical to the performance of an organisation, as are the other external and more tangible factors (environment, strategy, technology, etc.) which we discussed earlier.

Usually, different organisations are described as innovative, autocratic, paternalistic, stagnating, impersonal, achievement-oriented, professional, and so on. These are essentially descriptions of what we perceive to be the essence or the culture of these organisations. Such descriptions, however, portray culture as a static condition, which describes the state of affairs in the organisation. The essence of culture, on the other hand, is not static but dynamic. Indeed, the term culture actually means "to grow", which is a process. Thus, while it may be useful for the purpose of understanding, to look at the cultural "types" (as we will do later in this Chapter), to really appreciate the significance of culture in organisational functioning, it is necessary to focus on the organisational processes, which underlie and constitute its culture. In this Chapter, we will discuss these dynamic aspects of organisational culture: why and how it develops; what its functions are; how it is sustained, transmitted and managed; its impact on organisational effectiveness; the different types of organisational cultures; and, how they can be changed.

I. THE ESSENCE OF ORGANISATIONAL CULTURE

If one looks at different organisations, each appears to be unique in its own way; in some, the employees go through the whole day without even smiling once, while in others, there is an air of bonhomie and friendliness; in some, even free-time is filled up with shop-talks, while in the others, even during working hours, the employees only talk about personal gossips; in some, the employees are, by and large, active and ambitious, while in others, the atmosphere is passive and lethargic, and so on. It is almost as if, by some implicit agreement, organisational members start thinking, feeling and behaving in a similar manner. It is this underlying theme, which binds every organisation into a coherent whole, and creates its unique culture.

In a way, the culture of an organisation describes the submerged part of the organisational iceberg. It is pervasive, yet somewhat intangible. "From our point of view," wrote Pacanowsky and O'Donnell-Trujillo (1983), "a culture is not something an organisation has; a culture is something an organisation is." The organisational culture, thus, describes the personality of the organisation—its overall orientation, its unwritten codes and norms, the implicitly understood ways of relating and interacting among the organisational members, the values which are shared and practised by people, and so on—and thereby, infuses it with life and gives it a unique identity.

A. Defining Organisational Culture

One of the major problems in defining organisational culture is that it is a concept, i.e., it is something which is created and which resides in the minds of the people. It is not a thing which can be discovered and verified; rather, it has to be inferred, conjured, interpreted and defined. Not surprisingly, this has led to a proliferation of definitions and interpretation of what organisational culture is. Ott (1989) reviewed 58 books and journal's articles, and identified 73 key words/phrases, which were used by different authors to define organisational culture. These definitions attribute a variety of meanings to organisational culture, which range from behavioural to cognitive, from explicitly stated to tacitly followed, from being consciously enacted to being unconsciously felt, and so on (see Exhibit 10.1). Instead of looking for a "comprehensive" definition of organisational culture, an appreciation of the different definitions may contribute much more to our understanding of it.

Exhibit 10.1

What is Organisational Culture?

"...a set of common understandings for organising actions and language and other symbolic vehicles for expressing common understanding." (Louis, 1980)

"A quality of perceived organisational specialness—that it possesses some unusual quality that distinguishes it from others in the field." (Gold, 1982)

"A strong culture is a system of informal rules that spell out how people are to behave most of the time." (Deal and Kennedy, 1982)

"....a general constellation of beliefs, morals, value systems, behavioral norms and ways of doing business that are unique to each corporation." (Turnstall, 1983)

"...organisational culture can be thought of as the.glue that holds the organisation together, through a sharing of patterns of meaning. The culture focuses on the values, beliefs, and expectations that members come to share." (Siehl and Martin, 1984)

"The links between language, metaphor, and ritual and their celebration of particular social ideals or myths, form the essential administrative culture of the school. The culture is a translation of myths into action and relationship." (Bates, 1984)

"Every organisation will have its own words and phrases to describe what it means by culture. Some of these are: being, core, culture, ethos, identity, ideology, manner, patterns, philosophy, purpose, roots, spirit, style, vision, and way. To most managers, these mean pretty much the same thing." (Davis, 1984)

"Culture governs what is worth for a particular group and how group members should think, feel and behave. The stuff of culture includes customs and traditions, historical accounts be they mythical or actual, tacit understandings, habits, norms and expectations, common meanings associated with fixed objects and established rites, shared assumptions, and intersubjective meanings." (Sergiovanni and Corbally, 1984)

"A pattern of basic assumptions—invented, discovered, or developed by a given group as it learns to cope with its problems of external adaptation and internal integration—that has worked well enough to be considered valid and, therefore, to be taught to new members as the correct way to perceive, think, and feel in relation to those problems." (Schein, 1985)

While such a state of affairs makes it difficult to achieve conceptual clarity about organisational culture, it is also indicative of the richness of meanings, which the term carries. Based on a review of various definitions proposed by management theorists and practitioners, Schein (1985) concluded that there are, at least, six popular meanings which are ascribed to organisational culture.

1. Observed behavioural regularities in the interactions, language and rituals of the organisational members.

2. The norms which evolve over a period of time in working groups.

3. The dominant values which are espoused by the organisation (or by the dominant members of the organisation).

4. The philosophy which guides the decisions and policies of an organisation.

5. The rules of the game ("the ropes") one must learn in order to survive and be accepted in the organisation.

6. The feeling and climate that pervades and gets conveyed in the day-to-day functioning of the organisation.

One can, thus, understand organisational culture as a pervasive underlying set of beliefs, assumptions, values, shared feelings and perceptions, which influence the actions and decisions taken by the organisational members. This constellation, not only shapes the overt behaviour, but also determines the manner in which people normally interpret and respond to any given organisational situation. For instance, if the culture encourages innovativeness, any problem will stimulate people to take initiative and risks, and try out new ways of doing things. On the other hand, if the organisational culture is security-oriented, the same problem-situation would cause people to start looking for rules, procedures and precedences as a mode of response.

B. Functions of Organisational Culture

We saw in the previous Chapters that the life in organisations is far from always being stable and predictable, and definitely not totally rational. The experience of working in any organisation, involves coming to terms with uncertain (and sometimes turbulent) environments, mutually contradictory objectives, complex technologies, lack of availability of adequate information, threatening political climates, etc. The challenge for organisational members is to make sense out of such changing, incomplete and conflicting observations, opinions and information, so that they can relate to each other and act in a logically coherent and mutually consistent manner. Cultures, by providing a common interpretative system (assumptions and beliefs), help the organisational members in reducing ambiguity, resolving confusion, increasing predictability, and achieving coherence and uniformity of purpose (Bolman and Deal, 1984). As Boje et al. (1982) noted:

> This milieu of uncertainty is the foundation upon which organisational cultures arise, to provide a framework within which shared meanings are developed. Organisational culture, as used here, includes the unique language, symbols, metaphors, and myths that arise from the organisation's situation and the interaction of its participants. These particular components of culture, facilitate the feelings of rational action, in the midst of otherwise overpowering uncertainty and political maneuvering.

Thus, essentially organisational culture can be seen as an integrative mechanism, which serves to tie up the diversity of organisational experiences into a meaningful whole. By providing a coherent interpretative framework, it becomes a basis for the organisational members to attribute and arrive at common meanings of their own identity, and of organisational activities and events. In creating this system of logic, it also legitimises and provides a rationale for present and future actions. Based on a review of studies on organisational culture, Ott (1989) summarised the following four functions of organisational culture:

1. It provides shared patterns of cognitive interpretations or perceptions, thus, communicating to the organisational members how they are expected to think and behave.

2. It provides shared patterns of feelings, i.e., an emotional sense of involvement and commitment to organisational values and moral codes—of things worth working for or believing in—so that the organisational members know what they are expected to value and how they are expected to feel.

3. It defines and maintains boundaries, allowing identification of members and non-members.

4. It functions as an implicit organisational control system, prescribing and prohibiting certain behaviours.

One must also appreciate that the cultural influences on organisational behaviour operate more implicitly than explicitly. In fact, the power of culture lies in this very invisibility of forces. An effective culture guarantees that the organisational members would not only interpret and respond to a situation in a specific manner, but would also believe their understanding to be "factual" and not merely representing one of the many possible interpretations. For instance, in an autocratic culture, where power-inequalities between superiors and subordinates are taken for granted, a manager's attempts to be participative and to form equalitarian relationships would be seen as a factual evidence of his lack of self-confidence.

C. The "Stuff" of Organisational Culture

In our discussion so far, we have referred to culture as an implicit, invisible and unconscious influence. This, however, does not imply that organisational culture has no conscious and visible rootings or manifestations. For instance, in many organisations (Maruti Udyog, Petrofils Ltd., etc.) all employees in the organisation, from the chief executive to the operators, wear a uniform. This behaviour is a part of the culture of these organisations, even though it may have arisen from a conscious decision. Thus, while the essence of culture may lie in the subconscious levels of the organisation, the expression of culture can be manifested, and studied, in many different ways, and at many different conscious or subconscious levels.

An understanding of these different manifestations is crucial for not only comprehending, but also for managing and changing, the organisational culture. As Schein (1985) observed: "...the only thing of real importance that leaders do, is to create and manage culture, and that the unique talent of leaders is their ability to work with culture." To follow this goal of creating, working with, managing and changing organisational culture, there are two aspects which are essential to bear in mind. Firstly, that the strong cultures are characterised by a congruence and consistency in the variety of ways in which they manifest themselves. For instance, if the "espoused values" (Argyris and Schoen, 1978), i.e., what people *say* in the organisation, are reasonably congruent with the practised values, i.e., what people actually *do* in the organisation, then articulation of these values can help in bringing the group efforts together which would serve as a source of common identity. If, on the other hand, the professed and practised values contradict each other, they can become a major source of confusion and fragmentation of culture.

Secondly, these manifestations are also the mechanisms through which culture perpetuates itself and gets transmitted to new employees. Since by their very nature, cultural influences operate at the subconscious/unconscious levels, the dynamics of their self-perpetuation is subtle and remains largely hidden to innocent eyes. For the manager who aims to make cultural interventions, these expressions of culture also provide the answer to the critical question: how can one communicate, transmit and teach the members about something which remains largely out of awareness? (see Exhibit 10.2)

Exhibit 10.2

Some Cultural Artifacts in Indian Organisations

- NIIT, the premier computer education institute gives a "dating allowance" to its employees.
- In the headquarters of Marico Industries, there is a popcorn vending machine for the employees.
- When Tapan Mitra became the CEO of Indian Aluminium, he installed his small work-table (on which he used to work as a young manager in the company) in his new office.
- Work in Maruti Udyog starts every morning with all employees assembling and doing yoga.
- In CMC offices, people don't work in cabins but in a common hall, in which the work-spaces are divided by shoulder-high partitions.
- TISCO encourages its employees to go for mountain-trekking in groups.
- IPCL invites artists and painters of repute to stay in its township in Baroda and make paintings for the company.
- In the annual conference of the branch and depot managers of Transport Corporation of India, the high performing managers are often gifted a suit-length material by the CEO.

A number of theorists and researchers (e.g., Schein, 1985; Dyer, 1986; Lundberg, 1985, etc.) have conceptualised the cultural processes as operating at different levels, ranging from conscious artifacts to unconscious assumptions. They have identified the numerous ways in which culture expresses itself in the day-to-day organisational life. In the following sections, we will look at some of the most common expressions of organisational culture.

1. Physical artifacts. These are the most tangible and visible manifestations of organisational culture. If one moves around different organisations, it is easy to notice that each is different in terms of its physical layout and decor, nature of availability and use of facilities, centralisation or dispersion of common utilities, format of office stationary, and so on. These uniquenesses are neither merely incidental nor meant for serving some rational functional purposes; rather, they represent symbolic expressions of an underlying meaning, value or belief, which is shared by the people in the organisation. Organisational artifacts (shared office space or availability of recreational facilities in the working place) intentionally or unintentionally communicate information about the organisation's beliefs, values, assumptions and ways of doing things.

One of the distinctive features of cultural artifacts is their symbolic nature. Their value lies not in what they are, but in what they mean to people. In fact, often from a rational point of view, they may even appear to be non-functional (e.g., old photographs adorning the walls, gossip-sessions in which almost invariably similar stories are told, or a room occupied with old useless files which nobody needs to consult). But they survive, and are cherished, because they are symbolically important. As Ott (1989) noted:

> Symbols embody and represent wider patterns of meaning and cause people to associate conscious and unconscious ideas that in turn endow them with their deeper, fuller, and often emotion-invoking meaning.

This symbolic nature of cultural artifacts is most apparent in the behavioural patterns, which are typical to each organisation. In their normal life all organisations are characterised by recurring themes, which get expressed through what their members talk about, and how they do things. Thus, artifacts can also be non-material (behavioural) in nature.

2. Language, jargons and metaphors. The language, jargon and metaphors are an integral part of any organisation's culture. While language is a means of universal communication, most organisations tend to develop their own unique terminologies, phrases and acronym. For instance, in one organisation, members of the corporate office were referred to as *nawabs;* similarly, in another organisation, the acronym J.I.T. (Just-In-Time) was jokingly used to describe all badly planned fire-fighting jobs. Thus, in the organisational linguistics code, "Kremlin" may mean the headquarters, "special assignment" may be the corporate euphemism for Siberia, "early retirement" may denote being fired from the job, and, all new recruits may have to be "broken in". Such specialised and idiosyncratic usage of words and phrases makes an organisation's language incomprehensible to those who do not belong to that culture. And so, language becomes a means of identifying members from non-members, and of reinforcing a group's unique cultural identity.

3. Stories, myths and legends. The organisational stories, myths and legends are, in a way, an extension of organisational language. Like language, they epitomise the unwritten values and morals of the organisational life, and serve to validate unspoken thoughts, intentions and feelings of its members—only they do it in a more elaborate and effective manner. If one collects the various stories, anecdotes and jokes which are being shared in an organisation, they often read like plots and themes, in which nothing changes except the characters. Even the protagonists (the heroes and the outlaws) represent similar characteristics, though their names may change. One may find, for instance, that the popular jokes and stories in an organisation invariably narrate a situation in which a subordinate makes a fool of a superior authority, or, that how the superior was bribed by a subordinate to get a promotion, or how a new department was formed to accommodate a relative, or a new procedure was promoted to benefit the superior's secretary. All these stories predictably revolve around a decision-making situation, in which irrationality and violation of formal rules and procedures is encouraged.

What is most remarkable about these stories is that often they depict pure fantasy; people know that they are factually inaccurate but continue to narrate and listen to them with relish. "Myths", Ott (1989) noted, "are too important for people to be embarrassed about factual inaccuracy." Their importance lies not in the factual information they impart, but in the thematic coherence they provide to the members' experience of the organisational life. They also very effectively and implicitly communicate important cultural assumptions, beliefs, values and norms to the new members. In fact, their effectiveness lies in the fact that often the messages implied in the stories, myths and legends are more clearly remembered, believed in and followed. Boje et al. (1982) identified four basic functions which organisational myths fulfil:

(a) they create, maintain and legitimise past, present or future actions and consequences;

(b) they maintain and conceal political interests and value systems;

(c) they help explain and create, cause and effect relationships under conditions of incomplete knowledge; and,

(d) they rationalise the complexity and turbulence of activities and events to allow for predictable action-taking.

4. Ceremonies and celebrations. Ceremonies and celebrations are consciously enacted behavioural artifacts, which help in reinforcing an organisation's cultural values and assumptions. For instance, every year TISCO celebrates Founder's Day, to commemorate and reiterate its adherence to the company's original values; similarly, in the early '90's, the 60 odd senior managers of INDAL went into a "retreat", closeting themselves in a hotel for a week, with the sole agenda of thrashing out a strategic plan for the company. Such events are vividly remembered by people. They put the culture on display, and help the organisations to celebrate their values, heroes, myths and symbols. As Deal and Kennedy (1982) noted:

> Without expressive events, any culture will die. In the absence of ceremony..., important values have no impact. Ceremonies are to culture what movie is to script, the concert is to score, or dance is to values that are difficult to express in any other way.

5. Routines, rites and rituals. While ceremonies and celebrations are conscious efforts to enact the culture, there are many routinised activities in the organisation, which are carried out by its members repetitively, often without even giving them a second thought. They are ritualistic, because the organisational members have either forgotten about their original purpose, or, at least, consider the activities to be more important than the purpose they are supposed to serve. For example, organisations have staff meetings, training programmes, rituals of filling out performance appraisal forms, superiors' annual visits, etc., which often acquire a life of their own. Such rituals serve the purpose of providing a sense of security and personal identity, giving meaning to members' actions, and serving as mechanisms of control (Bernstein, 1975; Popkerwitz, 1982).

The ritualistic nature of these activities becomes apparent, if one wants to take them away, or substitute them with better and more effective mechanisms. For instance, in one department, it was a tradition that the manager would hold fortnightly group meetings with the employees, with the stated purpose of soliciting suggestions. When a new manager took over, he went through the old minutes and found that nothing of any significance was achieved in these meetings. Much of the time was spent in gossiping, or in ingratiating the boss. He decided to discontinue the meetings, and to substitute them with an incentive-based suggestion scheme. Not only did the scheme never take off, the new manager also started facing major resistance from the employees in getting the work done. He was blamed for being autocratic, insensitive to the employees' needs, and for following a divide-and-rule policy.

Many organisational researchers (e.g., Deal and Kennedy, 1982) have even considered some of the established management methods and techniques as cultural rituals, which serve more to provide a meaning to actions and efforts than to actually achieve any functional purpose. In many organisations, for instance, managers employ techniques such as PERT/CPM, complex modelling and simulation, dissemination of regular updates on projects, brainstorming sessions, etc., while the work continues to be done in the same manner as it was being done earlier. Deal and Kennedy (1982) noted:

> The literature on management is full of treatise on optimisation and conceptual strategic frameworks such as portfolio analysis and cost curve. But are these tools really involved in decision-making? They are... rituals that give individual managers a comfortable feeling... How managers really take decisions is to gather people in a room, review *available* information and data, and if pressed "decide" as best as they can.

6. Behavioural norms. Behavioural norms are an important indicator of an organisation's culture, since they describe the nature of expectations which impinge on the members' behaviour. Mostly, the norms evolve over a period of time in the groups' functioning. They determine and control how the members would behave, interact and relate with each other. Thus, the group norms determine whether or not one can openly disagree with a superior, or whether or not people can be friendly with employees in another department. Norms help in the patterning of members' behaviour, and so, create predictability in the organisational life. As Schmuck (1971) noted, "norms are strong stabilisers of organisational behaviour."

The behavioural norms are transmitted to new members through a process of socialisation. Learning of these norms (and the values, beliefs and assumptions underlying them) permits the new members to participate effectively in the organisational milieu. This process involves, for the new members, shedding a part of their identity as the price of membership. In many organisations, the socialisation process is coercive and unconscious (e.g., the new entrants are sent out on the most difficult of assignments, so that they can be "broken in"), but it can also be done in a more conscious and targeted manner (through induction programme, identification building exercises, mentoring, etc.).

Enforcement of behavioural norms also ensures the weeding out of those members who do not "fit" in the organisation. Wanous (1980) noted that the "deviant" members invariably leave the organisation, either voluntarily or involuntarily. This ensures that the cultural identity of the group remains uncontaminated. Ott (1989) observed that:

> Such departures usually are cause of celebrations, and the circumstances leading to them become cherished organisational stories. In these ways, the departure of people who do not buy into the organisational culture transmits an important symbolic message about cultural expectations and the price of "deviance" to all who remain.

7. Shared beliefs and values. All organisations have a set of basic beliefs and values (often also termed as ethical/moral codes or ideologies), which are shared by most of its members. These are consciously held, mental pictures of the nature of (organisational) reality, and form the basis of defining the right or wrong in the organisation. Essentially, these beliefs and values provide justifications for behaviours in the organisation. In an organisation, for example, if the predominant belief is that meeting customers' demand is essential for success, any behaviour which supposedly meets this criteria is acceptable, even if it violates established rules and procedures. Similarly, if the shared belief is that one must please the boss to get promoted, individual initiative and result-oriented behaviour will be discredited and discouraged. Thus, values and beliefs, guide and focus organisational energies towards certain actions, while discouraging other behavioural patterns.

8. Basic assumptions. While values and beliefs are conscious frameworks for interpreting and evaluating organisational reality, the basic assumptions are unconscious values and beliefs held by the members of the organisation. They exist at such a subliminal level that members are rarely aware of them. Ott (1989) noted that "basic assumptions are likely to have dropped out of awareness—they are there but have moved back into the recesses of the mind." This unconscious nature of basic assumptions, makes them quite a potent and change-resistant influence on members' behaviour. More so because, being unconscious they can neither be confronted nor debated upon.

People in organisations develop such basic unconscious assumptions about the reality, because of the repeated occurrence of certain events, situations and behaviours. If one finds, repeatedly that competent senior professionals have been leaving the organisation, the assumption may get built up that competent people are not valued in the organisation. Describing the dynamics of how certain values and beliefs become unconscious, Schein (1985) observed:

> When a solution to a problem works repeatedly, it comes to be taken for granted. What was once a hypothesis, supported by only a hunch or a value, comes gradually to be treated as a reality. We come to believe that nature really works that way.

II. ORGANISATIONAL CULTURE AND SUCCESS

The strength and influence of any organisation's culture depends upon how intensely and universally its core values, beliefs and assumptions are shared and practised by its members. It seems logical to assume that if the organisational culture is strong and influential, people will share common goals and priorities, and so, will show more coordinated efforts for achieving the organisational goals. In this section, we will discuss (a) how culture influences organisational strategy, and (b) how strong and weak cultures contribute to organisational success.

A. Organisational Culture and Strategy

In many ways, culture and strategy perform very similar functions in the organisation. As one would recall, in our discussion on strategy (refer to Chapter 5), we had noted that an organisational strategy can be viewed more as a perspective than a plan, which expresses the core values and "personality" of the organisation. Similarly, in Chapter 9, we discussed how strategies often evolve through the internal political dynamics, and also how effective strategic leaders develop viable strategies through "consensus-building" processes, which reflect, integrate and sometimes change the dominant cultural values of the organisation. Thus, the strategic orientation of an organisation is often just another expression of its dominant cultural values. Burgleman (1983) defined corporate strategy as a theory held by the organisation which:

> ...defines the identity of the firm at any moment of time. It provides a basis for the maintenance of this identity and for the continuity in the strategic activity.

Such a definition of strategy comes very close to our understanding of organisational culture. Weick (1985) also compared the concepts of culture and strategy, and concluded:

> ...both may serve a common function. That function is imposing coherence, order, and meaning. Strategy and culture resemble one another because they both gather bits and pieces of action and find coherence in them. Both assign action to well-adjusted categories, categories that are outgrowths of interactions.

Many studies (e.g., Walter, 1985; Despande and Parasuraman, 1986; Zammuto and O'Connor, 1992) have shown that culture has a major influence on the success of strategic choices. Walter (1985) highlighted that the success of acquisitions and mergers is critically dependent on the integration of cultural parameters in the acquisition plans. Similarly, Despande and Parasuraman (1986) related culture to business portfolio management practices. They found that the strategic success of the organisation would depend on the manner in which its culture encourages risk-taking and acceptance of feedback in the organisation.

Zammuto and O'Connor (1992) also proposed that acceptance and effective implementation of advanced manufacturing technologies in the organisation is influenced by its cultural characteristics.

B. Strong and Weak Cultures

Obviously, if the culture is strong, it would act as an effective integrative mechanism. More than just coordinating the efforts and activities, it would also replace many formalised and bureaucratic systems (e.g., rules, procedures, plans, and programs) and make the organisation more spontaneous in its manner of performing. Bresser and Bishop (1983) noted that:

> If values, beliefs, and exemplars are widely shared, formal symbolic generalisations (strategic plans) can be parsimonious. In effect, a well developed organisational culture directs and coordinates activities. By contrast, if an organisation is characterised by many different conflicting values, beliefs, and exemplars... considerable direction and coordination will be required, resulting in a symbolic generalisation formalised in plans, procedures, programmes, budgets, and so on.

Many authors have proposed that strong cultures are a necessary condition for corporate success. Deal and Kennedy (1982) argued that successful organisations tend to rely more on cultural mechanisms than on bureaucratic systems for achieving high performances. Peters and Waterman (1982) in their book *In Search for Excellence* noted that well-managed and high-performing companies had uniformly strong cultures. They also identified certain core values, which were common to the cultures of these companies. These were:

- Action-orientation
- Customer-orientation
- Sticking to what they do best
- Placing high value on their people
- Giving autonomy to their employees, and
- Encouraging entrepreneurial behaviour.

In his study of successful "excellent" Indian companies, Bhattacharya (1989) also found similar cultural attributes. He identified the three dimensions of organisational culture, which these successful companies had in common, "in a varying mix", as:

(a) An orientation towards managerial values, which sharply focus on *implementation* of plans and *actions* (rather than on decision-making alone);

(b) *Achievement orientation,* i.e., organisation-wide acceptance of achievement, rather than efforts alone, as the reference point for measuring success; and,

(c) A spirit of continuing *introspection, innovation* and *experimentation.*

These findings highlight the importance of strong cultures (and the nature of cultural attributes) in determining organisational success. Successful companies do appear to have a commonality in their cultures. But they are also dissimilar in a number of ways. This point becomes apparent if one compares the cultures of organisations, such as TISCO, HCL-HP, Larsen & Toubro, Lintas, etc. They are all successful in their own right, and yet are very different from each other in their cultural characteristics. It is these dissimilarities, also, which make each of these companies unique.

Moreover, for an organisation to have a strong culture may not always be the ideal state of affairs. The same values, which may be very healthy for the organisation in one set of circumstances, may become totally inoperative (if not dysfunctional) in another set of circumstances. A highly innovative organisational culture may be very useful for dealing with the demands of a dynamic environment; but, it would also become the reason for unnecessary wastage of organisational energy and resources, when the market has stabilised. As Weick (1985) noted:

> A coherent statement of who we are, makes it harder to become something else. Strong cultures are tenacious cultures. Because a tenacious culture can be a rigid culture, that is slow to detect changes in opportunities and slow to change once opportunities are sensed, strong cultures can be backward, conservative instruments of adaptation.

Likewise, Scully (1987) made the same point when he wrote:

> ...culture limits us by an emphasis on tradition, on yesterday's heroes, on myths and rituals whose sole value is that they derive from an earlier time... Businesses that define reality in such terms, similarly create closed systems for themselves. They excessively—perhaps unconsciously—venerate traditions and worship habits: 'the way we do things here'. Culture is a feel-good tool, a set of behavioral blinkers; it makes the corporation comfortable with its habits.

One may also mention here, that one of the criticisms of *In Search of Excellence* was that within five years of publication of Peters and Waterman's findings, many of their "excellent" companies did not remain excellent in terms of profitability, market-share and even liquidity!

Thus, to say that certain attributes of organisational culture contribute to their *success* in a given environment (with which these attribute match) is apparently true. But for identifying cultural determinants of organisational *effectiveness* (that is, its ability to succeed in a diversity of environmental demands over time), one will need to develop a more analytical appreciation of how cultures differ from one another. In the next section, we will look at one such conceptual framework, for understanding the diversities of organisational cultures.

III. HOW CULTURES DIFFER: THE COMPETING VALUES PERSPECTIVE

The competing values perspective (Quinn and McGrath, 1985) emerged from a series of studies done at the State University of New York at Albany. It was proposed as a metatheory for integrating the literature on organisational culture (Quinn and Kimberly, 1984), organisational effectiveness (Quinn and Rohrbaugh, 1983), organisational change (Quinn and Cameron, 1983), leadership (Quinn,

1984), organisational decision-making (Quinn and Anderson, 1984), and information processing (Quinn and Hall, 1983) in a comprehensive manner. Underlying this approach is a view of organisational culture as representing the similarities in the way in which its members perceive and interpret the corporate reality. The shared meanings, which constitute the organisational culture, impel people to behave in a similar manner in any given situation. Thus, the various ways in which people process information and make sense of their perceptions, is the key to understanding the differences in organisational cultures.

A. Two Dimensions of Human Information-Processing

The human perceptual processes can be seen as structured around two dimensions. Perceptions differ in terms of (a) the extent of familiarity or certainty of the cues, and (b) the extent of urgency for actions communicated by the cues.

1. The degree of certainty. The *familiarity-unfamiliarity* dimension deals with the extent of recognition, predictability and understanding of the environment. When people scan their environment, they would notice whether the patterns are familiar and predictable, or new, uncertain and unrecognisable. If the cues given by the environment are familiar, one tends to rely on previous strategies for dealing with it. On the other hand, if the environment highlights the novelty of the situations, one would have to rely on a more adaptive strategy.

The perceived novelty (or lack of it) of the environment, would depend not only on the objective qualities of the environment, but also on the characteristics of the perceivers. Certain groups of people (e.g., young, conceptually sophisticated, creative people) are more likely to be sensitive to novel cues. Similarly, certain organisational environments emit more unfamiliar cues than others (e.g., compare an advertising agency with a manufacturing firm in a stable environment).

2. The action perspective. This dimension focuses on the nature of actions necessitated by the perceived reality: does the reality call for immediate action or are the cues such that a response can wait? An organisation which is facing a competitive market, for example, is likely to convey a sense of urgency of action to its employees. In contrast, an educational institution is likely to be perceived as a more complacent place by its employees. It also follows, by implication, that organisations which have an external focus (i.e., which are open to influences from the external environment) will experience a greater urgency for immediate action as compared to organisations with internal focus (i.e., organisations which are insulated from environmental influences).

B. Types of Organisational Cultures

Given these two dimensions on which people differentiate their perceptions, one can conceptualise four basic perceptual systems (see Figure 10.1). Each of

	Long-term/ Internal cues	Short-term/ External cues
Novel cues/ Low certainty	**Consensual culture** *Information-processing strategy:* • Reduce uncertainty through interactions *Stimulates/Is sustained by:* • Affiliation • Mutual dependence	**Developmental/ Ideological culture** *Information-processing strategy:* • Use hunches; learn and adapt as you go *Stimulates/Is sustained by:* • Intensity • Growth
Familiar cues/High certainty	**Hierarchical culture** *Information-processing strategy:* • Maintain the present behaviour patterns *Stimulates/Is sustained by:* • Predictability • Security	**Rational culture** *Information-processing strategy:* • Analyse the pattern and select appropriate past strategy *Stimulates/Is sustained by:* • Independent action • Achievement

Figure 10.1 Illustrating the primary perceptual differentiations and related information-processing strategies (based on Quinn and McGrath, 1985).

these perceptual systems calls for a specific information-processing strategy which, in turn, stimulates specific patterns of needs and behaviours among the organisational members. These different information-processing strategies, when collectively employed by the organisational members, culminate in the development of specific cultural milieus. In the following discussion, we will focus on the characteristics of these cultural types, and how they are manifested in various organisational practices and systems (Tables 10.1 and 10.2 summarise the salient correspondences):

1. Rational culture. When perceptual cues suggest the need for immediate action and the certainty is high, one tends to rely on and uses already tried and tested successful strategies. Since one knows what is to be done, and the action is almost immediate, this stance involves a feeling of independence and achievement. This is an instrumental outlook, relying upon logical relationships among decisions, actions and outcomes. This systematic and goal-oriented strategy also becomes the basis of a *rational culture.*

Rational cultures are task-oriented environments, which emphasise performance, productivity and efficiency. Organisational goals are conceived of

Table 10.1 Characteristics of Four Types of Organisational Cultures

	Rational culture	Developmental culture	Consensual culture	Hierarchical culture
Organisational purpose	Pursuit of rational objectives	Creation; development	Group-maintenance; team-building	Execution; regulation
Performance criteria	Productivity; efficiency	Growth; innovation	Cohesion; morale	Control; stability
Authority	Boss	Charisma	Membership	Rules; seniority
Bases of power	Competence	Values	Informal status	Knowledge of regulations
Motives	Achievement	Growth	Affiliation; mutual dependence	Security
Decision-making	Planned; decisive	Intuitive; insightful	Participative	Factual; routine
Leadership style	Goal-oriented	Innovative; risk-taking	Supportive; concerned	Conservative; cautious
Compliance style	Contractual agreement	Commitment to values	Commitment to group	Control and surveillance
Appraisal	Tangible results	Intensity of efforts	Quality of relationships	Formal and impersonal criteria

Table 10.2 Correspondences between Organisational Cultures and Formal Characteristics of the Organisations (Adapted from Quinn and McGrath, 1985)

Organisational cultures	Organisational forms	Strategic types	Technology
Rational	Market-based; divisional	Analyser	Engineering
Ideological/ developmental	Adhocracy	Prospector	Non-routine
Consensual	Clan; simple structure	Implementer	Craft
Hierarchical	Machine bureaucracy	Defender	Routine

as achievement of set objectives, which are strategically planned. People with goal-relevant competencies and skills are encouraged and they normally exert a greater influence on organisational decision-making processes. Since this culture is based on the requirements of an immediate response under rationally predictable circumstances, the individual gets a quick feedback on his performance. This helps achievement motives to surface and get manifested in the behaviours of the members.

These cultures also correspond to specific formal characteristics of the organisation. Rational cultures are more often found in organisations which exist in a competitive environment (consumer products, banking and financial services, etc.). The competition makes them alert in planning and implementing their strategies. These organisations continuously scan the environment to detect trends and changes. This environmental scanning (and matching it with internal resources) becomes the basis of setting organisational, departmental and individual targets. However, while the organisations are able to fix the targets, due to their interface with the market environment, the jobs are characterised by many exceptions. Even though not requiring exceptional creativity, they are far from routinised. The employee has to tackle a myriad of non-routine exceptions in his day-to-day job. This makes it very difficult to monitor and control the activities of the employees. Thus, the only viable basis for evaluating performance in the rational cultures is in terms of target achievement.

2. Ideological/developmental culture. When the cues suggest immediate action, but the situation is uncertain, what is required is to act according to one's hunches and intuition. Also, to reduce uncertainty, openness to new information and ideas should be high; one learns and adapts on a continuous basis. Since the required information-processing strategy calls for generating ideas and alternatives, this perceptual system promotes (and is sustained by) creativity, growth, subjectivity and risk-taking. This outlook also becomes the basis of a *developmental/ideological culture*.

Ideological cultures are future-oriented, innovative environments, which give a high priority to growth and development (of people, ideas and society). Such organisations encourage people to look at each job-situation as an opportunity to be creative, to develop multiple perspectives and to take risks. The uncertainties and quick response-time inherent in the job, predisposes people to rely more on their individual insights and hunches, and to try out new ways of doing things. The viable leadership style which suits/promotes this kind of culture comes from a person who exemplifies these values of growth and innovation (e.g., Steve Jobs was a hero for Apple Computer employees, as was Dr. Kurien for the NDDB employees in its earlier days—because they personified the values for which these organisations stood for).

Obviously, such a culture can exist only when organisational members see their jobs as allowing for divergence of approaches. In fact, most often organisations which have non-routine jobs (e.g., creative advertising firms, software agencies and R&D departments) are more conducive for nurturing ideological/developmental cultures. The non-routineness and complexity of job-requirements also create organisations which are loosely structured, so that they allow people with different competencies to interact with each other.

3. Consensual culture. When perceptual cues suggest novelty, but there is no urgency of response, one tends to reduce uncertainty by interacting with and seeking the opinions of others. An example of such a situation would be that of an inter-disciplinary team of researchers engaged in basic research. The team members need to interact with each other to find a meaning of their experiences (e.g., research results). To do so, they tend to develop an openness for each other's views. The aim is to arrive at a mutual understanding and harmony, which becomes the basis of development of a *consensual culture.*

These are highly team-oriented, affiliative cultures. The primary purpose of an organisation, as seen by the members, is to build and maintain effective relationships, which allow for openness and spontaneity of interactions. The overall environment is informal, and individual issues are considered more important than strict implementation of rules. Similarly, in organisational decision-making process, the relationships play a more crucial role than the rules or the official position of members. Naturally, leaders who are adept in maintaining relationships, i.e., who are supportive and participative, are more effective in managing these cultures. Such leaders are able to tap the needs of affiliation and mutual dependence among the members, and channelise them towards the achievement of organisational objectives.

Such cultures are more likely to exist in organisations, where team-work is an essential requirement for organisational effectiveness. Particularly, in jobs requiring mutual interdependence, and which provide enough time for interactions. Most often, these are simple organisational entities, which one comes across, such as small sized project teams, workshops, and educational institutions. Members' perception of the aims of these organisations is not so much as achievement of some objectives in a set time-limit, but to maintain a stable and harmonious system.

4. Hierarchical culture. When the cues suggest no necessity for immediate action as the certainty of achievement is high, the appropriate strategy is to maintain and continue with the present modes of behaviour. Since urgent response is not very important, time is utilised for meticulously gathering information and for systematically analyzing it. The method of information processing is repetitive and with a single focus. This mode, perpetuates a sense of continuity, security and predictability, and forms the basis of *hierarchical culture.*

These cultures evolve around a shared perception among organisational members that tasks can be achieved through established rules in an environment which is static and unchanging. Thus, skills required for doing jobs can be formalised by transforming them into rules, procedures and standard operating techniques. Once this is accomplished, the task of managing lies in ensuring that people follow the prescribed rules and regulations. Obviously, people who have spent more time in the organisation (i.e., the seniors) have more knowledge about these rules and regulations (this is also because, as the environment keeps on changing, organisations evolve greater number of rules to deal with each situation, thus, making the rule-manuals voluminous and more complicated). Due to their knowledge of the rules, the seniors exert more power and influence in the organisation. Correspondingly, the leadership role in such cultures is characterised by a bureaucratic, cautious and rule-bound approach.

The formal characteristics of these organisations also reflect and endorse these cultural attributes. Strategically, these organisations focus on a narrow segment of the market and try to capitalise on a traditional low-risk product or service. Since success is conceived in terms of efficiently operating along the known and established methods, the jobs are formalised and provide very few opportunities for discretion.

IV. THE "EFFECTIVE" ORGANISATIONAL CULTURE

The obvious question is: which of these organisational cultures makes an organisation effective? We discussed earlier, that organisational success may not be the same as organisational effectiveness. An organisation may be at the pinnacle of success one season, and may altogether disappear from the scene (or, be reduced to a negligible entity), once confronted with forces of change. An effective organisation, on the other hand, would weather the changes in its internal and external environment, and would continue to flourish.

The contingency-theory perspective of organisation views effectiveness as congruence among different design elements of the organisation. That is, organisational effectiveness can be seen as the degree of fit among the characteristics of its operating environment, its strategic orientation, structural configurations, technology, leadership styles, etc. The previous descriptions of the four types of organisational cultures also identify the contingent design variables, which accompany each cultural type. This also helps in explaining why organisations with vastly different orientations can perform with equal excellence.

However, as we noted earlier, this same congruence which helps the organisation to act as an integrated and homogenous system, can also become its straitjacket and reduce its capacity to give an appropriate response in changed circumstances. The competing value perspective proposes that as organisations grow, they show spontaneous emergence of "opposite" needs. For instance, as the achievement-oriented values of the rational culture reach their optimum level, the need to develop values of the opposite quadrant (i.e., consensual culture) would become more and more emergent. Such dynamics is quite apparent if one follows the history of different organisations. In the 80's, for example, many Indian pharmaceutical companies, which were facing a competitive environment, found that many of their own territory sales offices were eating into each other's markets. For the organisations as such, while the expenditure on resources was increasing, there was no significant increase in their market-share. The need for these territories was to work like a team. Similarly, highly innovative, growth-oriented organisations, as they grow, experience the need to stabilise themselves, i.e., to formalise and routinise some of their significant operations. If unable to do so, they are likely to spread themselves too thin.

The seeds of organisational effectiveness, therefore, lie in the ability of the organisations to deal with, and integrate, these emergent contradictory values and needs. Actually, it is not as if the contradictory (or complementary) values arise out of nowhere; they are always there in the organisations. Organisations are never in a *perfect* state of congruence. While an organisation may have a dominant culture, it still has pockets where sub-cultures, with very different values, persist. In the same organisation, for example, while the marketing and manufacturing departments may have a rational culture, the finance department may be characterised by a hierarchical culture, and the HRD and product-development departments may have consensual and ideological cultures, respectively. When due to various external or internal reasons (e.g., changes in the market or leadership), the dominant cultural values undergo a change, the values of some other sub-culture would strive to become more dominant. Effective organisations tend to successfully negotiate these changes and make a shift to new values. Thus, effectiveness of a particular culture is not in its internal consistency or its congruence with other design elements, but in its ability to integrate its own opposites and to transcend itself.

V. IMPLICATIONS FOR MANAGERS

The above discussion would be incomplete if one does not also consider its implications for the managers. If culture is a critical determinant of organisational (and therefore, managerial) effectiveness, then it is essential for the organisational leaders to understand the critical aspects of managing and changing the organisational culture. While we will discuss strategies for organisational change in detail in Chapter 12, here we will have a quick look at the conditions which facilitate change and some broad guidelines for initiating cultural change.

A. Conditions for Cultural Change

The ideal condition for changing culture is the one when change becomes almost inevitable. Dyer (1984) observed that "...culture change is precipitated by unanticipated crisis that stimulate leadership transitions and major shifts within a firm." The crisis may be due to a financial setback, loss of a major customer, or a dramatic technological breakthrough which can change the market structure. For example, once the *Maruti* car was introduced in the Indian market, it shook up the otherwise sedate passenger car market, and forced other companies to take a more proactive stance. Similarly, the economic reforms initiated during the 1990's, as well as the opening up of the global market, forced many companies to attempt changing their cultural orientation. Deal and Kennedy (1982) identified five situations which facilitate change in the culture:

1. When the environment is undergoing fundamental changes, and the company has always been highly value-driven.

2. When the industry is highly competitive and the environment changes quickly.

3. When the company is mediocre, or worse.

4. When the company is truly at the threshold of becoming a large corporation.

5. When the company is growing very rapidly.

Such dramatic changes help in raising questions about the existing culture within the organisation, and force people to introspect about the relevance of the same.

Among the major shifts which create the right conditions for change, is the change in the leadership. New leadership at the organisational apex heralds signals of change. The kind of expected changes would, of course, depend on the vision and reputation of the new leader(s). Davis (1984) contended that dominant, charismatic and visionary CEOs can act as the primary sources, transmitters, and maintainers of organisational cultures. But even otherwise, new leadership situations heighten expectations and receptivity, and so, create conditions which are ripe for cultural change. For example, many Indian companies like MMTC, SAIL and ACC, saw major changes occurring after new CEOs took over.

Lastly, it is easier to change the culture of an organisation or department, when it is young and small. Since in such organisations, the cultural values and assumptions have still not taken deep roots, and because they are relatively informal, it is easy to communicate new values to the employees.

B. Suggestions for Changing Culture

It is important to appreciate that changing the organisational culture is not an easy task. As we saw earlier, while the culture may manifest itself in many obvious and conscious ways, its roots lie deep in the unconscious of the organisation. Since, these roots are highly emotionally and ethically charged, often representing a deep underlying and unconscious purpose for the organisation and its members, "to control the corporate culture by changing the stories (or) myths... is undoubtedly a very difficult, if not an impossible, task (Kilmann, 1982)." However, as Boje et al. (1982) proposed, corporate myths can be manipulated, and "mythmaking" can be an active and effective instrument for cultural change.

There are a number of things which managers can do to facilitate cultural change. Some of the specific suggestions are:

1. Managers can act as positive role models for the cultural values. It is not enough to merely describe the sought-for cultural values; the message must also get conveyed through the behaviour of the managers.

2. New symbols and rituals can replace (but should not contradict) the earlier ones. For example, many organisations introduce a new dress code for its members to create changes in the organisational identity.

3. The reward system must encourage the acceptance of new set of values. Employees espousing and practising new values must be identified, supported and rewarded. For instance, if the new values emphasise team-spirit,

the performance system must reinforce group efforts, rather than individual achievement only.

4. The selection, placement and socialisation systems must be redesigned to align with the new values.

5. Since the major resistance to cultural change comes from the sub-cultures, the efforts of the manager must focus on either diluting their influence in the organisation (e.g., through extensive job rotation), or should aim at integrating them in the mainstream organisational culture.

6. Most importantly, do not forget that culture is something which is shared and not imposed. Employee acceptance must be solicited through participation around the new values.

11 Why Organisations Fail

1. During the 1980's, Remington Rand of India Ltd., had a rough time. Once the leader in the typewriter market, it kept on losing to competitors. Reasons: while the market had shifted to electronic typewriters, Remington had continued with its manual versions; its attempts to enter into collaboration with Olivetti of Italy, and to enter into the push-button telephone market, had been a non-starter; the spread of its operations at the three factories at Howrah, Faridabad and Mysore added to the problems. In March 1990, Mahindra and Mahindra increased their equity in the company and took over its control. They formed a management committee, brought in an outside consultant, but soon found the venture unviable. In 1990-91, Remington registered losses, and in February, 1991, the Mahindras sold off their stakes in the company to the RPG Enterprises.
2. Hyderabad Allwyn would be remembered for many "firsts". Established in 1942, it was the first in the country to produce a double-decker bus, refrigerators, and quartz watches. It had technical collaborations with companies like Mitsubishi, Hitachi, Seiko and Nissan for its diverse range of products—buses, watches, refrigerators, sewing machines, LPG cylinders, compressors, office furniture, etc. With an emphasis on growth, the company kept on expanding and diversifying. By the end of the 1980's, the problems of consolidation and coordination became apparent: the diversifications had spread the company too thin, making it difficult for it to compete in the market either by volumes or niche; lack of synergy among interrelated production divisions had lead to high inventories of finished goods; workforce had swelled; plants were working at low capacities. By 1993, the company had an accumulated loss of Rs 168 crores, and its various divisions were up for sales.
3. Premier Automobiles Ltd. (PAL) was probably the worst recession-hit company in the automobile industry during early 90's. Reasons: the inability of the organisation to respond to early signals of the impending crisis, and take appropriate decisions, which only aggravated the damage. Even when the demand was slack, the company kept up the production at full steam, resulting in large stocks, and a cash-flow problem. To liquidate its stocks, the dealers were offered a longer credit period, which further increased the cash-flow problem. This also limited the company's efforts to capitalise on its diesel engine cars, which were still in demand, since it didn't have cash to produce enough of these cars. And so, in 1992-93, PAL showed a loss of more than Rs 20 crores, and its market-share had fallen from 23 percent in 1989-90 to around 11 percent.

The above examples of organisational failures, while varied in nature, have a common underlying message: organisations, like human beings, have the potential of losing touch with reality. If one looks at the history of organisations (business or otherwise), one is struck by how more or less successful and healthy organisations (e.g., Kamani Engineering, Binny, Scooters India and Murphy), which were often leaders in their field, ended up creating crisis for themselves. So many, among these well-established enterprises, disintegrated and vanished from the scene, over a period of time. Of course, organisations do not always die; many have the capacity of bouncing back after going through a period of crisis and failure. But such revivals are not always comfortable; those which survive often have to undergo a painful process of transformation (e.g., surgical turnarounds, takeovers, mergers) and are forced to acquire an altogether changed identity. It is almost as if some organisations programme themselves for failure.

So far, in the previous Chapters, our focus has been on factors which contribute to organisational success and effectiveness. We also discussed how the same factors, which contribute to an organisation's success (e.g., a strong culture, a particular alignment with the environment), can also contribute to its downfall. Understanding the nature and reasons for organisational failures is another way of understanding what makes organisations successful and effective.

There is another reason for focusing on organisational failures. Studies on factors contributing to organisational effectiveness fall into two broad categories. On the one hand, we have those approaches which measure organisational effectiveness on one or a combination of a few criteria (efficiency, productivity, return on investment, employee satisfaction, etc.). The problem with this approach is the sheer number of such criteria, which can be identified. Campbell (1977), for instance, provided a list of 30 measures of organisational effectiveness. A composite measure becomes even more difficult, since many of these criteria may even be contradictory.

On the other hand, we have the systems approach to organisational effectiveness (Katz and Kahn, 1978; Yuchtman and Seashore, 1967), which defines the effectiveness as the extent of alignment and "fit" between the organisation and its environment. To understand why organisations often fail to achieve this alignment, however, this is too limited a generalisation; there appear to be (as the above examples show) numerous reasons and ways in which organisations may lose their alignment with their task-environment, and create conditions for failure. One can say that while all successful organisations are successful in more or less in the same way, the paths to failure are different and varied.

I. REASONS OF ORGANISATIONAL FAILURES

It seems obvious that organisational failures occur when organisations do not adapt to changes. Such a perspective also implies that, to survive and grow, organisations must have an infinite capacity to continuously adapt themselves to changing circumstances. One can argue, however, whether such an adaptability to varying situations is really possible in all cases. After all, certain things (aims, processes, structures) in any organisations would be inviolable, because they would refer to the core identity issues of an organisation. As Loasby (1983) noted:

> Some principles an organisation must have, if it is to remain an organisation; some principles a person must cling to, whatever the evidence, if he is to remain a person. Some changes are simply not possible, even if the alternative is death.

While somewhat pessimistic, such an approach does point to the obvious and inherent limitations of any organisation to change and adapt to new circumstances. Within the historical, cultural, and human constraints, which circumscribe an organisation's response to change, to look for a perfect formula for guaranteed organisational success and effectiveness may be an unrealistic exercise. In the following discussion, we will focus on four inherent constraints—the trap of past success, inability to detect gradual changes, bounded rationality and organisational defenses against anxiety—which predispose organisations toward failures.

A. The Trap of Success

Talking of organisational failures and crisis, somehow gives an impression that failure-prone organisations would be fundamentally different from the successful organisations. Ironically, the processes and strategies, which produce successes are substantially similar to those which produce failures (Hedberg et al., 1976). For instance, the exclusive focus on CAD/CAM market, which gave Hyderabad-based OMC Computers a niche in the market (and a meteoric growth in the initial years) also became the reason for its failure when new competitors, with greater synergy in their product range, entered the field. Similarly, in the early 1980's, Intercraft, the creator of FU's jeans, hit upon the success formula of increasing the product range (to provide something for all ages and tastes) and expanding the number of sales outlets, which helped it capture the denim jeans market. But it was this very strategy which also became the source its subsequent troubles—a wide product range diffused brand identity, and a large number of franchisee outlets created logistic problems of control.

To understand why success produces failures, it is necessary to look at how organisations use their successes. Once having succeeded, their natural response is to create standardised programmes around the successful strategy or process, which would ensure a consistent success experience. They segment their markets/ customers, create inventories, formalise the work processes, standardise their products/services, make capital investments in technology to achieve economies, and so on. They also create buffers and slack resources so that their activities do not get affected by every minor environmental fluctuation. The aim of this programming, buffering, and creation of slack resources is to reduce the necessity of having to make a conscious analytical response every time, and to increase the efficiency of success (Thompson, 1967).

But the process of decreasing dependence on the environment has another repercussion: organisations tend to lose touch with their environment and become less and less sensitive to changes in their circumstances. Their responses become more focused on an imagined or fantasised environment, and less relevant to the reality. Even when they do perceive reality, they often believe so much in the rightness of their formalised (and now, rigid) approach, and in their ability to operate autonomously, that they fail to reflect before responding (Starbuck, Greve and Hedberg, 1978). Moreover, as we saw in Chapters 8 and 9, people who hold power in the current setup also resist a strategic reorientation, thus, further reducing the chances for the organisations to overcome the crisis.

The success-induced programming is not confined to merely the work-related practices and processes. Success experiences also reinforce and programme the informal cultural processes and attitudes in the organisations. We had noted earlier how strong cultures can often reduce an organisation's flexibility in responding to situations. Kotter and Heskett (1992) found that low-performing cultures invariably had a history of past success. They noted that the experience of success in terms of growth and profits has two cultural consequences. Firstly, the managers begin to feel that they and their cultural traditions are superior, and should not be changed. This makes the organisations culturally and psychologically insulated from the environment. Secondly, the need to cope with growth results in building and staffing a large bureaucracy. This implies hiring and promotion of a large number of people whose main competence is in maintaining status quo, rather than in creating and managing change. Thus, even culturally, success experiences have the potential of restricting and reducing the organisation's capacity to change with the environment.

B. Insensitivity to Gradual Change

Another major reason for organisational failures, is their almost inherent inability to sense, detect, and respond to gradual changes in their task-environment. Senge (1990) observed that primary threats to organisational survival come not so much from sudden and drastic events, as from the slow, gradual processes of change. The failure-prone organisations tend to behave in a manner, which is remarkably similar to the "boiled frog". If one puts a frog in a pan of water, and gradually heats the water, the frog does not respond to the increasing temperature; it fails to notice the change, becomes groggier and groggier, but does not try to escape, and ultimately dies. Like our boiled frog, most organisations are also not designed to notice and respond to slow and gradual changes.

As an essential precondition, organisations must be able to perceive the slow and gradual environmental changes before they can respond to them. This is not possible in most cases, because in formalising their information-processing and reporting procedures, organisations inevitably tend to focus on discrete, quantifiable, and communicable events of certain magnitude and nature. Commenting on this filtering of information, perceived and processed by the organisations, Starbuck, Greve and Hedberg (1978) observed:

> Many unanticipated events are never perceived at all; others are only perceived after they have been developing for some time... organisations overlook the earliest signs that crisis are developing, because the earliest signals are poorly observed variables and they are communicated orally in informal reports.

Actually, there are ample early warning signals of impending threats which the organisations can rely upon, if only they are sensitive to these minute changes (Lurie and Ahearn, 1990). Many of these also manifest themselves in a tangibly perceptible manner, e.g., a deteriorating cash-flow situation, growth of a competitive small scale sector, high managerial turnover, increase in overhead costs, growing discontent in the workforce, etc. Unfortunately, however, organisations often tend to ignore and rationalise them. For instance, in the case of Hyderabad Allwyn (quoted at the beginning of this Chapter), there were enough warning signals about the lack of coordination among the production facilities; while the watch manufacturing plant had a capacity of producing only 0.6 million balancing sets, 1.2 million watch parts were ordered; similarly, when the capacity of the refrigerator manufacturing unit was increased, it did not coincide with a corresponding increase in the capacity of the compressor plant, resulting in a high inventory of unfinished refrigerators. And all the while, the organisation continued to follow the targets of 30 percent growth for all its diversified units.

C. Bounded Rationality

Related to the above are the inherent limitations of rational human information-processing capabilities (we had made a passing mention of these limitations at the end of Chapter 1). Organisational decisions, ultimately, are decisions taken by managers, and so would be moulded by the limitations of their capacities. March and Simon (1958) put forward the argument that it is impossible for managers to take optimally rational decisions. This is so, because (a) limitations of time do not permit any manager to consider all possible alternatives and all their possible consequences, and (b) since the outcomes of many decisions are indefinable (or, at best, probabilistic), the manager cannot really evaluate the outcomes of his decision, prior to taking the decision. Thus, the rational managerial efforts are inevitably flawed and contaminated by the ambiguities inherent in the manager's existential situation.

A somewhat unsettling implication of the concept of "bounded rationality" is that managers do not, and cannot, take decisions based on an accurate picture of reality. Rather, their decisions emerge from, to use March and Simon's phrase, their "limited, approximate, simplified model" of reality. The reality does not exist 'out there', but is perceptually constructed by the person, by attributing to it characteristics and meanings (Kelly, 1955). For instance, decisions about whether an investment proposal is 'safe' or 'dangerous', whether the 'relevant' market-segmentation should be according to income, life-style or rural-urban background, or whether a job-applicant would be 'reliable' or not, etc., would depend on the assumptions or 'theories' held by the decision-maker. These implicit theories (or assumptions/models/personal constructs/cognitive maps) are essential to arrive at decisions, since they help in relating the perceived causes with probable effects.

One would assume that even if managers take decisions within the confines of a subjectively interpreted world, developing a capacity to generate and deal with multiple interpretations would give their decisions greater validity.

Unfortunately, stuaies also suggest that the number of interpretations, which people can successfully deal with are rather limited. In the late 1960's and 70's, the Shell Company developed the planning technique based on 'scenarios'. Scenarios are detailed alternative futures which are internally consistent, though each is based on a different set of assumptions about the probable environmental changes. Jefferson (1983) found that if managers were required to deal with more than two or three scenarios of the future, they became confused. He noted:

> Most people want to know what the future will be, what the result of a decision will be, and they dislike being confronted with the realities of uncertainty... For many people the opportunity of working with more than one scenario... is not perceived as offering scope of choice and responsibility but as opening up the risk of error.

More rigorous empirical studies also show similar limitations of human cognitive abilities. The findings of these studies, indicate that it would be unusual for people to use more than two dimensions, and about 15 constructs (kind of mental/perceptual pigeon-holes) in making sense of the reality. Axford (1983, quoted in Earl, 1984), for instance, found that 30 of her subjects, between themselves, had just a total of 101 constructs (or mental pigeon-holes) for viewing people. Similarly, Miller (1956) found that people can, at a time, focus on only "seven, plus or minus two", separate variables. In their study on personal constructs, Kumar and Singh (1978) also found that there are basically two dimensions, personal-impersonal and own-other, on which Indian managers perceive people. (It is also worth noting, that most of the managerial tools and techniques for interpreting and taking decisions about reality, ranging from Johari Window to product portfolio analysis, are based on just two dimensions).

Reflecting on the implications of such findings, Earl (1984) concluded:

> Managerial decisions are apt to be bad, not merely because relevant dimensions and constructs somehow were not on the perceptual agendas of those involved; with the result that problems can be mis-identified and solutions mis-appraised, but also because the number of options considered is restricted. The boundedly rational decision-maker, furthermore, is not guaranteed even to recognise that it is time to change his/her behaviour.

D. Organisations as Defenses against Anxiety

The most popular view of organisations is that they are socio-economic entities, which are meant for producing goods or providing services in the most efficient and effective manner. Moreover, so pervasive is their influence in our lives that one tends to unquestioningly accept their existence as almost natural and given. In accepting this view, however, we neglect the basic truth that, organisations are man-made, simulated, controlled and 'artificial' environments, which also serve some deep psychological purposes in the lives of their members (managers, staff members and workers).

At the most obvious level (as we noticed in Jefferson's observation about the Shell executives), organisations, with their emphasis on rationality, reliability, control, etc., provide excellent mechanisms for warding off uncertainties and ambiguities of human condition. They help people to regulate their lives, to experience a feeling of predictability, and to derive a sense of mastery over themselves. In this sense, they serve as useful psychological defenses, which are often quite functional (in a task-related sense) as well. Menzies (1960), for instance, described how the depersonalised work systems, procedures and practices related to a nurses' job (e.g., strict "professionalism", structuring work in precise routines, referring to patients as "bed number", etc.) are aimed at increasing their interpersonal distance from the patients. Such psychological distancing may also be necessary for the nurses to do their jobs effectively.

The fact, nevertheless, is that organisations do provide legitimacy to defensive behaviours, and so help people to avoid coming in touch with their deep-seated emotional or existential anxieties and dilemmas (Jaques, 1970; Chattopadhyay, 1986). Kets de Vries (1980) noted how people create structures and roles to avoid coming in touch with their deeply experienced feelings of alienation and emptiness. Behind the conscious concerns with tasks, responsibilities, obedience, etc., may lie the unconscious interpersonal anxieties aroused by close contact with people. In fact, Morgan (1986) showed through his analysis of the life of Frederick Taylor, the father of scientific management, how the unconscious concerns for controlling one's impulses can get translated into socially legitimate aims of controlling organisations (see also Chowdhry and Kakar, 1971). He points out how Taylor's life provides:

> ...a splendid illustration of how unconscious concerns and preoccupations can have an effect on organisation. For it is clear that his whole theory of scientific management was the product of a disturbed and neurotic personality. His attempt to organise and control the world, whether in childhood games or in systems of scientific management, was really an attempt to organise and control himself.

At a much deeper level, the very construction of organisations can be seen as a social defense against the anxiety of death. In his book, *The Denial of Death*, Becker (1973) argued that all the efforts of mankind (religions, ideologies, institutions, culture, etc.) are aimed at denying the finite and transient fact of human existence. The fact that we will all die is a fact which makes our existence devoid of any permanent meaning, and creates anxiety. In building organisations and institutions, and in identifying with them, we create something which is more durable and larger than life. Our roles and work activities, give us a sense of continuity, and make our existence real to us. In the introduction of their book, *In Search of Excellence*, Peters and Waterman (1982) quoted Becker: "What man really fears is not so much extinction, but extinction with insignificance... Ritual is a technique for giving life." They go on to say: "In other words, men willingly shackle themselves to the nine-to-five, if only, the cause is perceived to be in some sense great."

The implication of this defensive nature of organisations, is again for the accuracy of the perception of reality. If the involvement of the decision-makers and organisational members is based on the unconscious motives of warding off deep-seated anxieties, then they are less likely to accept psychologically threatening realities. Janis (1982) pointed out how decision-making groups develop filters and shields (illusions of invulnerability, stance of self-righteousness, stereotyped perception of the problem and the "enemy out there", etc.), which do not allow the members to come in contact with an unacceptable reality, and reinforce a process of groupthink. Similarly, Argyris (1970) noted how in the organisational change process, managers tend to neglect, deny, and distort dissonant information:

> ...the clients may tend to forget controversial information suggested by the interventionist and recall in its place the information from the past substitutes for the controversial information. It means clients will expose themselves to learning the information that maintains their present degree of self-acceptance... (and) will tend to interpret relatively threatening information in line with their values...

According to Pauchant and Mitroff (1992), these distortions result from the bounded emotionality of the managers, i.e., from the defects in their capacity to feel and experience certain emotions. They found that these inadequacies in the emotional capacity of the decision-makers (i.e., their faulty and unhealthy mechanisms of dealing with their own feeling and impulses) were significant contributors in making organisations crisis-prone. One only has to look at some of the major industrial disasters and organisational failures (e.g., Bhopal gas tragedy and the Challenger shuttle accident) to realise that in all these cases, there were individuals (sometimes, even everyone involved) who were aware of the possibility (or certainty) of the crisis, but somehow they "decided" to ignore it. What is also significant is the fact that these defenses are, by nature, unconscious, and do not yield (in fact, often become more rigid) in the face of crisis and failure. As Starbuck, Greve and Hedberg (1978) noted:

> Denials that crises are developing and that strategic reorientation is needed arise, to no small degree, from sincere conviction... (managers) really do believe that they should act only on the basis of reliable information and that communications should flow through channels... it is a normal human characteristic to adhere to one's prior beliefs, inspite of evidence that they are incorrect.

II. PATTERNS OF ORGANISATIONAL FAILURES

The above discussion, helps us become more aware of the natural propensity of all organisations towards failure. It does not, however, really enable one to identify the warning signals of a failure-prone organisation. After all, while all organisations share the above characteristics, not all of them fail (just like all of us, by our biological makeup, are susceptible to cancer, but only a few actually suffer from the disease). For a practising manager, it is important to have frameworks for diagnosing the symptoms of organisational failures.

Mostly, when organisations fail (i.e., go bankrupt, lose the market share or show low profits or losses for long periods), one tends to assign some single, and mostly external, event (e.g., a long-drawn labour strike, failure of a major product or a bad investment) as the root cause. In fact, even most of the empirical studies (Smith, 1966; Cohen, 1973; Argenti, 1976; Kibel, 1982; Lurie and Ahearn, 1990) list down a number of probable reasons, which are likely to cause failures. The fact that it is difficult to identify a consensus among such lists, further reduces their usefulness for the practising manager.

It may be more useful to look for deeper patterns underlying organizational failures. After all, as our discussion in the previous section shows, the roots of failure are mostly outside the range of organisational conscious awareness. The nature of the failures, as well as the few singular causes normally assigned to them, mostly only reflect the tip of the iceberg. Underlying them are the more basic and deeper failure-prone patterns, which characterise the organisations. Miller (1977), in a study of 40 cases of organisational failure, found that the patterns which make organisations more susceptible to failures are something like organic illnesses: they are created by a multitude of symptoms or characteristics; these symptoms cluster together to form a holistic unhealthy syndrome; and, more than the specific clustering, it is the extreme nature of the clusterings which causes the failures. He also found that barely four such basic patterns of organisational functioning could account for almost 80 percent of these cases.

Looking for similar patterns Kets de Vries and Miller (1984, 1987) arrived at five "neurotic" organisational styles, which overlapped with Miller's (1977) four common patterns of organisational failures. According to Kets de Vries and Miller, each of these neurotic syndromes emerges from a specific clustering of various aspects of organisational functioning: the style of corporate leadership, the nature of strategic orientation, the organisational structure, the peculiarities of its culture, etc. Based on a number of cases, they also provided evidence how these deep-rooted neurotic syndromes create problematic situations for the organisations. In the following sections, we will discuss these five neurotic patterns, and how they predispose the organisations towards failure (see Table 11.1).

Table 11.1 Comparisons among Failure-Prone Patterns (based on Kets de Vries and Miller, 1984, 1987)

	Strategy	Structure	Culture
Dramatic organisation	Hyperactive; over-ambitious and inconsistent goals	Primitive and rudimentary; weak second-tier management; over-centralised	Dependency; passivity among subordinates
Suspicious organisation	Reactive and conservative; analytical and diversified	Elaborate information-processing; centralised	Lack of trust; "fight or flight" power oriented
Compulsive organisation	Narrow, focused and tightly calculated	Rigid, formal and segmented; hierarchical	Rigid, inward and insecure; bureaucratic
Depressive organisation	Lack of focus and direction; antiquated	Ritualistic and bureaucratic; poor internal communication	Inward; lack of initiative and leadership
Detached organisation	Vacillating; narrow and parochial	Blocks to smooth communication; no scanning mechanisms	Lack of warmth; conflicts; inward

A. The Dramatic Organisation

Miller (1977) described such organisations as "impulsive", being dominated by an over-ambitious, dominating and power-hoarding CEO. The leader's narcissistic need for attention extends into dramatic organisational actions. At a personal level, one finds such leaders seeking attention through life-styles which are somewhat larger than life (a fleet of cars, personal luxury yacht or aircraft, large villas and vacation-houses around the world, and so on). They are showmen who seek excitement and take unconventional risks. Their fantasies about unlimited personal power, success or brilliance also makes them bend towards extremes. They mostly fluctuate between over-idealising something at one moment, while totally devaluing it in the next. At times they may appear to be generous, magnanimous and charming. There is, however, an egoistical streak in them, which makes them take others for granted, and even exploit them if it suits their purpose.

The failure pattern emerges because these personal qualities and aspirations, start influencing the organisational functioning, and the organisation merely becomes an extension of the CEO's personality. The strategy is characterised by bold, dangerously risky and unconventional "mega" moves (mega-issues, mega-projects, mega-investments). One may find the organisation going in for diversifications into unrelated markets and products, indiscriminate acquisitions, widely publicised wild schemes, and so on.

As long as these organisations (or their CEOs) survive, they expand and diversify rapidly, and sometimes randomly. This creates pressures on them to develop better integrating mechanisms, e.g., a better information system, more delegation and better systems and structures for coordination. The problem, however, is that such corporate leaders are more inclined to run their own show, than to rely upon or consult their managers. The power remains concentrated with the CEO, who likes to maintain his/her say in the operational matters, and to manage the organisation personally and informally. The structures and systems of such organisations remain at a rudimentary and primitive stage. Thus, while the organisation grows and expands, its structure and systems lag behind, unable to control and coordinate the diverse demands created by the growth.

The problem is further compounded because centralisation does not help the middle-level managers to feel empowered. In fact, often these corporate leaders also carry a charismatic image, and are idealised by the subordinates. While the leader's presence does bolster the enthusiasm and confidence, the dependence is also extreme. Those who can act autonomously often leave the organisation for more responsible jobs, while the organisation is left with people with low personal initiative.

These conditions increase the pressure on the chief executive, since, over a period of time, he is forced to do what he otherwise loves to do, viz., exercise limitless control. But his responsibilities also start exceeding his limits. Not only has he to formulate the long-term strategies, but he also must supervise the short-term implementation of these strategies in the increasingly diverse operations. The end-result is inconsistencies among vision, plans and implementations. The expansions and grand plans further weaken the systems and structures for coordination and control. Mostly, such organisations end in the same manner as they grow—all of a sudden, with a bang.

B. The Suspicious Organisation

The suspicious organisations are like suspicious people—always alert and ready to fight. They are, therefore, characterised by elaborate mechanisms for collecting and analysing information, a very reactive posture to threats, and an extremely low level of trust/delegation. Kets de Vries and Miller (1987) described seven characteristics of suspicious persons. These also apply as well, to these organisations:

1. They are ever-vigilant to counter any and all attacks and personal threats;
2. They are hypersensitive about neatness, maintaining clarity, following rules and regulations to letter, etc.;
3. They are characterised by lack of emotional expression, which makes them watchful, reserved, precise and calculating persons/cultures;
4. They are inherently suspicious and distrustful of people, and insist on loyalty as a mode of relating;
5. They are characterised by an over-involvement with rules and details to secure complete control;
6. They are vindictive, and over-react to situations which threaten them; and,
7. They show an extreme craving for information in order to feel secure.

In a sense, one would view such organisations as competitive, "professional" and disciplined. In fact, many of the above characteristics can be found in some of the highly effective organisations: they are vigilant to competition, have properly laid out detailed systems for control which must be followed, they deal with problems in a rational task-oriented manner, and often are also centralised in varying degree. The point, however, is that these same characteristics become the reasons for failure, specially when (a) they are carried to the extremes, and (b) when the organisations institutionalise suspicion, as a way of working.

In an organisation, suspicion gets institutionalised when people start treating information as an instrument of power, and not merely as an input for organisational problem-solving. Suspicious organisations are characterised by an abundance of formal and informal mechanisms for gathering (as well as withholding and distorting) information. Organisational leaders rely on elaborate and sophisticated information systems (e.g., budgetary reviews, audits, cost--reports, profit accountability, weekly performance reports, informal surveillance mechanisms, etc.) for identifying potential threats within and outside the organisation. Knowing minute details about what is happening in the organisation, gives them a sense of security as well as helps them in maintaining a tight centralised control over the internal working of the organisation.

The most predominant cultural theme pervading these organisations is that of distrust. Kets de Vries and Miller (1987) attributed this cultural propensity to the impact of the chief executive's insecure and paranoid personality. Obviously, if the CEO himself divides the organisation along those who are "with him" and those who are "not with him" (and therefore "against him"), managers down the line also align themselves (and their superiors, colleagues and subordinates) along this division. The prevalence of suspicion, however, can also be due to other reasons, such as memory of an earlier organisational disaster, or a recent hostile takeover by a new management. In any case, the consequence of this suspicion is that people become reluctant to discuss common problems, do not share relevant and accurate information, view dissent as disloyalty, develop adversary relationships and become over-obsessed with "protecting oneself".

The internal theme of suspicion often gets displaced in the organisations' response to the external world, splitting it along a "we vs. they" dimension. This gives these organisations a semblance of a competitive strategic posture. However, their scanning mechanisms are aimed more at alerting them to environmental threats than to opportunities. In fact, these organisations are often quite slow, conservative and risk-averse in their strategic moves. Even when they diversify, the main reason is to decrease their dependence on one particular product-market segment, and not to seize an opportunity. Moreover, the internal distrust also blocks or distorts the flow of relevant information within the organisation. This results in strategies getting formulated, without an accurate picture of the internal resources and competencies. Thus, in spite of the apparent competitive posture, the strategies of suspicious organisations end up as inconsistent (and often unrealistic), piecemeal and knee-jerk reactions, which lack an overall integrated vision and goal-orientation.

C. The Compulsive Organisation

These organisations are the "stagnant bureaucracies" (Miller, 1977), which have lost touch with their customers, competitors, and with the relevant developments in the technological field. Ironically, this losing touch with reality is not because they don't have a well-defined strategy; rather, they become obsolete, precisely because they have a tightly calculated and focused strategy. This excessive reliance on a narrow, and often archaic strategic focus, with the exclusion of all other factors, makes these organisations out of tune with a changed environment.

Most often, the current strategy is also the one which had contributed to the organisation's success in the earlier years. By formalising the mechanisms of past success, however, these organisations become straitjacketed, with a dogmatic adherence to traditions and norms. Correspondingly, their structure also shows a similar aversion to change and a bias towards maintaining status quo. Three characteristics dominate these organisations:

1. They develop elaborate sets of rigid and formal rules and procedures. The focus is on exactness, creation and maintenance of routines and order, and ensuring high levels of efficiency and reliability, in all forms of organisational life. It is the rules, not people, which dictate issues ranging from major operational/administrative decisions to dress codes or where one can take a client for lunch. While such formalisation and regimentation often results in discontent (owing

to lack of discretion), people often also get acclimatised to operating in a programmed manner. By creating such "bureaupathic" personalities, these organisations further reduce their options for changing.

2. To ensure that the stipulated rules and procedures are being followed, these organisations develop elaborate information systems. The information is gathered with a ritualistic thoroughness, and is used, not for taking decisions, but to control and evaluate the extent of adherence to the rules. While providing stability and control over organisational functioning, organisations squander away a sizeable amount of their resources for the sake of unnecessary details and perfectionism.

3. Lastly, the compulsive organisations are highly centralised organisations. The control over operations is exercised through a control-oriented hierarchical structure, which is based on an extreme division of roles and functions and clear lines of authority. The organisational chart is the most powerful document in these organisations, since it determines the status of the person, identifies the people who he can communicate with, and the kind of tasks he can (or cannot) do, etc. Hierarchies, unfortunately, also block the flow of relevant information within the organisation. Thus, if managers down the line, identify threats or opportunities requiring the organisation to change, this information rarely reaches the top. Similarly, if the top management identifies new visions for change, people at the grassroots levels refuse to acknowledge the necessity of change, and continue to operate in their traditional manners.

As one would anticipate, these organisations fail, because they are trapped in a glorious past. They programme their successes with such perfectionism, and in such detail, that their activities become inflexible and inappropriate for dealing with changed environmental demands. Moreover, their structures and systems do not permit them to even recognise the need for change. Even if they accept the need for change, the complacency and frustration characterising their culture, does not leave them with enough resources to master and manage the change process.

D. The Depressive Organisation

Depressive organisations are another form of stagnant bureaucracies. However, they differ from the compulsive organisations in that they are worn-out, purposeless enterprises, which continue to drift amidst a plethora of out-dated administrative rules, procedures and systems. In a way, these organisations almost run by themselves, in a listless and apathetic manner, with no reference to the changed environmental conditions. Underlying this scenario of hopelessness is an implicitly shared meaning among the members that nothing can be changed, and so, it is not worth making any efforts.

This stance of passivity and lack of initiative finds reflection in many facets of organisational functioning. The most conspicuous among these is the extreme lack of self-confidence and self-esteem, which characterises the behaviour of its members. Members of depressive organisations perceive their lives and work as inferior and tend to resign themselves to mediocrity, ineptitude and failures. The corporate leaders feel powerless to manage and revitalise the organisation, and let the organisation drift aimlessly, following its own rituals and routines without any sense of direction. They suffer from "decidiphobia", i.e, a fear of deciding and committing themselves, and their organisations, to any specific goals and programmes (lest they fail and increase their sense of hopelessness). Often this lack of self-confidence leads to the organisation's excessive reliance on outside "messiahs", e.g., consultants, bankers, government subsidies, even politicians, to solve their problems. This is one way, in which they avoid facing the reality and taking responsibility for change.

Another distinctive characteristic of these organisations is their total neglect of the need for gathering and disseminating information. They rarely engage in collecting information about the markets, often completely insulating themselves from the environment. Even internally, there is a complete breakdown of communication, partly because of the bureaucratic layers, but mostly due to the prevailing climate of apathy and cynicism. Managers (*if* they take decisions) have to rely on vague and incomplete information. The decisions and strategies of these organisations, correspondingly, are characterised by a lack of focus, and reflect a concern for minor trivial issues, while excluding the significant problems.

One is most likely to find depressive organisations in stable environments. Typically, these organisations have a past record of being well-established in a mature market, in which the customer requirements, basic technology and competitive patterns never changed. Large bureaucracies existing in protected economies, like in our country, are most likely to fall into this self-destructive pattern. Due to the past stability of market and competition, these organisations never learn to adapt their strategies with the changing markets. But when changes do take place (e.g., liberalisation of economy, changes in customer preferences and profile, entry of competitors and technological changes), they find themselves unable to redefine their strategies to suit a broadened market. In fact, having never learned to adapt, often they are even unable to immediately identify what their problem is. Thus, when they experience significant losses, the prevalent feeling is that of inadequacy and powerlessness.

E. The Detached Organisation

These organisations share one characteristic in common with the depressive organisations: they are both "headless" (Miller, 1977), and their major crises arise due to the leadership vacuum at the top. Kets de Vries and Miller (1984) characterised the detached organisations as being "led" by a schizoid chief executive, who is withdrawn and indifferent, lacks enthusiasm and emotional warmth, and is incapable of getting involved and committed to organisational realities. Such CEOs show a lack of interest both in the day-to-day operational details, as well as in the company's future. The organisation, thus, is left to float rudderless aimlessly, without a unifying and directional effect.

The detached attitude of the chief executive has quite dysfunctional repercussions on the organisational processes, systems and structure. The lack of exercise of power by the CEO, encourages the second-line executives to try to fill up the leadership vacuum. If they work as a team, it can be quite beneficial for the organisation. Mostly, the absence of a strong leadership unleashes forces of conflicts and competition for greater influence among these managers. The result is that coalitions, power struggle, politicking, etc., become a way of organisational life, and start affecting its functioning in an adverse manner. The organisation becomes a collection of fragmented fiefdoms, whose parochial (personal or divisional) interests often supersede those of the organisation as a whole. That is why, one is most likely to find symptoms of a detached organisation in large, highly diversified conglomerates.

The decisions and strategies of these organisations also reflect the effects of the leadership vacuum. They emerge out of a precarious act of balancing of power among the various political constituencies, within the organisation. The organisation goes in one direction, as one group of managers succeed in persuading their detached and (for all practical purposes) indecisive leader to accept their pet projects—till this influence is mitigated and neutralised by an opposing coalition. The instability and insularity to environment, which characterises such political equilibriums also gets reflected in the organisational decisions and strategy, which show inconsistency, and a focus, which is more internal, than adaptive to environmental demands.

It is important to note that the detached behaviour of the CEO may not always be due to any enduring personality problem, as the term schizoid suggests (Kets de Vries and Miller, 1987). Often, conditions, such as a major personal crisis in his life, greater interest in other aspects of his personal life, an explicit knowledge of his short-term involvement with the organisation, etc., can also encourage similar behaviour from the chief executive. For many CEO's, the knowledge that he/she is going to retire or get transferred within a year or so, can also be a reason for lessened involvement with the organisation. Whatever may be the reasons for the leader's detached behaviour, the results are more or less the same: an inconsistent, vacillating and internally-focused strategy, political fragmentation of the organisation, a climate of conflicts, conspiracy and suspicion, and lack of collaboration among the various units of the organisation.

III. IMPLICATIONS FOR MANAGERS: DIAGNOSING ORGANISATIONAL ILLNESSES

In this Chapter, we have discussed various origins and patterns of organisational failures. Of course, organisations rarely die; they make turnarounds, get merged or are taken over, and continue to survive. Many, in fact, flourish more after undergoing a crisis period. For the manager, however, the effectiveness would lie in being able to identify the impending crisis, and in taking precautionary steps. Therefore, it is necessary to draw the implications, for diagnosing failure patterns in organisations. The following are some of the broad conclusions one can derive from the preceding discussion:

1. There are no singular, isolated causes to failure. Organisations do not fail because of a few scattered incidental reasons. A major strike, failure of a plant, collapse of the market, an environmental disaster, etc., seem to be the most obvious causes one can assign to failures. However, these are only the precipitating causes. They only bring out the weaknesses, which were already existing in the system. The actual causes are the ones which predispose the organisation to failures. These are many, and exist as a definable pattern, which is discernable in all facets of the organisation's functioning (its systems and structures, culture, decision-making procedures, managerial practices, etc.). Thus, for managers it is important to focus his/her efforts on identifying the failure-prone patterns, rather than on isolated factors.

2. The patterns of failures exist outside the organisational consciousness. Failure and its obvious symptoms are only the tip of the iceberg. The formal practices of the organisation, tend more to hide these patterns than to deal with them (e.g., stringent accounting practices may cover the implicit assumption of distrust on/among people). Harvey and Albertson (1971) observed that the existence of an underlying organisational problem is often apparent from the behaviour of its members. These behavioural symptoms, which show that a failure-prone pattern exists, can be useful guides for managers in their diagnosis:

(a) Organisational members do not own and accept responsibility for existence of problems, but tend to blame it on others (other managers, environmental factors, etc.);

(b) The organisation is divided into more or less permanent and often mutually exclusive, sub-groups, which consistently meet informally to exchange rumours, grievances, fantasies, or solve problems;

(c) In general, members are individually aware of problems being faced by the organisation. This awareness and concern, however, is limited to the privacy of their sub-groups, and is never shared and openly discussed (often there may be large areas of agreement among these private definitions of the problem, though the members may not be aware of this agreement);

(d) Members act in a manner, which is incongruent and contrary to the information which they possess, and the understanding of the problem which they privately confess; and,

(e) There is a marked difference in the way members behave within and outside the work-related situations (e.g., during and after the meeting).

3. The problem of failure-prone organisations is their problem of inability to change. Organisations are not inevitably doomed to fail. But they become failure-prone because of their inability to adapt and change with the circumstances. As we saw earlier, getting stuck in a past pattern of success, itself can be a failure-prone pattern. It is important for the manager, therefore, to focus his/her efforts on identifying organisational blockages to change. How one can deal with these organisational forces resisting the change, is a topic requiring more in-depth deliberations. In the next Chapter, we will deal with the issues that should be dealt with in managing organisational change.

12 Managing Organisational Change

1. In 1971, in response to its increasing size, and the nationalisation of the banking sector, the State Bank of India embarked on an organisation-wide restructuring exercise. Taking the help of external consultants, and through the involvement of a top management steering group, it managed to implement major changes in the organisation: a shift from a functional structure to a market segment-based structure; introduction of a budgeting and performance review system; differentiation and strengthening of planning and staff functions; and, creation of more unified channels of command of branches from the local head offices.
2. In 1981, when Gurucharan Das took over as the President of Richardson-Hindustan Ltd. (now, Proctor & Gamble India), the company was in a bad shape. Profitability was low, return on equity had gone down from 25.2 percent in 1977 to 11.4 percent, industrial relations were poor, and inter-departmental relations were marred by politics and rivalry. To improve the situation, Das went ahead creating a "people oriented culture" where "new ideas thrive and people develop their full potential; otherwise good people do not stay." What followed was a massive OD exercise for changing the values and attitudes of people at all levels. In 1984, RHL had a committed management team, the union-management relations had improved, profits had more than doubled and the sales had gone up by almost 30 percent.
3. The Steel Authority of India (SAIL) had suffered losses of Rs. 2760 million during 1980–84. When V Krishnamurthy became the CEO, he met almost 25,000 employees, either individually or in groups and, based on the discussions with them, prepared a list of priorities of action. Company-wide discussions on these priorities were initiated by calling meetings and mailing the list to all its 2.5 lacs employees. As a result a greater amount of decentralisation was introduced, cost savings were made on overtime payments and fuel consumption, a flatter organisational structure was introduced at plant-levels, more efforts were put in to develop human resources, and so on. In 1988-89, the company registered a profit of Rs. 3600 million.

What these examples depict, is that organisations do not remain the same over a period of time. Either through deliberate and planned efforts, or through a process of adapting to changes in internal or external circumstances, they change. In fact, change is not only inevitable, but also essential if the organisation aspires to grow and excel. In order to cope with the economic, socio-political and technological changes, any organisation must, by necessity, adapt itself by aligning its goals and strategies, optimising the balance among its various sub-systems, and structuring itself for a more effective interface with the environment. That is, the organisation must behave like an open system (Saxena, 1985).

One of the most important requirements of the managerial role is the ability to initiate, facilitate and manage changes in the organisation. In this Chapter, we will focus on the essential elements involved in the organisational change processes; that is, why changes occur, the nature of the change process, characteristics of successful and unsuccessful changes, and strategies for a planned organisational change.

I. WHY ORGANISATIONS CHANGE?

To understand why organisations change, it may be useful to think about why individuals change. One of the reasons why most of us change is because we need to adjust and adapt to the changing life-circumstances (e.g., loss of money, offer of a new job, sickness or work pressures). These are situational reasons which impel us to readjust ourselves to new conditions, either through consciously questioning, reflecting upon, and redefining our present habits and orientations, or by forcing, coercing and overpowering ourselves to start behaving in certain manners. There are, however, also certain more inherent reasons for change, which are related to our life-cycles. Even if nothing changes in our external environments, we do not remain the same always or forever because of the growth and aging processes. As we grow, the circumstances of our life automatically keep on changing (adulthood, aging, family responsibilities, etc.), often quite predictably.

Like human beings, organisations are also open systems. They are also characterised by openness of environmental influences, and the processes of differentiation and negative entropy. Thus, these same reasons also apply to organisational changes. That is, organisations change both because of situational fluctuations in the environmental demands, as well as because it is in their nature to grow and develop.

A. Situational Reasons for Change

One of the implications of viewing organisations through the systemic perspective is that all the systemic elements of the organisation (its environment, goals and strategy, technology and tasks, structure, culture, etc.) are not isolated, but interrelated. Thus, change in any one sub-system would have an impact on the other sub-systems as well. This in turn, would also affect the characteristics of the total system. As Khandwalla (1982) pointed out:

> Organisational change means significant change in any one or more of the tasks, techniques, structure, and the people of the organisation. Changes in these, however, tend to be correlated. A change in tasks can often lead to changes in people, structure, and techniques.

The changes in any of the sub-systems, of course, can originate from a diverse number of sources. Very broadly, one can classify these reasons as external or internal (see Table 12.1). One must note, however, that these reasons are not mutually exclusive, and affect each other. An internal change in corporate

Table 12.1 Some of the Significant External and Internal Factors Initiating Organisational Change

External reasons	Internal reasons
• Government regulations	• Changes in corporate leadership
• Changes in economy	• Implementation of new technology
• Competition	• Decline in corporate performance
• Raw material prices	• Changes in employee profile
• Raw material availability	• Union actions
• Pressure groups	• Low morale and motivation etc.
• Technology push	
• Scarcity of labour etc.	

leadership, for example, may ultimately result in changes in organisational goals and strategy, and correspondingly change the texture of its operating environment. Similarly, changes in consumer demands may force organisations to develop new systems and structures for coping with them.

1. External reasons for change. Organisations do not exist in a vacuum. Changes in the environment necessarily affect them, since they change the very nature of relationship between the organisation and its environment. In order to remain effective and to survive, the organisation must find new ways of relating to its environment. The organisation may respond to these changes in a healthy adaptive manner (i.e., by converting a potential threat into an opportunity) or reactively (i.e., by succumbing to the new pressures and demands), depending upon its preparedness to change. In either case, however, they change.

It would be almost impossible to build a comprehensive list of the external situational triggers to change. Sometimes even minor and apparently unrelated changes in the external environment can cause major shifts in the organisation. In order to convey the relevance of these factors, we are listing some of the most common and obvious external determinants of change:

(a) *Government regulations*: The slashing of subsidies by the government to the professional institutes (IIMs and IITs) during the 1990s, created pressure on these organisations to generate funds for themselves. Correspondingly, they were forced to strengthen their revenue-generating functions, such as training programmes, consultancy, etc. Similarly, the privatisation of the power sector, encouraged many industries (e.g., Jayprakash Industries) to diversify into this sector.

(b) *Economic changes*: The recession in the consumer-durable industry forced many organisations to reduce their manpower (e.g., Premier Automobiles reducing its workforce by 2,200), find out and institutionalise methods for cost-cutting (e.g., Crompton-Greaves trying to reduce the inventory carrying cost), or diversify into other markets (e.g., Andrew Yule & Co. diversifying into tea business).

(c) *Competitors' actions*: In 1993, to counter the threat, particularly to its Bombay operations, from its competitors Lintas and HTA, the advertising agency Mudra Communication decided to reorganise itself.

(d) *Raw materials price and availability*: Fluctuations in prices and erratic availability of raw materials, often impel organisations to create buffers, strengthen their purchasing functions, or gain control over raw material sources through backward integration.

(e) *Changes in consumer preferences/profile*: With business travellers gradually becoming a major customer segment for hotels, many five-star hotels had to not only include new infrastructural facilities (e.g., telecommunications, fax, voice mail, etc.), but also start new services (e.g., business centres, conference hall facilities, secretarial services, etc.).

(f) *Pressure groups*: Consumer right forums, unions, environmental protection groups, etc., although often not very much organised, also influence organisations to change themselves. For instance, the Rs. 700 crores copper-smelting project of Sterlite Industries (India) at Ratnagiri, had to be stalled due to active opposition from the environmentalist groups.

(g) *Technological advances*: The proliferation of communication technology (communication satellites, cable networking, dish antenna, etc.) was a major influence (apart from competition from satellite services) on Doordarshan to restructure itself, segment its services to different kinds of viewers, and become more competitive.

2. Internal reasons for change. External changes do not always affect the organisations directly. They create changes in some of the internal sub-systems, leading to a realignment of all other sub-systems. For instance, in an organisation, external factors (such as increased domestic competition, government regulations encouraging exports, opening up of an integrated European market, etc.) may have a primary relevance only for the production, quality control and marketing functions. However, changes in these functions, to achieve ISO 9000 certification, would have wide-ranging ramifications for all other functions (purchase, training, etc.) in the organisation.

Moreover, certain changes in the organisations take place primarily due to internal decisions, which may or may not be directly affected by the external situational factors. Once again, it would be difficult to comprehensively list all such internal factors. Some of these changes, however, are part of a familiar experience for most practising executives, which we will briefly discuss below:

(a) *Implementation of new technology*: A decision to purchase and implement new technology is bound to have consequences for other functions as well. The computerisation of railway reservations, for instance, also resulted in changes (or pressure for changes) in the reporting relationships, span of control, coordination mechanisms, etc.

(b) *Change in corporate leadership*: A new chief executive may not only introduce new systems and structures, but may also symbolically, communicate new values and culture in the organisation. One can think of numerous examples (e.g, V. Krishnamurthy-SAIL, Tapan Mitra-INDAL, Gurucharan Das-RHL, Ratan Tata-Tata Sons, etc.), where change of leadership also led to major internal changes within the organisation.

(c) *Union actions*: Unionisation of workforce creates a major power coalition in the organisation, which would have its impact on organisational decisions. In our country, the political affiliation of unions (and the party in power) also affect the kinds of actions organisations can or cannot take. In 1992, for instance, the Philips Employees' Union successfully pressurised the management to stop sale of debentures to Tata Sons.

(d) *Changes in employee profile and attitudes*: Over a period, people in organisations grow and change. Also, fresh recruitment brings in new kinds of employees. Structural and systemic changes become necessary to retain and get work out of this changing set of employees. With the young professionally qualified managerial workforce becoming more mobile and ambitious, many companies in our country are changing their recruitment policies, developing better compensation packages, redesigning work to provide more challenge and autonomy, and so on.

(e) *Setback in corporate performance*: A setback often shakes up the organisation out of complacency, and forces it have a relook at itself. For instance, a downward trend in profits and market-share, compelled Hindustan Motors to start contemplating changes in its management structure and style, its inventory control system, investment plans, etc. Similarly, the Bhopal disaster forced Union Carbide to introduce major changes in its business structure.

(f) *Mergers, acquisitions and alliances*: A meeting of two distinct corporate cultures, obviously, creates new demands on the organisation. These changes become apparent in the new strategic emphasis, new lines of control, new systems, new set of employees (also departure of some old personnel), etc. The teaming up of HCL with Hewlett-Packard, for instance, brought in new systems, with emphasis on quality, after-sales service, cash-flow management, etc., in the organisation.

B. Organisational Evolution and Life-Cycle

As we mentioned in our discussion on the determinants of organisational design (refer to Chapter 2), the processes of growth and aging themselves create new demands for adjustment for the organisation, and so, act as potent forces of organisational change. Based on his observation that organisations grow in a relatively predictable manner, Greiner (1972) proposed a developmental model for organisational growth. He contended that, just as individuals grow through sequentially confronting and resolving developmental crisis (Erikson, 1968), so do the organisations. He described five phases of organisational evolution (see Figure 12.1), each culminating in a crisis (or "revolution"), which the organisation must overcome before graduating to the next phase. Let us have a more detailed look at this model.

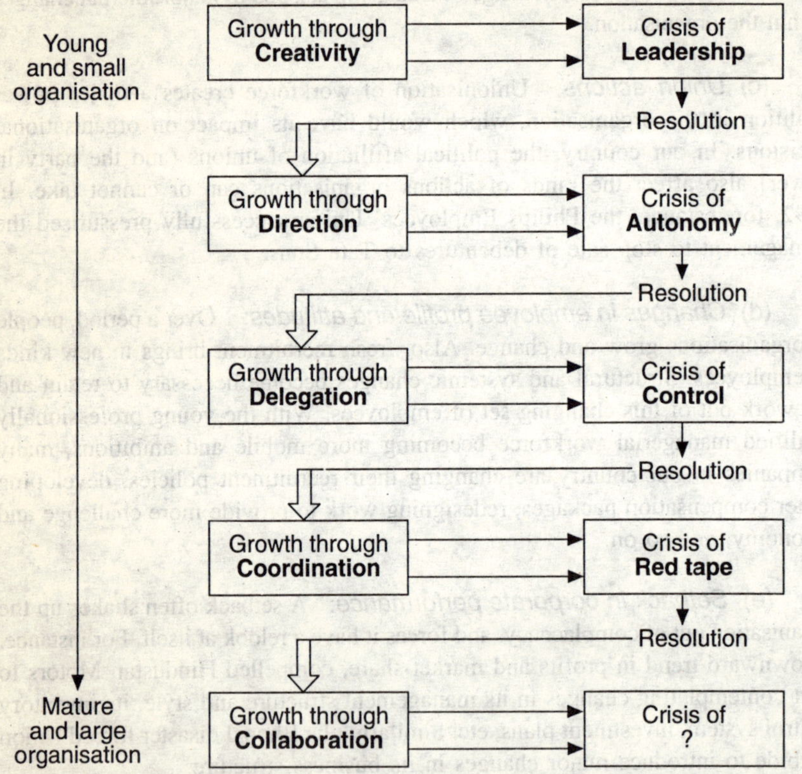

Figure 12.1 Illustration of the five phases of organisational evolution (Greiner, 1972).

1. Phase 1: Growth through creativity... crisis of leadership. The first phase of organisational growth is marked by creativity and entrepreneurship. The organisation is usually small and informal. Leadership and decision-making is concentrated in the hands of the dominant, and often charismatic, owner-entrepreneur(s). The structure and control systems are simple and primitive, since the organisational emphasis is mainly on a "make and sell' strategy. In a way, the organisation prospers through highly individualistic efforts of a few persons who control, inspire and command a high-level of performance from the employees.

As the organisation grows and becomes larger, it becomes more and more difficult to control and manage it through informal and individualistic methods. Increased volumes call for a better planning and control; larger size makes it difficult to communicate and control the organisation informally; new employees do not share the same dedication to and involvement with the organisation as the old ones do, etc. This leads to a leadership crisis, the resolution of which may involve the replacement of the entrepreneur by a professional manager. The crisis occurs because the founder must step aside and make way for the business manager.

2. Phase 2: Growth through direction... crisis of autonomy. If the organisation is able to survive the first crisis, the tasks for the business manager would involve pulling the organisation together, by streamlining its activities. This phase is characterised by the implementation of a functional structure, in which hierarchies, responsibilities and jobs are clearly differentiated, focus is on operational efficiency, and communication is done formally through proper channels.

This centralised and formalised management style, however, turns out to be inappropriate, as the organisation grows and becomes more complex and diverse. The gap between the decision-makers and the implementers becomes wider; multiplicity of organisational objectives create conflicts among functions; the lower-level employees feel constrained by procedures and orders from the top, which they find increasingly inappropriate for performing their tasks in the market, shopfloor or office. This leads to the crisis of autonomy, which can be resolved only by the delegation of authority and responsibility to the lower-levels.

3. Phase 3: Growth through delegation... crisis of control. This phase is characterised by a decentralised structure, with responsibilities delegated down the line. Control over the operating units is held by the creation of profit centres, and the managers are autonomously responsible (and accountable) for their own plants, departments or market territories. Executives at the apex, manage more by exception, relying on periodic reports from the units. Their major energy is focused on expansion and acquisitions, to strengthen the other decentralised units.

Continued over a period of time, this state of affairs leads towards a crisis of control. Decentralisation and autonomy, results in a parochial attitude among the field managers, who prefer to run their affairs without coordinating with each other or with the corporate office. The consequent loss of synergy, and increase in redundancy of efforts and expenditure, starts hurting the overall organisational interests. At this stage, many organisations tend to regress back to centralisation as a means to control. The solution, however, lies in developing more sophisticated integrating mechanisms to achieve better coordination among the units.

4. Phase 4: Growth through coordination...crisis of red tape. During this phase, the organisation evolves formal systems for achieving greater coordination among units. Numerous staff personnel are inducted in the headquarters, tc create, review and monitor these coordination mechanisms. Companies often merge the decentralised units into product or market-based groups and plan and review capital expenditures judiciously before allocating funds. While field managers still have decision-making powers, they are required to justify their actions to the "watch-dog" functions at the headquarters.

While these steps help the organisation in achieving better coordination and more efficient allocation of limited corporate resources among the units, they also make the organisations increasingly bureaucratic. The line managers resent receiving directions from the staff functionaries who may not be familiar with local conditions, while the corporate staff starts finding the line managers uncooperative and uninformed. This staff-line conflict also signifies that the complexity and size of organisation can no longer be managed by formal and rigid programmes and systems. The need is to build a more interactive and collaborative system of working.

5. Phase 5: Growth through collaboration... crisis of?. This last "observable" phase of organisational evolution, focuses on development of more interactive, spontaneous and collaborative systems of achieving integration among the decentralised units. Managerial actions and decisions are characterised by the resolution of interpersonal differences, negotiations, problem-solving through teamwork, and social/self control. Organisation works through cross-functional/ unit task-forces, meetings and conferences, and frequent interpersonal interactions. The staff strength at the headquarters is reduced, and the role of the corporate staff is to facilitate a cultural integration within the organisation.

Even such a growth phase would have its crisis. At the time of writing, Greiner (1972) could not find any observable evidence about the nature of the ensuing crisis. He hypothesised, however, that the crisis following this stage would centre around "the psychological saturation of employees who (would) grow emotionally and physically exhausted by the intensity of teamwork and the heavy pressure for innovative solutions." He also suggested, that organisations would attempt to solve this crisis by allowing the employees to rest, reflect and revitalise themselves. Twenty years later, we do find in many organisations (particularly those dealing with information/communication technology, marketing and advertising, etc.) a high rate of burnout, and organisations using yoga, sabbatical, re-education, flexi-time, etc., as means of coping with the crisis.

Greiner's model holds significant implications for managing organisational change. Besides providing an insight into how evolutionary forces influence organisational change, it is also a map which provides broad guidelines for facilitating the change efforts. Specifically:

(a) Since there is some amount of predictability in the way organisations change and grow, the manager's sensitivity to the particular phase in which the organisation is, would not only prepare him better for the change, but also help him in devising strategies for a smooth transition to the next phase.

(b) Each phase of growth, and the possible subsequent crisis, requires specific solutions. Since different kinds of change interventions are likely to be successful only during particular developmental phases, one must recognise that the range of solutions is limited.

(c) Lastly, one must appreciate that there are no permanent solutions. A solution that may help the organisation overcome a particular crisis itself becomes the problem, which generates the next crisis.

II. THE PROCESS OF ORGANISATIONAL CHANGE

One obvious conclusion, which gets reiterated in the preceding discussion is that change is an inescapable fact of organisational life. Whether due to change in external or internal environments, or due to change in the age and size, the organisations are constantly changing. Morgan (1986), in fact, proposed that the metaphor of flux and transformation can itself be a meaningful conceptual framework in understanding the basic nature of the organisation. While it may be possible to change the nature of change, one cannot possibly stop the organisation from changing over a period of time.

It is for this reason that an insight into the nature of organisational change process becomes an essential requirement for managerial effectiveness. Managing an organisation, in this perspective, is nothing but management of change. A good manager is a person who has mastered the change process.

But how do organisations change? What human processes take place within the organisations, when they change in terms diversifying, growing in size, implementing an MIS system (or a new performance appraisal system, new control system, incentive scheme or a new technology), getting a new CEO/departmental head, or moving into new markets and so on? In this section, we will focus on these behavioural processes, which get stimulated by/during the change process, and so, act to facilitate or resist it.

A. A Model of Organisational Change

Consider the two cases presented in Exhibit 12.1.

Both are dissimilar in many ways. While one deals with an academic institution, the other deals with a corporate setting; one focuses on how problems were created, while the other deals with the problem-solving process; one describes the imposition of change, while the other narrates a process of change through participation; one involved a spontaneous occurrence, while the change process in the other was professionally managed, and so on.

Inspite of these differences, however, they also share many similarities in terms of the change process. At the beginning of the change process, both systems (the academic institution and the senior management group of the construction company) were in a state of equilibrium. In both the systems jobs were performed in a manner which was sort of unquestioningly accepted and shared by the members. The change process started when this equilibrium got disturbed, due to the entry of something which was alien to the system. In one case, it was a person defining new rules of the game; in the other, it was a dissonant feedback. In both cases, the result was that the system lost its

Exhibit 12.1

Two Cases of Organisational Change

CASE 1: **The Zealous Reformer**

In one academic institute, a new person took over as the Dean (Academic affairs). In his zeal to reform the system, he centralised many powers, which till then were vested with the departments and faculty (e.g., number of courses a faculty must teach, registration of students for electives, whether the same course could be offered twice if more students wanted to take it, whether the students could be given a make-up exam or not, etc.). These rules were imposed suddenly, and initially they created a lot of confusion; some faculty members welcomed the changes while others resented them. Protests were ignored by the new Dean, and problem were mostly brushed under the carpet. Over a period of an year, some of the more rebellious faculty joined together and formed a faculty association. The climate of the organisation became political, with both the faculty and the Dean using pressure tactics to arrive at decisions. Even the faculty group was divided, because even though a large number of them joined the association, some of them had refused to do so.

CASE 2: **The Reluctant Change-Masters**

A construction company invited OD consultants to help in improving its operating effectiveness. After a thorough diagnosis, through interviews and questionnaire surveys, the consultants shared their finding with the senior management group in a workshop. These findings highlighted that the managerial styles at the senior levels were bureaucratic and control-oriented, and were blocking initiatives from the lower-levels. Most of the executives refused to accept these findings; only a handful amongst them were prepared to believe them. In the ensuing discussions between the "refusers" and the "believers", the OD consultants also pointed out how the methods adapted by the group to resolve the differences, corroborated the findings (e.g., the old-timers would refuse to listen to the new managers, and argue them out). Such observations, magnified the polarisation of views, and much heat was generated. The consultants encouraged the group members to resolve their differences by starting to discuss their views about these findings. Gradually, people started feeling comfortable about discussing the implications of their styles. By the end of the workshop, they had developed detailed action-plans, with deadlines and accountabilities, for implementing significant systemic changes in the organisation.

---

equilibrium: in responding to the arrival of the alien, views got polarised and were expressed; people became emotional; in comparison to earlier position, different kinds of interactions started taking place; and, people started discussing the underlying basics of the system itself. This process finally led to the system finding a new way of aligning itself. In the academic institution, the re-establishment of a new equilibrium was achieved by the faculty defining new ways of relating to the Dean and with each other. In the case of the construction company, the group of executives arrived at a new and shared understanding of the organisation's problems (which became the basis of their action plans).

These parallels between the two cases, refer to the commonalities of the change process, which underlie all kinds of healthy and unhealthy systemic changes. Lewin (1947, 1951) was the first social scientist to point out that all changes follow an identical sequence, which can be described by four specific stages (see also Figure 12.2):

Equilibrium --> Unfreezing --> Movement or change --> Refreezing

Figure 12.2 Showing a schematic view of the change process.

1. Equilibrium. This is the first stage when the system is in a steady state, which may be apparent in terms of a stable culture, a set of practices, certain shared norms, or a particular mental set.

2. Unfreezing. In this second stage the steady state gets affected due to intrusion of an alien element in the system. This may be a new person, a piece of information, a new rule of procedure, or a new technology.

3. Movement or change. In the third stage the system moves to find a new equilibrium through a variety of exploratory maneuvers. This process may be done consciously or unconsciously.

4. Refreezing. In this final stage the system re-establishes an equilibrium. It may do so, either by integrating the new element within the system (e.g., new plans based on the feedback), or by psychologically or physically rejecting the new element (e.g., employees ganging up together to protest against a new control procedure).

Efforts to manage change, therefore, must focus on each stage of this sequence. It is also important to note here that often managers unwittingly ignore the unfreezing effect of many of their actions and decisions. This is often so, because managers look at the implementation of change in a piecemeal tangible manner. They neglect that a new rule or a new technology also has fallouts in the other, particularly the intangible human and cultural sub-system of the organisation. When not attended to, the "unfrozen" cultural sub-system moves, changes and refreezes in manners, which may not be in the desired direction (as happened in the case of our zealous reformer—see Exhibit 12.1). And so, the managers lose control over the change process. While we will be discussing what managers can do to manage and facilitate the total change process, let us first look at why people resist changes.

B. Resistance to Change

Most of the reasons why people resist change can be seen as problems associated with the processes of unfreezing, movement and refreezing. Many management researchers (e.g., Zaltman and Duncan, 1977; Nadler, 1981; Beer, Eisenstat and

Spector, 1990, etc.) have identified numerous reasons why organisations and people resist change. In the following paragraphs, we will discuss some of these reasons:

1. Structural inertia. Most organisations are designed to perpetuate stability. To change is a requirement, which is alien to the purpose for which these organisations are programmed, and the manner in which they are supposed to operate. Thus, when needed to change, the rigidity of the structures and systems, itself poses a major obstacle. This is more so with large, functional and bureaucratic organisations than with the small, simple structures (although they may have other reasons for not changing). In any case, all organisations have some semblance of structure, and once having structured their activities, they prefer to maintain the status quo.

2. Limited focus of change efforts. As mentioned earlier, changes in the organisations are often attempted in an isolated and piecemeal manner. Managers initiating and implementing them, ignore the impact which the change may have in other organisational sub-systems. For instance, a decision to computerise the inventory control system would not only affect the work procedures and practices of the Materials and Stores Department, but also influence the working of other departments, such as production, purchase, finance, etc. If these parallel changes are not managed properly, they often become a hinderance to change.

3. Disruption of existing power relationships. We had discussed in Chapters 8 and 9, how organisations, apart from being many other things, are also an arena for play of power and politics. In a stable organisation, the power relationships and coalitions are, more or less, in a state of equilibrium. A change in the formal structure and tasks of the organisation, however, tends to disrupt this, often precarious, balance of power. Certain departments, coalitions and roles, which were more powerful in the earlier scheme of things, may now have to yield their place in the hierarchy of influence for others. These power constituencies naturally resist the change efforts on account of their vested interests.

4. Group norms and pressures. As we had discussed in Chapter 10, the norms and values of a group, are a powerful influence on the behaviour of its members. If the change efforts contradict some of the implicit or explicit cultural norms, people are likely to reject the change. For instance, if the cultural norm is that employees interact informally with each other while working, a new and more efficient work system, which involves their working alone for long stretches of time would be resisted (even though by working under this system, the employees may stand to benefit through incentives).

5. Fear of loss of expertise. Any organisational change involves a change in certain tasks performed by the organisation. Thus, it would always entail the replacement of certain skills (technical or behavioural) by others. For people who have developed expertise over certain skills and competencies, such changes would be most threatening. For instance, automation would be perceived as a threat by traditional operators, since it can make them and their skills, obsolete in the organisation.

6. Fear of loss of need-fulfilment. People are committed and motivated to work in an organisation, because it helps them to satisfy their various needs. They earn their livelihood, meet and relate to people, feel part of a larger entity, get a feeling of job satisfaction, and so on. Various researchers (Maslow, 1943; McGregor, 1960; Alderfer, 1969) have commented on this need-fulfilling aspect of work in our life. People also tend to develop ways and means by which they can optimally satisfy most of their needs from their jobs. A change in the characteristics and context of the job would also imply changes in the manner and level of fulfilment of these needs for the person (one may lose social status, earn less, feel less secure, etc.). This implication for one's overall need-satisfaction is often a major reason for people to reject changes.

7. Loss of self-control. Probably, one of the most existential consequence of change is the sense of having lost control over one's life. People do not always resist change, but they certainly do resist *being* changed. Certain kinds of changes (e.g., mechanisation of work), which hamper with the individuals' or groups' autonomy, very obviously create this threat of losing control over one's choices; but even other kinds of changes, when imposed or implemented without preparing people, also generate similar feelings. For instance, the despondency which follows the acquisition of one's company is often rooted in a perception that one is a pawn and not an active contributor to the organisation's evolution.

8. Differences in ideology. Often, people resist change because they are ideologically opposed to the direction or means of change. Such differences are deep-seated in the values, which these people cherish. When the management proposes a change for the benefit of the organisation, the question "change to whose concept of the organisation?" becomes relevant. A change which may be good for the organisation-as-a-profit-making-enterprise, may not always meet the goals of organisation-as-a-socially-responsible-unit. For instance, people may resist technological changes, which may be economically sound, but which are not eco-friendly, because they may clash with their values.

C. Force-Field Analysis

The force-field analysis (Lewin, 1947, 1951; French and Bell, 1991) provides a useful framework for understanding the change process, as well as for planning strategies for implementing change. To understand the force-field analysis, one must start with a very basic question: if the human systems (e.g., individuals, groups and organisations) are constantly targeted by such a variety of forces of change, why don't they keep on changing? why do they remain in a state of quasi-equilibrium, and not in a state of continuous flux?

From the preceding discussion, one can gather that at any point of time, there are forces, both within and outside the organisation, which drive it towards change. Simultaneously, there are also forces, which restrain the organisation from changing. We can term these two kinds of forces as driving and restraining forces. Whether the organisation changes or not would depend on which one of these two forces is stronger, and the whole process of change can be understood as the interplay between the driving and restraining forces.

When the organisation is in a state of equilibrium, apparently, the driving and retraining forces sort of cancel out each other. For instance, if the capacity utilisation of a plant is low, driving it to increase the utilisation level would be forces such as, the need for profits, management's pressure, fear of a takeover, increasing competition, fear of large-scale retrenchment, etc. The reason why, inspite of these pressures, the capacity utilisation has not increased, is because there are also restraining forces (e.g., poor maintenance of machinery, ineffective management systems, autocratic supervisory style, etc.), which counter-balance the forces of change (see Figure 12.3). Similarly, one can look at all organisationally and socially stable conditions (productivity level, morale, level of prejudice

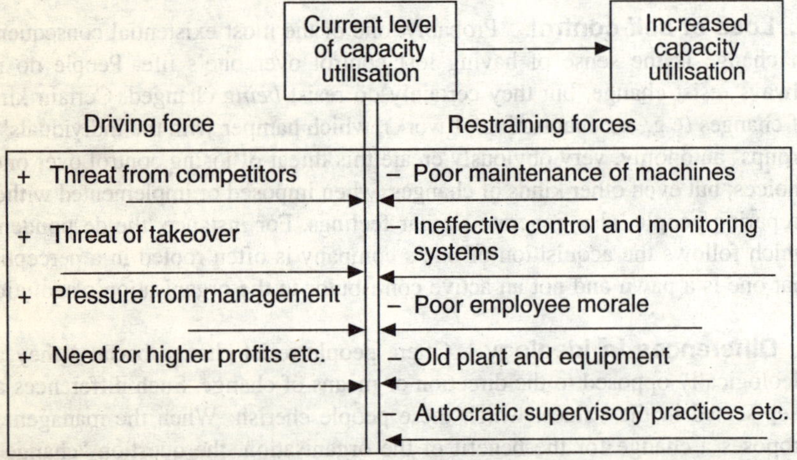

Note: The length of the arrows indicates the strength of that force.

Figure 12.3 An example of force-field analysis.

in a society, etc.) as being expressed by a balance between the driving and restraining forces.

One of the implications of the force-field analysis is that changes occur only when this balance is somehow disrupted. If the driving force increases (either because the pressure for change has increased, or because the resistance to change has decreased), then the conditions may improve towards the desired direction. On the other hand, if the forces of resistance increase, the situation may further deteriorate.

This understanding can also be used by the managers for planning changes. If a change in a desired direction (e.g., increase in capacity utilisation, decrease in employee turnover, improvement in morale or a change in the absenteeism rate) is to be brought about, then the manager must identify the driving and the restraining forces, which are keeping the situation in the present state of equilibrium. This equilibrium can then be shifted towards the desired condition either by increasing the driving forces or by decreasing the restraining forces.

While increasing the driving forces (i.e., increasing the pressure for change) is sometimes effective, in practice, however, reducing the restraining forces is usually a more effective method for bringing about changes. There are two reasons for this: firstly, often the driving forces are external (e.g., increasing competition), and therefore, outside one's influence; and secondly, by increasing pressure for change, one may create more resisting forces, which may nullify the pressure. For instance, as seen in the example given earlier, in the case of the educational institution (see Exhibit 12.1), the pressure for change created by the Dean only created further resistance. In contrast, in the second case, facilitation of the process in the group meeting decreased the resistance, thereby, making it possible for changes to occur in the desired direction.

III. MANAGERIAL OPTIONS FOR IMPLEMENTING CHANGE

So far we have been focusing on the processes involved in organisational change. We have largely dealt with changes as something which "happen" to the organisations (more or less as a sort of spontaneous occurrence), the origins of these occurrences, and the kind of response they invoke from people and organisations. Managing change, however, is more than reacting to changes and doing damage control. Besides reacting to changes, a manager must also consciously initiate and implement changes to meet the new demands created by the changed circumstances.

In this section, we will review three broad approaches, which are popularly used in organisations to create changes. This classification aims to integrate the findings on change management (Greiner, 1967; Chin and Benne, 1976; Kotter and Schlesinger, 1979, etc.). These approaches differ from each other in terms of the assumptions about people and systems change, the specific strategies used for making the change successful, and the kind of response they are more likely to stimulate (see Exhibit 12.2).

A. Top-Down Approach

One of the most common ways in which organisations attempt to introduce changes is by pushing the changes down the hierarchy. In this approach, the solutions or decisions are arrived at by people at the top, and then are passed down the formal channels of communication and control in a unilateral manner (Greiner, 1967). Mostly these changes focus on the tangibles, e.g., changes in structure and reporting systems, replacement of executives, announcement of concrete plans and procedures, etc.

There appear to be two assumptions underlying this approach to organisational change: first, the reasons for the existing behaviours in an organisation (e.g., low performance, high absenteeism, low productivity rate) can be traced to single tangible factors. Correspondingly, the overall system can be changed by changing these tangible causes of existing behaviours. Thus, if one changes the existing structures, systems and procedures, or if one replaces

Exhibit 12.2

How to Decrease Absenteeism Rate

Top-Down Approach	Collaborative Approach	Laissez-Faire Approach
Assumptions about people and change:		
People change by complying to standards set by more powerful ones.	People change when their normative attitudes change self-interest.	People change by making rational choices about their own relevant issues.
Focus of change efforts:		
Coercion; manipulation; gaining compliance	Change of perceptions and attitudes; gaining commitment.	Informing people; Increasing their options.
Likely change strategy:		
Create rules/systems to check and control absenteeism.	Re-educate people through workshops, discussion forums, participation, etc.	Disseminate information about what people lose by being absent.
Likely outcomes of change efforts:		
Quick control of absenteeism, but may create other problems in long term.	No short-term change; would be lasting if successful.	Absenteeism may go down; but change may not last due to group pressures.

the strategically located people in the system, it should lead to basic changes in the organisation.

The second assumption underlying this approach is that change can be understood as a coercion-compliance phenomenon, i.e., change consists of compliance of those less powerful, to the desire of those with more power (Chin and Benne, 1976). The change process is approached with the basic assumption that some people initiate changes while others get changed. The strategies used for accomplishing change are often coercive and manipulative (Kotter and Schlesinger, 1979). For instance, the management may threaten a lock-out if the unions do not fall in line. In this situation, they may also resort to using covert, and sometimes unethical, influence practices (e.g., creating false rumours or buying out potentially threatening people).

A top-down strategy of change can be quite effective, provided the change initiator has considerable power (not necessarily coercive, but even from other sources, e.g., charismatic). The advantage of this strategy is that the resulting change is quick and speedy. Sometimes, when other strategies don't work, this may be the only option left to the manager. However, as one would notice, the top-down approach focuses primarily on the unfreezing (by issuing a decree) and the refreezing (by installing systems) stages of the change process. Since it ignores the intervening behavioural and socio-cultural process of transition, the refreezing is not successful—people obey the new system, but also informally organise efforts to subvert it. People do not like to be coerced. The changes in behaviour which do occur, are often only superficial. Moreover, in coercing people to change, certain relevant change-related issues (e.g., interests of coalitions, fears of losing control over self) may get ignored, and may create problems in the long run.

B. Laissez-Faire Approach

The laissez-faire approach to change is just the reverse of the top-down approach. It presupposes that systems can change only when its members change. Moreover, it is also based on the assumption that people are primarily rational beings who follow their rational self-interests. They will change (and in a particular direction) only when they realise that it is advantageous for them to change (Chin and Benne, 1976). Thus, the most one can do to create change is to provide enough information for people to make rational choices. For instance, if an organisation is facing a problem of decreasing sales, it may try to improve the situation by increasing feedback on sales figures to the sales-force, building an awareness about company's problems among them, conducting training programmes on selling skills, and so on.

One of the consequences of this approach, is that it delegates much responsibility for defining and acting upon problems to the subordinates (Greiner, 1967). The most common forms this approach takes in the organisations are communication meetings and workshops, conferences, training programmes, etc. An organisation conducting company-wide training programmes on, for instance, decision-making skills is assuming that participants would learn these skills, and would later be able to use them in concrete organisational situations. Many organisations also use annual conferences and meetings, in which executives can exchange information and clarify issues, with the assumption that such an exercise would improve overall organisational performance.

Such an approach to change can be quite effective if the hinderance to change is coming from lack of adequate and accurate information, or lack of relevant skills. Organisations do change when its people change. Many organisations, which successfully implemented a Total Quality Management Programme, did benefit from conducting awareness workshops. However, this may not be the most appropriate strategy in all cases. The assumption that organisational change is a sum of individual changes is a tenuous one. Developing decision-making skills may not yield improved decision-making in the organisation, if the problem is with the management information system, or with the power struggle among coalitions. Merely unfreezing the system by feeding in more information, may not necessarily lead to change in the desired direction. Moreover, it is a rather slow, uneconomical and time-consuming approach. This would be particularly so, if the organisation is large, with large number of people, who should be affected to bring about change.

C. Collaborative Approach

This third approach to change falls somewhere between the previous two approaches. Neither does it involve dictating the nature and steps of change from the top, nor does it leave the change process entirely in the hands of the functionaries. Rather, it involves sharing of power between the superiors and subordinates, in terms of jointly defining the problems and developing the solutions (Greiner, 1967).

The underlying assumption of this approach is that the organisational systems and structures, which need to be changed, are not mere mechanical procedures, or Exhibits in the organisational chart. Rather, they are defined by the patterns of behaviours and practices, which are rooted in the socio-cultural norms, values and attitudes of people. An effective change can come only when these underpinnings of the existing ineffective behaviours and practices are discarded and replaced by new and more effective ones (Chin and Benne, 1976). Such deep-rooted changes, however, cannot be achieved either by force or by leaving them to chance. They are achieved only when people feel secure, motivated and empowered enough to review and question the existing practices, and to experiment, evolve and develop commitment, with the new ones. That is, they have an active role in the design, direction and implementation of the change process.

The collaboration between the superior and subordinates in creating change, however, does not necessarily mean that the superiors have no distinctive role to play in the process, or that the subordinates completely take over the mantle of change. They have to play different roles in the process. Mostly, the role of the superior consists of providing a broad perspective to guide the process and direction of change (see Exhibit 12.3). He may highlight the problems which need the organisation's attention, and invite participation from others in solving

---

Exhibit 12.3

Six Steps to Effective Organisational Change

In their study of successful organisational changes, Beer, Eisenstat, and Spector (1990) identified overlapping but distinctive steps, which executives used for aligning tasks with the change process. These were:

- Mobilising commitment to change by jointly diagnosing what the major problems with the organisation are, and what can be done about them.
- Based on the analysis, developing a shared and task-aligned vision of how to manage and organise new role and processes to deal with the problems.
- Fostering a consensus for this new vision, helping people to develop competencies for managing this vision, and developing a cohesion and bonding among people to help in achieving this vision.
- Replicating and spreading this revitalisation to all other departments and units, without pushing it from the top, i.e, supporting other departments and units to experiment with the change.
- Institutionalising the change by developing formal policies, structures and systems.
- Monitoring and making adjustments in response to problems encountered during the process of implementation of changes.

---

them. This approach, besides increasing the commitment of people to change, also provides an opportunity for bringing out and working on those underlying factors, which are likely to cause resistance to change. For instance, if departmental heads have to collectively arrive at a decision about a change which involves reallocation of resources, working on this decision would also give them an opportunity to negotiate the underlying issues of power-parity.

A large amount of research evidence (Greiner, 1967; Beer, Eisenstat and Spector, 1990) on organisational change shows that a collaborative approach is more likely to be successful than the other two. The OD approaches to planned organisational change (French and Bell, 1991, see also Exhibit 12.4) are also

---

Exhibit 12.4

What is Organisational Development?

Organisational Development (OD) is a planned and collaborative effort to organisational change, which aims at improving the organisation's capabilities to diagnose, and solve problems and learn how to change.

The steps of OD can be described as follows:

Entry of the change agent: The change agent, usually a behavioural sciences consultant is invited to help the organisation to change.

⇓

Preliminary diagnosis by the change agent: The change agent interacts with the members and diagnoses the relevant problem issues.

⇓

→ **Feedback to the client system:** The findings of the diagnosis are presented to the client group.

⇓

Discussion and action planning by the client system: Members of client system discuss the diagnosis and decide on an action plan.

⇓

Action implementation: The action plans are implemented by the client group.

⇓

Further data gathering and diagnosis: Implementation of action plans generates new data, which is collected by the change agent/client group.

As can be seen from the arrows connecting the steps, OD is a cyclic process, which helps the system to develop competencies for diagnosing and solving its own problems—a stage when the change agent disengages himself from the system.

---

primarily based on the principle of a collaborative strategy. Nevertheless, even this approach has its pitfalls. Firstly, it is a time-consuming and often quite expensive approach to change. Of course, one realises that large-scale and basic changes in the organisations cannot be achieved overnight, but an undue emphasis on collaboration and sharing can also deter the organisation from its primary economic goals. Secondly, this approach requires sophisticated social and behavioural process skills from the managers, which, in many cases can be an unrealistic expectation.

IV. GUIDELINES FOR FACILITATING CHANGE

If, as we said earlier, the basic task of management is to manage change, then it follows that the change strategy must incorporate and manage all the three stages (i.e., unfreezing-movement-refreezing) of the change process. It is for this reason also that the collaborative approach is the most viable strategy for successfully implementing organisational change. Greiner (1967) found that while there was an inconsistency of pattern among the unsuccessful changes, the successful organisational changes seemed to be achieved in a reliably consistent manner (see Exhibit 12.5). In this section we will look at some specific guidelines which can be used by managers to collaboratively manage changes.

Exhibit 12.5

Patterns of Successful Organisational Change Process

Greiner (1967) in his study of successful and unsuccessful change processes in the organisations, found that successful changes appeared to follow a more or less similar pattern. He identified the following eight stages through which organisations achieve successful implementation of change.

- Internal or external pressures create a need for change, which is shared in the organisation, but particularly felt by the top management.
- An outsider, either a new executive or a consultant, who has a reputation for creating change, enters the organisation.
- This change agent encourages the organisation to re-examine its past practices and present problems.
- The top team assumes a direct and highly involved role in conducting this examination.
- The change agent, with the help of the top team, involves different levels in this diagnosis.
- The change agent provides people at different levels with new ideas and methods for developing solutions for the organisational problems.
- The initial solutions are tested/implemented at a small scale, and, if found successful, applied at a larger scale.
- As the change efforts spread, they get absorbed permanently as the organisation's way of life.

A. Unfreezing the System

In order to change, the system needs to be shaken up. Unless people see a need for change and start questioning the status quo, no energies would get mobilised for movement towards change. In addition, people in the organisations must also feel secure and supported enough to do this kind of self-critiquing. Some of the following strategies have been found quite useful in creating the conditions for change.

1. Creating dissonance. Very often people are quite aware of the discrepancies between "what is" and "what should be". But if the organisation is complacent, highlighting the deficiencies in its performance (sales and production figures, customer complaints and perceptions, findings of satisfaction surveys, etc.) stimulates people to start questioning the present ways of functioning (Nadler, 1977).

2. Sharing information. In his book, *Moments of Truth* on the turnaround of SAS, Jan Carlzon (1987) observed: "An individual without information cannot take responsibility; and the individual who is given information cannot help but take responsibility." Sharing information, besides making people aware of the problems, serves another very important function; it makes them feel more secure and empowered to look at themselves as proactive agents of change, and not merely recipients of the impact of change.

3. Creating contacts with the external world. One of the stimuli which encourages people to look at themselves is an exposure to what is happening in the outside world. Such information provides comparisons around which people can focus their problem-sensing/solving energies. Many organisations, for example, depute their executives to external conferences and training courses, invite outside experts from various fields to share their experiences and encourage executives to subscribe to management and technical journals to remain in touch with the state-of-art practices and technologies, etc.

4. Enlisting top management support. This is important since the commitment of corporate leaders increases the sense of comfort with change among people (Bennis, 1969; Zand and Sorensen, 1975; Lee, 1977). Strong leaders can increase pressure within the organisation to unfreeze. Some studies (e.g., King, 1974) also imply that expectations for change by leaders have a determining influence on the outcomes of change.

5. Reward for change efforts. To make the proposition for change look more attractive, it is often useful to build in rewards for change efforts (e.g, suggestions, proposals) put in by the employees. It is not necessary to give tangible rewards; even the intangible ones have an encouraging impact. Moreover, since rewards are viewed as a formal recognition of efforts by the organisation, they also give credibility to the organisation's resolve to change.

B. Facilitating the Movement

Once the organisation has started identifying and reflecting on the change-related issues, the next task of the manager is to give this energy a direction, and support to move in a desired direction. This is an important task, because otherwise, the change may take place, but in a dysfunctional direction. Managers may find the following strategies useful in managing this transition.

1. Establishing clear goals. Goals provide a picture of what the future should be like, and give a direction to change efforts. Many studies (e.g., Nadler, 1981) have noted that people change only when there is a clear purpose for changing. Beer, Eisenstat and Spector (1990) noted that this requirement places the managers in a paradox of "directing a non-directive change". They suggested that goals should be defined in a manner which specifies the broad direction of change without insisting on a specific solution.

2. Involving people in change. If the goal is expressed as a broad vision, and is evolved through participation, it is likely to attract greater commitment for change (Barczak, Smith and Wilemon, 1987; Peters, 1987). By encouraging people to participate in the process of diagnosing and discovering solutions for problems (e.g., through task-forces or project teams), one not only empowers people, but also helps them to surface and work through the cultural and political fallouts of change.

3. Focusing on the total system. Any change in one department would have repercussions in other departments and sub-systems as well. It is essential, therefore, for the manager to focus his/her efforts on the total organisation. In considering a change in the technology, for example, it is necessary to also integrate the consequent changes which are likely to occur in the roles and structure, culture, relationships, informal power hierarchy, and so on.

4. Developing support systems. One of the most unsettling experience of being in the midst of a change process is the ambiguity and uncertainty of the situation. It is necessary to create systems to help people, both psychologically and professionally, and to help them feel at-ease with the changes. It is also necessary to develop competencies for dealing with change. Development of various skills, opening of multiple channels of two-way communication, role-negotiation forums, counselling, etc., are some of the examples of the popularly used support systems.

C. Re-establishing the Equilibrium

This last stage of the change process is as important as the first two. Not only should change take place, but the new form must also become a stable and continuous part of organisational processes. If the change process has been properly managed so far, it would be relatively easy for the organisation to refreeze into a new equilibrium. A few key points, however, still need attention at this stage.

1. Rewarding/celebrating desired behaviour. It would seem obvious that reinforcing desired behaviours and ignoring or discouraging undesirable behaviours would help organisations and people to adapt to and accept change.

It is remarkable, however, how often managers and organisations inadvertently encourage people to continue practising old patterns. For instance, if the change has been towards developing systems for better customer-service orientation, the organisation may still persist with promoting people from those marketing offices, which overshoot their sales target, even though there are maximum number of customer complaints from these regions.

2. Planning for incremental success. Major organisation-wide changes do not occur overnight. Rather, they occur in incremental small steps (Quinn, 1980a). Managers must plan for built-in incrementalism in their change efforts. Beer, Eisenstat and Spector (1990) also suggested that the initial success of change in some units/departments can become a "developmental laboratory" for other units. This incremental approach also keeps the costs of failure low and within control.

3. Creating social bonds. Most organisational changes have the potential of disrupting the existing patterns of group dynamics. Changes in structure, location, shifts, reporting relationships, etc., do change the existing nature of social relationships, which can create a sense of discomfort with the new set-up. It is important, therefore, to take care of these ruptured social bonds. Team-building exercises and increased social interactions (e.g., office parties) can be quite useful for building and strengthening the social bonds.

4. Institutionalising the change. Lastly, the most important aspect of managing change is the activity of formalisation of the new practices and processes into stable systems. While changes are initiated and achieved through more or less non-directive and informal means, for them to become a part of organisational life, it is essential to structure them. For instance, many organisations expose their executives to training programmes on creative skills. Unless the use of these skills is given a focus and form in organisational systems and procedures (e.g., formation of idea generation forums, or a norm that in all meetings called for solving problems, half an hour would be spent on brainstorming, etc.), people may lose interest in using these skills, or they may be lost to the organisation along with their leaving. It is important to note, however, that the formalisation and institutionalisation of change outcomes, is the end-product of the change process, and early efforts to structure the change are likely to be unsuccessful.

13 Organisations: A Future Perspective

In the previous Chapters, we had been focusing on the nature of organisations, as they exist at present. One must appreciate, however, that organisations are merely man-made mechanisms which are devised for dealing with the uncertainties of a particular social context and era. The large bureaucratic structures emerged as an offshoot of industrialisation, and were appropriate for mass-production of products and services. The growth and proliferation of divisional form can also be seen as an organisational response to increasing complexity in the business environment. Similarly, in the 50's and 60's, the need for groups and people to work together to accomplish complex tasks (e.g., the Apollo Programme, which required NASA, academic institutions and manufacturing firms to work together) triggered the emergence of structures such as matrix and project organisations, task-forces, etc.

Thus, with changes occurring in the society (technology, market, politics, values, etc.), it may not be surprising to find new organisational forms, structures and processes being implemented and practised in the coming years. In fact, indications are that alternative forms of organisations, more capable of coping with the emerging environmental demands, have already started emerging (Stewart, 1992). In this Chapter, we will discuss the nature of these environmental changes, their implications for managers and organisations, and how organisations can design themselves to cope with these emergent changes.

I. THE CHANGING ENVIRONMENT

The environment, both in our country and the worldover, is undergoing critical changes. These changes are significant, not only because of the pace at which they are occurring, but also because of their impact on the very quality and texture of the business environment. Within the last few years, we have witnessed major changes taking place in the politico-economic sphere (breakdown of marxist economies, creation of European Market, liberalisation of economies of many third world nations, etc.), technology (revolution in information technology, materials research, genetic engineering, etc.), markets (product diversity, increase in volumes of transactions, globalisation, etc.), social values (rise of consumerism, environmental consciousness, sex-roles, etc.), and so on.

In India too, the emergence of similar patterns of change can now be noticed (Business Today, 1992). The recent changes toward a more liberal and deregulated economy have created multiple and simultaneous pressures for the business organisations. There are greater demands on the organisations now, to deal with intensifying competition; develop a quality-conscious customer orientation; globalise, grow, diversify and modernise; decrease overheads, increase cash-flow and equity-base; shed corporate fat, restructure and professionalise; develop, upgrade and acquire new technologies, and so on. Such pervasive changes are making it more and more imperative for organisations to develop capacities for coping with, what Toffler (1981) describes as the "Third Wave", and the consequent "corporate identity crisis".

Obviously, such changes will have significant implications for the organisations and managers. But before we discuss those, let us first appreciate the nature and quantum of these changes.

A. Information/Communication

In the last decade or so, one of the most crucial change, with an impact on the very nature and concept of organisation, has been the proliferation of information/ communication technology (see Exhibit 13.1). Many writers have commented

---

Exhibit 13.1

How Information is Shaping Our World

- According to some estimates (Toffler, 1970; Naisbitt, 1984), even a decade or two ago, as many as 6000–7000 scientific articles and more than a thousand books were getting published every day, in the world.
- According to Naisbitt (1984), the estimated rate of growth of information (which itself was growing exponentially) in the mid-eighties as 13.5 percent, i.e., the information would get doubled every five years.
- In 1960s, there were just a few hundred computers in the whole world. By 1980s, this figure had grown to one million. In 1992, the annual worldwide sales of PCs alone (i.e., not counting the mainframes and minis) was 28 millions.
- In India, in 1984, there were approximately a hundred companies, which were producing about 3000 computers per year. In 1987, there were as many as 250 companies producing 45,000 computers every year. In 1992, 1.2 lacs PCs were sold in India (not accounting for the sales by the non-branded unorganised entrepreneurs).
- Globally, on-line database accounts for a business of $12 billion. In India, too, many organisations (e.g., NIC, DART, BIIT, UUNET, etc.) are offering such service.
- In June 1992, the world's first digital cellular telecom system, GSM (Global Standard for Mobile Communication) started operating in Germany. It allows internationally mobile travellers to communicate with each other across 20 countries.
- Between 1995 and 1997, Motorola is planning to launch 77 communication satellites to build its Iridium System, which will allow it to establish a universal globally mobile telecom system. These systems can even be hooked to a computer and allow transmission of electronic data.

---

upon the significant shift which is taking place the worldover, changing the existing industrial society to, what has often been described as the "post-industrial" (Bell, 1979) or "information" (Naisbitt, 1984; Naisbitt and Auburdene, 1985) society. We are generating, receiving and processing more information than at any other time in human history.

One of the factors, which has significantly contributed to this information explosion is the advent and growth of computer technology. In a span of less than a generation, computers have become increasingly popular, invading offices, factories, shops, institutions, and homes. The availability of increasingly sophisticated systems and softwares has enhanced our information-processing capacity manifolds. In the organisations, computers are now being used to perform many complex tasks, such as forecasting, managing costs, monitoring inventory and sales, product designing, production planning and process control, maintaining career records, planning job-rotations, handling performance appraisal data, etc. At Eicher Tractors, for instance, in case of a breakdown, the computerised fault tracking system can track down the particular supplier, the consignment, and even the supervisor who cleared the consignment. Similarly, at Asian Paints, computerisation makes it possible to keep track of 56 million packs (which contain 40 different types of paints in hundreds of shades) as they are sold through a network of thousands of distributors.

Such usages, however, can now be described as conventional, to which most organisations have become more or less adjusted. More staggering changes in the foreseeable future may involve, not only a greater capacity to process information, but also a greater capacity to communicate and interact around this information, instantaneously and simultaneously. Interactive and networked systems would also result in reducing the decision-time. For instance, the aircraft manufacturing firm, Boeing, used an interactive system TeamFocus for conducting a meeting to finalise a customer satisfaction strategy. In two and a half days, they were able to arrive at a consensus, a task which would have normally taken about seven weeks. In a study, which the company conducted on its 64 networked meetings, they found savings of an average of $ 6,700 per meeting, mainly in employee time (Kirkpatrick, 1992).

Systems networking would also allow people to globally interact with each other through terminals, thus, increasing their accessibility to different databases on a real-time basis. In the recent years, integration of computer technology with the advances in the field of telecommunication has opened up new possibilities in the area of processing and transmitting information. Thus, in the very near future, it may be quite possible for an executive, to collect sales figures from distributors on a palmtop computer, tabulate and analyse them, prepare a report, and send it by portable modem using the cellular telephone kept in his pocket—and all this, while travelling!

B. Technology

The other major source of influence on our age is the advances in technologies and processes in a variety of fields. Computerised systems, cellular phones, communication satellites, etc., of course, are part of this technological revolution.

For instance, computer-aided design (CAD), used with state-of-art communication system, helps engineers at Hitachi to design and produce new parts in just half a day. Similarly, computerised mixed-model assembly procedures, highly automated and flexible welding processes, sophisticated short-cycle stampings, etc., allow Mazda to make profits with a production-run of just about 40,000 cars.

But similar critical shifts are also occurring in other scientific and technological fields, e.g., materials sciences, fibre optics, energy, biotechnology, etc. In the increasingly networked world, knowledge gets disseminated faster, and so, shortens the gap between the scientific discovery and the commercial product launch (Toffler, 1970). These breakthroughs have enormous potentials for changing the very nature of production and design processes, products, markets, and, therefore, competition. New discoveries in materials science and condensed matter physics are helping industrial R&Ds to develop stronger materials with novel properties (e.g., tough ceramics, high-strength polymer alloys). Similarly, biotechnology is gradually revolutionising the chemical and agro-based industries i.e. fertilisers, food-processing, petroleum, pharmaceuticals, paper, distilleries, etc. (see Exhibit 13.2).

Exhibit 13.2

Technological Breakthroughs in India

- Indian Organic is going to import .5 million tonnes of used plastic soft-drink bottles from Pepsi Co of the US, and all for free (!), to use as raw material for polyester fibre.
- The Pune-based National Chemical Laboratory has developed a tissue culture which cuts short the flowering period of bamboo from 80 years to just a few weeks!
- Another breakthrough by the NCL is a strain of yeast that works continuously on molasses. Using this, a distillery can switch from batch-processing of alcohol to continuous processing, increasing its productivity by about 15 percent.
- Ballarpur Industries is planning to put up a plant for producing bricks and ceiling panels from flyash, a waste product which comes free from thermal power plants. The product would be better insulated, lighter and stronger—and while the cost of production is more, the raw material is for free.
- The National Metallurgical Laboratory, Jamshedpur, is working on developing a zero-effluent Resins process, which integrates three stages of steel production (reduction, sintering and electro-slag smelting), which will reduce the energy costs by about 20 percent.
- Using tissue culture technology, AV Thomas and Co. increased the yield of cardamom from 100 kg. per hectare to 1000 kg. per hectare.
- Thermax Ltd. uses earthworms for treating the 129 kg. of waste generated by its canteen.
- The Central Electronics Engineering Research Institute, Pilani, is developing a 1200 words speech-recognition system, which may make the secretarial pool redundant and transform the security system.
- Anand-based Amul factory uses a gravity-based conveyer system for transporting its products from the shopfloor to the stockpile.

These hard-core scientific discoveries have implications not only for new product developments, but also for developing more responsive, cost-effective and flexible processes of manufacturing. What makes the technological edge more relevant to the emerging business scene is that there is also a proliferation of the number of technologies which are relevant to developing/manufacturing the same product. As Clark (1989) noted:

> An expanding science base in communication, design and manufacturing puts enormous pressure on business... Markets are more fragmented and global, precisely because competitors have the means to cater to increasingly particular customers and deliver products worldwide almost instantaneously; computers, materials science, and biology offer numerous, powerful, even astounding ways to improve products and the processes that make them.

C. Globalisation and Competition

According to one report (quoted in Hax, 1989), the worldwide exports totalled $ 2.48 trillions in 1987. This amount showed an increase from 12 percent in 1962 to 30 percent in 1986. In other words, throughout the world about one-third of the goods are consumed in a country other than where they are produced. This change is only one indicator of an increasing trend towards a global economy. One can also discern similar trends in many politico-economic changes, e.g., liberalisation and removal of trade barriers in many developing nations, development of a global capital market, division of the world into economic zones (e.g., SAARC, EC, ASEAN, etc.) through alliances among countries, etc. The world, as Ohmae (1991) observed, is gradually turning into a borderless, global marketplace.

One can also notice similar changes occurring in the Indian business environment (see Exhibit 13.3). While India still plays a very minor role in the world market (accounting for less than a percent of the world's total exports), the rate at which the changes are occurring is quite fast. With the shift from a "protected" economy to a "market" economy in the early 90's, one finds many more foreign collaborations and alliances taking place. Likewise, most established Indian business houses have started floating off-shore ventures.

There are many significant implications of this global trend for organisations. The first, of course, is an increase in market competition. Not only do global markets make more products and brands available to the customer, but also, the availability of diverse forms of alternative technologies brings in competition from non-traditional sources. For instance, the competition to the Indian consumer electronics industry came, not only from foreign competitors in the same industry, but also from the Hong Kong-based Star TV. Moreover, since the new technologies are now becoming available at a faster pace, time has become a critical element for maintaining a competitive edge (Schmenner, 1988).

Secondly, operating and facing competition at a global scale has larger implications for the very nature of business. To meet the diverse local requirements of individual countries, organisations would need to develop more pluralistic and more consumer oriented product-market strategies (Kim and Mauborgne,

Exhibit 13.3

Globalisation Trends in India

- The world's top ten brands (Coca-Cola, Kellog's, McDonald, Kodak, Marlboro, IBM, American Express, Sony, Mercedes-Benz, and Nescafe) have either entered or are all set to enter the Indian market.
- While India's contribution to world trade is still minuscule, in terms of absolute growth, India's imports and exports have shown a remarkable increase. Between 1960-61 to 1990-91, India's imports increased (at 1990-91 prices) from about Rs. 600 crores to more than Rs. 42,000 crores. Similarly, the exports increased from about Rs. 500 crores to about Rs 32,000 crores.
- In 1981-82, there were only four international trading houses in India. Five years later, this number had merely gone up to eight. In 1991, however, there were 172 such trading firms.
- There are more than 2 lacs exporters in India.
- Between 1991 and 1993, the foreign investments in India from four major countries (USA, Japan, Germany and UK) increased from $ 127.4 million to $ 1,675 million.
- In 1987, the total foreign investments in India were merely Rs. 108 crores. In 1991, this figure had grown to Rs. 535 crores. In 1992, the amount of approved foreign investments suddenly increased to Rs. 3890 crores. And by the first half of 1993, foreign investments worth Rs. 3952 crores were already approved.
- The Chelliah Committee report on tax reforms suggests reduction in import duty to an average of 25 percent—also reduction, if not elimination of duty differentiation between raw materials, finished products, intermediates and finished goods—and all this by 1997. This would mean more foreign competition.

1987). Bartlett (1986) also noted the requirement of replacing multinational strategy (which serves the multiple needs of national markets through relatively independent organisations) by transnational strategy. According to him, if the global organisations have to remain responsive to local restrictions, demands and opportunities, they must move away from the headquarters-subsidiary mould; rather, their physical assets and managerial capabilities need to be networked as autonomous international units, while remaining interdependent. Similarly, Scully (1987) noted the need to develop "multi-local" (in contrast to multi-national) organisational forms. Obviously, such global strategies and structures would require more sophisticated and flexible culturally integrative processes to accommodate/offset the diverse local interests and concerns. As Ohmae (1991) noted:

> As companies become global,... problems take on even greater dimensions. First, the time and effort required to learn and maintain the organisation's culture reach a whole new order of magnitude. And second, the local aspects of shared values that once held things together now work to drive them apart.

Lastly, globalisation of economy would also necessitate working through alliances and collaborations (e.g., minority stakes, technological collaborations, resource-sharing, distribution agreements and trading relationships). Cooperative ventures between organisations across the national boundaries are becoming more popular for simple economic reasons: they ensure quicker entry into a market, are flexible to operate, involve lesser risks, and require lesser cash and other resources from the sponsors (Lynch, 1990). For instance, during the 80's, the entry of Japanese companies in India (as it was in countries like Taiwan and Malaysia) was through collaborations in auto and electronics goods industries. Similarly, in 1993, Continental Tyres formed an alliance with Modi Tyres to start its production facility. Apart from changing the rules of business from competition to collaboration, these changes also place new demands on the companies to evolve systems and structures for control, decision-making, coordination and adaptation.

D. Customer and Quality

Related to the changes in the competitive environment, are the shifts in the customer-preferences and a diversification of customer-base. Increased choices for products/services in the market (and a profusion of information leading to a greater awareness of these choices) have created a customer population which is more discerning and demanding. The pressure to maintain a customer-orientation is further aggravated by the fragmentation of the market, created by diverse changes in the socio-economic and demographic profile of customer-base. Consider, for instance, the following facts:

- In the 1980s, a new market segment, consisting of urban young adults (18–30 years old), with considerable purchasing power, emerged as a major purchasing power in India.
- Between 1984 and 1989, the rural markets almost tripled from Rs. 733 crores to Rs. 2083 crores. These account for more than a 50 percent market share (besides the traditional grocery items) for durables such as radios, cycles, motor-cycles, sewing machines, table fans, etc.
- While India has about a 250 million strong middle class population, which is larger than the total populations of many countries and economic trade zones, it would be inaccurate to assume that they constitute a homogenous mass. The needs of a middle class city-dweller obviously would be quite different than those of his counterpart in the villages.
- Between 1985 and 1990, there was a significant increase in the number of brands for many products. For example, brands of packaged tea increased from 31 to 81, brands of soaps from 92 to 135, brands of edible oil from 84 to 116, and so on.

Thus, to compete and survive, it is becoming increasingly imperative for organisations to put in extra efforts to retain their customers. In fact, many studies (e.g., Hart, Heskett and Sasser, Jr., 1990; Reichheld and Sasser, Jr. 1990) show that it is the retention and zero-defection of customers, and not just the size of customer population, which is essential for improving a company's profitability and competitive edge. In such a scenario, conventional hard-sell marketing strategies are not likely to suffice. What companies would require is a more holistic strategic reorientation, or, as Peters (1987) put it, they would need to develop a "total customer responsiveness" (see Exhibit 13.4 for some emerging examples).

Exhibit 13.4

Customer Responsiveness in Indian Organisations

- In 1992, HCL-HP, started maintaining a database on the service problems solutions, which helped it to bring down the solution time for such problems from three days to just four hours. Similarly, maintaining an inventory network of spares, and restructuring its customer services, helped bringing down the resolution time for critical problems from an average of 100 days to about 15 days.
- Escorts' after-sales services extend beyond dealers' showrooms. The company organises service camps in remote rural areas, and has added advice from agriculture experts to its service portfolio.
- Acknowledging the differences in preferences across the country, Lipton has customised its polypouched branded tea, *Taaza,* in seven blends to cater to regional tastes.
- To find a niche market in the recession-hit industry, in 1992-93, DCM Toyota started manufacturing LCVs based on customer specifications. They found that apart from meeting customer-requirements, customisation of vehicles also saved costs, since many components could be substituted locally.

A more customer-responsive strategy would entail at least three major changes for the organisations. These would be:

1. Organisations must ensure the quality of products/services being offered to the customer. Many organisations are finding that quality is not only an effective way of creating loyal customers, but contrary to the conventional wisdom, it also improves the bottom-line. Stimulated by the requirements of easy entry into the European markets, many Indian organisations have embarked upon a company-wide Total Quality Management (TQM) programme (between early 80's to 1992, the number of companies practising TQM had increased from just 6 to 144).

2. In order to maintain their share in a fragmented market, organisations must differentiate their products and services, and create niche markets. This would require greater "on-line" interactions with end-users, distributors and suppliers to help organisations devise strategies for value-added differentiations, re-launches, and so on.

3. Organisations would need to devise cost-effective strategies for mass-customisation of products/services, to tap high-end niche markets. This would necessitate bringing manufacturing closer to customers, instead of operating with buffers to protect it from market demands.

Such requirements, obviously, would have many significant implications for organisations' strategies, systems and practices. The future organisations may have to devise new capabilities for dealing with these emerging demands. In the next section, we will focus on these imperatives in greater detail.

II. ORGANISING FOR THE FUTURE

As would be apparent from the preceding discussion, the demands and imperatives on the future organisations would be very different from those, to which one is normally familiar. The need for organisations would not be merely to cope with an accelerated rate of environmental change; rather, the major pressures for adaptations are emerging from the qualitatively different nature of these changes. In the following section we will focus on three significant tasks which these changes emphasise for future organisational forms.

A. Managing Multiple Goals

In a way, all organisations have multiple goals to achieve, e.g., making profits, increasing the market-share, providing better quantity or quality of products/services, protecting health and environment, making product and technological innovations, maintaining quality of life, and so on. In the conventional organisational forms, however, all these activities and goals revolve around one core goal (which most often is financial performance and shareholders returns). A continuously changing and diversifying environment, on the other hand, has an altogether inescapable implication for the goal-structure of organisations, making it essential for them to give equal priority to all these goals. Increasingly, organisations are finding that focusing exclusively on financial indicators of corporate health and achievement, while neglecting and being complacent about others, can be a dangerous corporate stance. For instance, many manufacturing organisations have started realising that a greater emphasis on keeping the costs low, while neglecting the service is a certain way of losing customers. Similarly, neglect of safety functions, all but wiped out the Union Carbide after the Bhopal Gas tragedy.

In the emerging environment, there seems to be little choice for the organisations but to simultaneously pursue multiple, and often seemingly contradictory, goals (Kanter, 1990). One can observe this organisational necessity to cope with incompatible demands and goals in almost all its activities. For example:

- Becoming "lean and mean", while simultaneously offering employee-centred policies and job-security;
- To "stay close to your knitting", while encouraging creativity and innovation to grow in new directions;
- Taking risks in new ventures, while ensuring that no failures occur;
- Providing high quality customised products/services, while maintaining low costs;
- Decentralising tasks and responsibilities in small autonomous units, while maintaining centralised control for achieving efficiencies and better resource management, etc.

Thus, one of the most important requirements for the future-oriented organisations is to learn to manage these complexities and contradictions. It is becoming more imperative for organisations to organise and focus their resources in more innovative ways to achieve a wider range of goals.

B. Using Multiple Information-Processing Systems

Traditionally, organisations are designed to reduce their information needs. That is why, they segment themselves into functions and departments, create buffers and inventories, focus on tangible and quantifiable reality, and so on. The formal information channels are aimed at achieving better coordination and control by inhibiting the free-flow of information in the organisations. In the changed scenario, however, for the organisations to follow multiple goals, it is becoming necessary to receive and process diverse kinds of information. In a turbulent environment, organisations need to develop intensive communication systems, manage them participatively, utilise coordinative committees, and devote considerable efforts for scanning the environment (Miller and Friesen, 1977). Such activities are essential for two reasons:

1. to gain a closer and quicker contact with the environment, and
2. to gain more effective coordination among highly differentiated (i.e., strategically and geographically dispersed) sub-parts of the organisation.

As we saw earlier, the information/communication revolution makes it well within the reach of organisations to increase their information-processing capacity. However, as Savage (1992) pointed out, the existence of a networked infrastructure is no guarantee for meaningful communication. To cope with the future, organisations need to redesign themselves to facilitate the collection, processing and communication of relevant information from multiple sources. For instance, many organisations have already started institutionalising systems with the setting up of coordinating councils and customer focus groups and activities such as periodic attitudinal surveys, information sharing sessions, video-meetings, etc. Such mechanisms, besides enhancing environmental scanning and achieving cohesion, also increase organisational preparedness to cope with the complex and continuously changing condition.

C. Managing Resources

One critical demand of the emerging competitive environment is the essentiality of efficient resources utilisation. It is no longer viable to grow by creating slack resources or by passing on the costs of inefficiency to the customers. Organisations need to learn to work smarter and to "do more with less" (see Exhibit 13.5 for some emergent Indian examples). Such demands affect the future-oriented organisations in at least three ways: Firstly, they force the organisations to rely more on advances in automation, flexible manufacturing techniques and information-processing technologies. Leaner plants, for instance, would help the organisations to simultaneously achieve high levels of productivity, quality and complexity of product-mix (Krafcik, 1988). Similarly, reduction in throughput-

Exhibit 13.5

Some Examples of Resources Management in Indian Organisations

- In early 90's, after devaluation of the rupee, Modi Xerox found it difficult to compete with its imported photocopier with the low-priced suppliers in the domestic market. So, they used value engineering to eliminate some of the low-utility extra features in the model (e.g., built-in heating system, not useful in India), and redesigned the adjustable paper tray. This helped them in reducing their cost by more than Rs. 20,000 per machine.
- Eicher Tractor introduced Japanese systems of workers' participation, such as *Kaizen* (Continuous Improvement) and *Poka Yoke* (Zero Defect) in its Alwar plant. In three years, their production jumped up by 45 percent, productivity by 27.4 percent, and manpower requirements reduced from 320 to 277.
- For three years, Velvette International, producers of *Velvette shampoo* and *Nivarana cough syrup*, had a distribution agreement with Godrej Soaps, which gave it access to the latter's 4 lacs country-wide sales outlets (and saved it the cost of setting up its own distribution channels). In 1992, having gained substantial market share for its products, Velvette decided to set up its own distribution channels, since now it was cheaper than paying 12 percent commission to Godrej Soaps.
- In 1992, Godrej & Boyce furniture division, discovered that their inventory carrying costs for finished goods were almost twice as high as the salaries of the plant employees. Realising that the reasons for high inventories lay in poor quality and high rejections, they streamlined the production-to-marketing cycle on a Just-in-time basis. Results: 80 percent decrease in rejection rates in 10 months, and a 44 percent lowering of the inventory levels.
- In 1992-93, Asian Paints installed a computerised information system to check material wastage on the shopfloor. The system helped the company to do a stage-wise analysis of costs, identify causes and stages at which losses occurred, and develop appropriate controls. The company could bring down the materials consumption cost by more than Rs. 15 crores.

---

cycle time, through more sophisticated manufacturing technologies, permits the organisations to decrease inventories and overheads, improve quality and capital appreciation, and gain a strategic advantage through quicker response to the market (Schmenner, 1988).

Secondly, the need for more efficient utilisation of resources is also making it imperative for organisations to seek more synergistic solutions across organisational boundaries. Thus, one may see greater proliferation of joint ventures, trading and distribution agreements, strategic alliances, etc., to help organisations share their financial and technical resources as well as risks. It is important to note that these solutions also imply a change from the traditional competitive mindset to one which is collaborative, and necessitate the organisations to work as allies rather than as adversaries (Kanter, 1990).

Lastly, it is becoming increasingly important for the organisations to select, manage, utilise and develop their most important resource, namely, their employees, in a better manner. As would be apparent from the preceding discussions, the new designs of organisations require more sophisticated technical and interpersonal skills, greater commitment and intrinsic motivation, and more sharpened learning capacities from the employees. After all, if organisations have to become more responsive, flexible and adaptive, people must become the primary focus of value addition, and should not remain just a factor to be optimised, minimised or eliminated (Peters, 1987).

III. ORGANISATIONS AS LEARNING SYSTEMS

One underlying implication in the preceding discussion is the necessity for the organisations to develop mechanisms and capacities which would facilitate them to learn and change on a continuous basis. This would become increasingly essential because of the following implications, which the environmental changes hold for the organisations:

1. The emerging changes in the business environment are rendering many of the standard, "time-tested" managerial solutions and techniques obsolete. What worked earlier may not work for long now. As Kanter (1990) noted, the nature and pace of contemporary change makes it "harder and harder for executives... to succeed by traditional corporate methods when technology, customer preferences, employee loyalties, industry regulations and corporate ownership are constantly changing." Thus, with the environment becoming more complex, unpredictable and interconnected, there is an increasing need for the organisations to learn and develop new techniques and methods.

2. The need for developing new methods and problem-solving capabilities is placing a new requirement on the organisations to be effective—to learn and develop new capabilities on a continuous basis. The traditional corporate goals may even become secondary to the goals of organisational learning. As Owens (1990) noted: "Not that profits and products are no longer important, but without continuing learning, they will no longer be possible."

3. The diversity and volume of environmental changes, is making it impossible (and definitely, ineffective) for organisations to rely on only one person, hierarchical level, or department, to learn and solve problems on behalf of the organisation. Senge (1990) pointed out that, "It is no longer sufficient to have one person learning for the organisation...It's just not possible any longer to "figure it out" from the top." The need for contemporary organisations, thus, is to develop learning and problem-solving capabilities across all levels and departments.

It is in this context, that it becomes necessary to explore and study the mechanisms through which organisations learn. It is becoming increasingly essential to build *learning organisations,* where, to quote Senge (1992), "people continually expand their capacity to create the results they truly desire, where new patterns of thinking are nurtured, where collective aspiration is set free, and where people are continually learning how to learn together."

A. How Do Organisations Learn?

Obviously, one would say, all organisations learn from their experiences of successes and failures. They learn to pursue aims and strategies, which have given them results, and avoid those which proved to be failures. Such learnings help the organisations to adapt to their existing environments. But, as we saw earlier (refer Chapter 11), often organisations also become trapped in their own success patterns. "Adaptive learning" does help the organisations to change, but only within a narrow range. It does not give them the ability to envision new, and as yet untested, markets and products whose introduction can re-define the very nature of competitive environment (McGill, Slocum and Lei, 1992). Thus, in a changing and unstable environment, this kind of learning ability would be more of a liability for the organisation, than an asset.

Organisational learning, on the other hand, refers to a more basic "generative" ability of the organisation to question and change its unconscious assumptions (its theory-in-use), which determine the way in which it receives, processes and evaluates information. A learning organisation is like the intelligent computer, which is capable of, not merely responding to information according to its programmes, but also of altering the very nature of its programming in response to new information. Such an organisation learns from its experiences, rather than getting bound by them. Argyris and Schoen (1978) defined organisational learning as follows:

> Organisational learning occurs when members of the organisation act as learning agents for the organisation, responding to changes in the internal and external environments of the organisation by detecting and correcting errors in organisational theory-in-use, and embedding the results of their inquiry in private images and shared maps of organisation.

It is important to highlight two distinctive aspects of organisational learning. The first is that the key to organisational learning is not in *what* is learnt, but in *how* it is learnt. Torbert (1973) viewed the learning which arises from experiences, as a process, rather than an end-product. He noted: "Learning involves becoming aware of qualities, patterns, and consequences of one's own experiences as one experiences them." In the context of organisational learning, this would mean that organisations learn, not when they achieve a solution—that would be adaptation—but when they become aware of their processes of arriving at solutions, i.e., when they "learn how to learn".

The second aspect is that organisational learning is more than just the cumulative learning of its members (though that, of course, is important). Like individuals, organisations too have cognitive systems and memories, which are coded in the norms, values, interpretative frameworks, and operating practices of the organisation (Hedberg, 1981). While individuals do contribute to these, by and large, these organisational schemes are independent of individuals, and persist inspite of changes in the membership (often even in leadership).

In the management literature, the concept of organisational learning has been variously termed as double loop learning (Argyris, 1977), generative learning (Senge, 1990), and higher-level learning (Fiol & Lyles, 1985). The underlying theme in these conceptualisations is that organisational learning is essential to any kind of organisational transformation, renewal and innovation. It enables the organisation and its members to differentiate between the symptoms and the systemic sources of the problems, to collectively think of problems in a holistic manner, and to develop innovative and flexible solutions. Pareek (1988) defined organisational learning as "the process by which an organisation acquires, retains, and uses inputs for its development, and the process results in an enhanced capacity for continued self-learning and self-renewal."

The relevance of the concept of organisational learning has been seen in the context of a wide variety of organisational activities. De Geus (1988), for example, noted that the "ability to learn faster than your competitors may be the only sustainable competitive advantage". Organisational learning competencies, thus, would play an important role in the strategic planning/management processes. Likewise, Pucik (1988) noted that developing a comprehensive organisational learning strategy is essential to gain a competitive advantage in strategic alliances. Kaipa (1992) observed the common linkages between organisational learning and such organisational renewal activities as TQM and OD. Likewise, Denton and Wisdom (1991) drew implications of organisational learning for the role of organisational leaders/managers.

B. Processes and Practices in Learning Organisations

Designing an organisation capable of continuous learning is a somewhat paradoxical requirement, since, as we discussed in Chapter 11, in the very act of formalising a mechanism and developing a structure (even if it is for initiating change), the organisation is likely to make itself rigid and change-resistant. What one needs to focus on, therefore, is not so much the formal mechanisms, as the designing of the processes which facilitate continuous organisational change and build learning capacity. That is, the skills of the future organisational designer would focus more on designing organisational processes than on designing tasks.

Bartlett and Ghoshal (1990) pointed out complex organisational structures, which are capable of learning and innovation and are not mere designs of formal roles, departments and systems; rather they are specific frames of minds, and emerge from the shaping of mental structures. Or to use our analogy of "organisational iceberg", the change-facilitating structures would be "process structures" (Newman, 1973) which are shaped by integrating the submerged organisational processes with the visible and tangible parts of the organisation.

Learning organisations, likewise, are also process structures, which exists in the organisational mind—in its values, ideology, assumptions, norms, practices, etc. This, of course, does not mean that there are no specific structures which are typical to learning organisations. But, the concrete structural arrangements, which characterise learning organisations, are more like derivatives of the organisational processes, instead of vice-versa. Thus, to understand the learning organisations, it is essential to focus on the processes which help the organisations to learn.

Senge (1990) identified five learning disciplines, which enhance an organisations' capacity to learn. He used the term disciplines as "component technologies" which ensemble together, each providing a vital dimension in evolving the learning organisation. Each of these disciplines involve the stimulation and management of certain organisational practices and processes.

In the following sections, we will discuss these processes and practices, which characterise a learning organisation.

1. Systemic thinking. Organisations are dynamic systems, consisting of a continuous interplay of interrelated parts. In making sense of the reality, and in solving problems, people normally consider only the static and segmented 'snapshots' (the divisions and departments, the functional performance, the quarterly report, tabulated frequencies, etc.) and not the patterned continuities, which exist in the real systems. Systems thinking is the act of seeing patterns in the wholeness, rather than focusing on individual parts. It is a way of doing away with the mental boundaries, which people create for themselves.

In the organisational context, a stance and practice of systemic thinking offers many distinctive advantages for dealing with uncertainty and turbulence (Senge, 1990a):

(a) It encourages people to identify the systemic causes of problems, and not look for scapegoats to attribute blames on. For instance, a drop in sales is typically attributed to the lack of initiative by marketing people; this may not be always so, and systemic thinking would help people to identify more basic causes, e.g., the long order-production-delivery cycle time, which result in more dissatisfied customers.

(b) It helps people to identify those dynamic complexities, which arise because the causes and effects are separated in time and space. For instance, it may help people to perceive that the "minor" sources of dissatisfactions—e.g., inferior quality of food in the canteen, due to awarding the contract to cheaper quotation—can, in the long run, lead to strike, loss of production and even loss of competitive edge.

(c) It helps people to appreciate that small, well-focused actions can, and do, result in significant and enduring improvements. That is, it helps people to identify those subtle areas of high leverage, which often escape managers' attention in their search for solutions. For instance, the observation of small courtesies can win an airlines or an hotel many more regular clients than the costly advertising campaigns.

(d) A major implication of the above is that systemic thinking helps the organisations to focus their problem-solving efforts on tackling the underlying causes, instead of seeking only short-term symptomatic solutions.

Unfortunately, most organisations are not tuned to thinking systemically. Narrow specialisation, lack of adequate (and accurate) information-flow, and political power games inhibit executives from perceiving larger patterns, which describe the problems. The most essential requirement for systemic thinking is a view of the organisation as a dynamic network, rather than a collection of islands. That is, being conscious of the constantly shifting, yet patterned, interrelationships among the various parts (roles and departments) of the organisation. There are many organisational practices, which can encourage organisational members to think in such a systemic, and not a linear, manner (McGill, Slocum and Lei, 1992). Some of these practices are elaborated here.

(a) Sharing of complete and accurate (not nice-to-look-at, whitewashed and distorted) information helps people to build more realistic mental maps of how an organisation functions and what it aims to achieve. If the strategic intent is poorly communicated in the organisation, people give less importance to the learning requirements associated with strategy implementation, and continue to focus on their narrow tasks (Pucik, 1988).

(b) The greater the opportunities for members to interact across functional/divisional boundaries, the more they would be able to understand the distant causes and consequences of their actions. Practices such as working in cross-functional teams, inter-functional job-rotations, inter-departmental seminars, etc., are some examples of organisational actions which would promote this understanding.

(c) There needs to be an explicitly shared understanding among organisational members that meaningful work relationships can be formed only on the basis of sharing and exchanging information, goods and services; and that mutual respect and feelings (i.e., liking for each other) are more important than the traditional hierarchical relationships. Such an attitude is essential for building and working with cross-functional networks.

(d) Systems thinking also gets hampered by artificially created functional boundaries within the organisations. Minimising function-based jargons, expert domains and turfs (e.g. "this is a problem for finance guys"), and legitimisation of a wide variety of concepts, ideas and talents help in decreasing such segmentation. Greater acceptance of diversity in selection placement and promotion, therefore, would create right conditions for a more integrated approach to problem-solving efforts.

2. Developing personal mastery. Although individual learning does not guarantee organisational learning, it is a necessary precondition for creating learning organisations. Organisations aiming to develop learning capabilities, therefore, spend considerable efforts for developing a commitment to personal mastery among their members.

Personal mastery, however, is not merely the acquisition and learning of new competencies and skills. Rather, it involves a continuing urge and motivation for personal growth and learning. "People with high levels of personal mastery are continually expanding their ability to create the results in life, they truly seek. From their quest for continual learning comes the spirit of the learning organisation (Senge, 1990)." That is, personal mastery is living creatively, rather than reactively. It is not something which one possesses; it is a process which one is continually engaged in.

There are two underlying mechanisms of this process of personal mastery:

(a) It involves a continuous process of formulating and clarifying one's personal vision. Having a vision is more important than having goals and objectives. Most people have personal goals and objectives; and, they spend so much of their energies and efforts in coping with the problems encountered in achieving them, that they rarely question why they have those goals and objectives at all. Vision focuses on the ultimate intrinsic desire about what is important to oneself in life. It is something which is emotionally exciting and deeply fulfilling.

(b) The process of personal mastery also involves continuously clarifying one's perceptions to gain an accurate picture of the current reality. A vision would be meaningless if one does not have an accurate assessment of where one currently stands. Unfortunately, for most people, their present position is an inconvenient hurdle between the past glories and the future hopes; they tend to deny, distort, rationalise, or defend unpalatable truths (whether about one's self-image or about achievement of departmental targets) to maintain a comfortable, even if deceptive, understanding of the reality. An active self-awareness, however, is fundamental to developing personal mastery.

Developing personal mastery in organisations is a process of empowering employees, enabling them to gain self-awareness, formulate and express their visions, and feel adequate and competent enough to pursue these visions. This becomes a precondition for organisational learning, because it is only when people gain high-levels of personal mastery, that they would take more initiative, be more committed to their goals, and learn faster. Though organisations cannot force people to develop personal mastery, there are a number of steps they can take to help and encourage their members to develop it (McGill, Slocum and Lei, 1992; Senge, 1992):

(a) Build a climate where it is psychologically safe for people to create and articulate their personal visions, even if they challenge the organisational status quo while doing so.

(b) Reinforce the idea that personal growth and learning is valued in the organisation. That is, what people learn and envision about themselves is not limited to themselves; rather, they can legitimately enact and experiment with it within the organisational boundaries.

(c) Build principles of personal mastery into the daily life and practices of the organisation. For example, if the organisation is open to critiquing itself, and invites participation in reflecting about the gap between the corporate vision and the reality, it would provide a model and a supportive climate for people to risk similar exercises with themselves.

3. Surfacing and testing mental models. Mental models are our unconscious maps of the reality which, while helping one in understanding the terrain, also block us from seeing the reality in any other manner. They are deeply held assumptions about the world and how it operates, and so, exert a major influence on our decisions and actions. In organisations, these mental models determine the assessment of business opportunities and managerial options. This conception of what can and cannot be done is so deeply entrenched in the organisational practices, procedures and tradition, that organisational members are rarely aware of this mind-set. For instance, for a long time, most organisations functioned with an implicit belief that the better the quality of the product/

service, the greater will be the cost—till Japanese management systems and practices showed that it is possible to achieve high quality at low costs.

Mental models can sometimes kill some of the best business ideas. Many innovative insights about new organisational practices, markets and products fail to be put into practice because they contradict the existing powerful mental models. That is why, for organisational learning to take place, it is essential to provide conditions where these models can be brought to surface, tested and, if necessary, modified, without invoking defensive reactions from its members. Organisational efforts to do so focus on facilitating the following processes (Senge, 1990a):

(a) They point out the leaps of abstraction in managerial decision-making. Our mind moves fast, often paradoxically, slowing our learning. People often jump from data to conclusions, without sufficiently reflecting on the nature of data. The conclusions or generalisations are then treated as if they are the observable facts. For instance, the statement that "young MBAs are less committed to organisation" is actually a generalisation, which is often treated as if it were an observed fact. The fact may be the reason for the high rate of job-hopping among MBAs, which can be interpreted in a number of ways (e.g., most organisations do not know how to use the capabilities of MBAs).

(b) They seek to balance inquiry and advocacy. Most managers are conditioned and trained to be good debaters and advocates. They are seen as effective if they can work out solutions to problems and persuade others to accept them. Complex organisational problems, however, require the ability to tap resources of other, equally competent people from other disciplines, and to work out solutions jointly. Absence of the skills required for seeking other person's views (inquiring) becomes a major block to the learning process.

(c) They help in distinguishing the espoused theory from the theory-in-use. Organisations often contain contradictions between what they profess and the way they operate. Such contradictions are so much embedded in the organisational fabric that people even fail to notice them and take them as facts of life. Recognising this gap between the deeper mental models (i.e., the theory-in-use) and the espoused value is essential for learning to take place. Otherwise, what people may "learn" is only a new set of jargon, while continuing to behave in the same old manner. Systematic organisational diagnosis and feedback, followed by self-critiquing often helps organisations to gain greater awareness about these gaps.

(d) They help in recognising and defusing defensive organisational routines. Many organisational practices are unconsciously aimed at protecting people from coming in contact with embarrassing reality e.g., all information must go through proper hierarchical channels, even when it is acknowledged that such structures distort information (which, ironically, they are meant to communicate); it is an accepted (and acceptable) fact that people would talk about an issue differently inside and outside the meeting room; the visit of the senior officers from the headquarters are always announced, so that field offices have enough time to hide the ugly facts, and so on. Identifying, and then questioning the need for such defensive routines is essential for unshackling the learning potentials within the organisation.

4. Building shared vision. An organisation consisting only of a set of people with separate personal visions is more likely to become an arena of conflicts and chaos. Cohesion of efforts is vital for organisations to function effectively. Learning organisations attempt to develop this cohesion through building a shared vision, rather than relying on formalised systems and procedures. Shared vision is vital for organisational learning because it gives a focus and direction to the learning efforts, while, at the same time, ensuring a deep personal involvement and commitment of its members.

The process of building shared vision involves certain basic principles, which underlie the organisational practices:

(a) Sharing a vision is not necessarily contradictory to having a personal vision (to assume so, may be a result of succumbing to some unconscious mental model). A personal vision is not always focused only on issues of self-interests; people do care about and value issues which are larger than the boundaries of their individual self—family, society, organisation, nature, etc. And they have the capacity to care, feel and envision about these issues in an intense personal manner, while at the same time, sharing this care, feelings and vision with others. In other words, for building a shared vision, organisations must encourage personal visions among its members.

(b) A corporate vision cannot be imposed from the top. Acceptance of a vision does not necessarily mean that people also share it, and are deeply committed to it (or even agree with it). Organisations often fall into the trap of "writing the vision statement" without bothering about the process through which they arrived at the vision statement itself. In order to share a vision, people must feel personal about it. Thus, a continuous process of communicating, seeking and enroling support is essential for building shared vision.

(c) Building a shared vision is not a one-time exercise; rather, it is an ongoing process, which relies on continuous reevaluation and interaction among organisational members. In fact, truly shared visions take time to emerge. They grow out of interactions of individual visions, in an atmosphere where people can feel free to express and listen to each other's cherished dreams.

(d) Many highly involving and exciting shared visions are extrinsic in nature. That is, they focus on achieving a goal which is external to the organisation, e.g., beating a competitor. However, once this goal is achieved, the same vision may lose much of its potency, and may even become a defensive posture (thus losing its learning potential). Powerful visions blend the extrinsic with the intrinsic. That is, they are based as much on external necessities, as on the internal aspirations and values of the organisational members.

5. Institutionalising team learning. According to Senge (1990), team learning "is the process of aligning and developing the capacity of a team to create the results its members truly desire." It is a natural off-shoot of shared vision and personal mastery, enabling the members to enact their vision. In many ways, learning as a team is a neglected aspect of managerial efforts. In fact, in most other human endeavours (sports, performing arts, science) team learning is a popular practice. Sportsmen, stage artists, scientists, etc., not only perform as a team, but they also learn as a team. Their individual learning is deeply embedded in the team learning.

There are at least three reasons for the relevance of team learning in an organisation:

(a) While individual learning may not necessarily result in organisational learning, if a team learns, it becomes a microcosm for organisational learning. The learning easily gets translated into practice.

(b) Team learning is essential for thinking through complex organisational issues, which require tapping the potential of more than one, and diverse, talents. When people learn as a team, they have greater acceptance and respect for each others' views and ideas.

(c) When a team learns as a whole, it provides for more coordinated and spontaneous actions. When people learn together, they automatically align with each other, thus, reducing the need for external control, and shortening their response time.

Senge (1990) identified two basic processes which underlie most team learning efforts. The first, *discussion*, involves presenting and defending different points of views in search for the best solution. While this process of discourse may help the participants to arrive at a better analysis and understanding, the emphasis is on winning, i.e., making others accept one's views. In terms of facilitating group learning, this mechanism alone would have a limited utility. In contrast, the second process, *dialogue*, is an invitation to joint exploration, which is likely to promote a more synergistic team learning. Learning organisations, while consciously balancing these two processes, pay greater emphasis on building a culture of dialogue. That is, they promote a spirit of dispassionate mutual exploration of ideas, leading to a richer grasp of issues.

C. Structural Arrangements for Learning Organisations

Looking at organisations as systems for continuous learning and change has a crucial, and somewhat unsettling, aspect: it calls for fundamental transformation in our concept of the very nature of an organisation, i.e., the way tasks and processes need to be organised for the purpose of achieving organisational goals. Traditional organisational designs aim at creating stability and maintaining status quo, in which changes are anomalies requiring periodic (but not continuous) adjustments. To cope with a continuously changing environment (Toffler, 1970, 1981), however, it is equally essential for the organisational structures to be continuously flexible and adaptive. Thus, the assumptions underlying organisational learning, view structures not as permanent givens, but merely as temporary solutions for a set of current problems. Thus, structures can, and should, be changed and readjusted to fit changing strategies, tasks and environment

(Hedberg, Nystrom and Starbuck, 1976). In the following sections, we will discuss some characteristics of the emerging organisational forms and mechanisms, which help organisations to achieve this requirement.

1. Self-designing capability. It follows from the above that learning organisations need to design themselves in a manner, which permits the design to change on a continuous basis, i.e., they must have a capability for self-designing.

Hedberg, Nystrom and Starbuck (1976) proposed that organisations aiming to develop capabilities for self-designing must seek "minimal amounts of desirable characteristics". That is, if organisations have too much consensus, affluence and success, or are too consistent, rational or contented, they are likely to become prisoners of their design and customs. On the other hand, too less of these characteristics would lead the organisations towards chaos and failure. A capacity to continuously reappraise oneself would come only when there is an optimum balance between the structured and unstructured, the consensus and dissension, and the planned and the unplanned. Such a blend, they suggested, would stimulate processes, which would lead to spontaneous activities of self-designing:

> A self-designing organisation can attain dynamic balances through overlapping, unplanned, and non-rational proliferation of its processes; and these proliferating processes collide, contest, and interact with one another to generate wisdom.

Learning organisations, therefore, need to be more loosely coupled, giving greater opportunities for informal, though guided interactions among its incumbent.

2. Flatter network structures. Many studies (e.g., Galbraith, 1977; Cummings, 1978; Mohrman and Cummings, 1989; Lawler, 1992, etc.) have shown that flatter organisational structures, consisting of interdependent, but self-contained units, provide the organisations with greater capability for thriving in a changing environment. Similarly, Ross (1990) suggested that to meet the requirements of high flexibility, organisations would need to shift from the conventional pyramidical structure to a "molecular" design, i.e., to a clustering of interdependent, yet independent, units.

This change in the basics of organisational design is becoming easier to achieve with increasing computerisation of work-processes. Savage (1992) pointed out that wide-spread impact of information technology is bringing about six major shifts in the organisational processes and structures, which would ultimately replace hierarchies with human networking:

(a) The conventional *chain of command,* based on concepts of scientific management (planning, directing, controlling, organising, coordinating, etc.), is giving way to *networking*, which allows people to directly reach out and get in touch with others, for getting the tasks done.

(b) The core responsibilities of managing are shifting from *commanding and controlling* activities of employees, to *focusing and coordinating* their efforts.

(c) The basis of authority in organisations is becoming less and less dependent on *position and seniority* and is getting increasingly focussed on the *knowledge and expertise* of the incumbent.

(d) Use of group technologies, expert systems, parametric designs, etc., is helping the organisations to convert their conventional *sequential* patterning of jobs to *parallel, concurrent*, or *simultaneous* modes of operations.

(e) As people become knowledge resources, and not just a link in the chain of command, the predominant channels of organisational communication are shifting from *vertical* to *horizontal.*

(f) Perhaps most importantly, the assumptions and values underlying the designing and structuring of activities are changing from those of *distrust and compliance* to those of *trust and integrity.*

3. Self-managing teams. One of the essential precondition for networks to function effectively is the autonomy and independence of work-groups which form the teams. Peters (1987) noted that to achieve high-levels of involvement and flexibility, it is necessary to, as far as possible, organise tasks around autonomous and self-sufficient teams, and not individuals. Similarly, Lawler (1992) suggested that for people to feel responsible for the work they are doing, they must decide about how the work is to be done, and should have control over the work-process. Such decisions would even include many traditionally managerial activities, such as hiring, planning, scheduling, purchasing, etc. (Stewart, 1992).

Obviously, to facilitate the functioning of such autonomous teams, organisations would need to go beyond the conventional methods of delegation and decentralisation, and it would be necessary for them to completely "reengineer" (Hammer, 1990) their work-processes. For instance, self-managing teams imply minimisation, if not complete elimination of supervisory role. Based on studies of organisations which have experimented with work process innovation, many authors (e.g., Hammer, 1990; Ross, 1990; Stewart, 1992) have suggested guidelines for redesigning organisation processes for facilitating self-managing teams:

(a) *Organise around processes and outcomes, and not around tasks.* Performance objectives should be based on customer requirements, and the processes which meet these needs should become the basic design components.

(b) *Flatten the hierarchical layers of management* by avoiding subdivision of processes, and by moving head-office functions down-the-line.

(c) *Make teams, not individuals, the focus of organisational performance.* Relate rewards and accountability for team performance.

(d) *Make teams multi-functional, each individual having* multiple skills, and each team carrying out both managerial and non-managerial functions.

(e) *Empower teams by taking information-processing and decision-making to the point where the work is performed,* but build controls in the process/peer norms (not in hierarchy).

(f) *Build partnerships with the suppliers and customers,* including early involvement in design and production. Increase their contact with everyone in the organisation.

(g) *Build flexibility into the system.* Use automation in production and office, work on the basis of just-in-time with suppliers and members, capture and process information at source and only once.

It is important to note that such redesigning is a all-or-none activity. It cannot be planned and introduced in small incremental steps. As Hammer (1990) observed, "At the heart of reengineering is the notion of discontinuous thinking..."

IV. IMPLICATIONS FOR FUTURE MANAGERS

Obviously, if organisations are changing, the nature of managerial work would also change. As we saw in this Chapter, the transitions in organisational "structures" will make the manager's job more ambiguous and vague. After all, in a network organisation, consisting of self-managing units, and relying on intangible processes to organise organisational efforts, the traditional focus and meaning of managing would no longer be valid. Since influence within the organisation would shift from vertical to horizontal, channels and means for influencing would become diverse, managerial and non-managerial activities would become indistinguishable, and relationships across organisational boundaries (e.g., with customers and suppliers) would be sources of power within the organisation (Kanter, 1989), the conventional bases of managerial power would be considerably eroded.

Schein (1989) noted that implicit in the very concept of managing is the assumption of hierarchy. As organisations adapt non-hierarchical forms, the managerial concepts of power, influence, leadership, etc. will become obsolete and redundant. Malone (1987), in fact, suggested that the "electronic hierarchies" would exist without management, with everyone contributing to the coordination of organisational activities. Similarly, Zuboff (1988) observed:

> The twenty-first century company has to promote and nurture the capacity to improve and innovate. The idea has radical implications. It means learning becomes the axial principle of organisations. It replaces control as the fundamental job of managers.

Thus, the potential ambiguity of the future manager's role is simultaneously anxiety-provoking as well as exciting, due to the new opportunities it contains. Let us look at what new role these opportunities offer to managers:

1. The effectiveness of the future manager would depend less on managing tasks, and more on managing processes. In that sense, the role of the manager would shift from that of a "line" functionary to that of a "staff" functionary.

2. The increase in diversity and need for dealing with perpetual change,

would place greater responsibilities on managers to design processes for integrating organisational efforts towards learning and change.

3. At the interpersonal level, the task of the manager would be that of empowering, guiding, facilitating and coaching people, rather than that of monitoring and controlling their activities.

4. Lastly, with greater external organisational focus, the competence of the manager would be indicated as much as by his/her ability to form external linkages (with suppliers, customers, collaborators, pressure groups, etc.) as by his ability to feel comfortable with internal social and professional diversity.

References

Ackoff, R.L., A Concept of Corporate Planning. New York: Wiley-Interscience, 1970.

Adler, A., Understanding Human Nature. New York: Greenburg, 1927.

Agor, W., The logic of intuition: How top executives make important decisions, *Organisational Dynamics,* 5–18, Winter 1986.

Alderfer, C.P., A new theory of human needs, *Organizational Behaviour and Human Performance*, **4,** 142–75, 1969.

Andrews, Kenneth, R., The Concept of Corporate Strategy. Bombay: D.B. Taraporevala, 1972.

Ansoff, H.I., Corporate Strategy: An analytic approach to business policy for growth and expansion. New York: McGraw-Hill, 1965.

Argenti, J., Corporate Collapse: The causes and symptoms. New York: McGraw-Hill, 1976.

Argyris, C., Double loop learning in organisations, *Harvard Business Review,* 115–25, Sept.–Oct. 1977.

Argyris, C., Intervention Theory and Method. Reading (Mass.): Addison-Wesley, 1970.

Argyris, C. and Schoen, D.A., Organisational Learning: A theory of action perspective. Reading (Mass.): Addison-Wesley, 1978.

Astley, W.G. and Sachdeva, P.S., Structural sources of intra-organisational power: A theoretical synthesis, *Academy of Management Review,* **9,** 104–13, 1984.

Axford, The attitude of depressives: A comparative examination using Beck's questionnaires and Repertory Grid Technique. Unpublished Dissertation, University of Sterling Library, 1983.

Bacharach, S.B. and Lawler, E.J., Power and Politics in Organisations. San Francisco: Jossey-Bass, 1981.

Bachman, J.G., Bowers, D. and Marcus, P.M., Basis of supervisory power: A comparative study in five organizational settings. *In* A.S. Tannenbaum (Ed.), Control in Organisations. New York: McGraw-Hill, 1968.

Barczak, G., Smith C. and Wilemon, D., Managing large-scale organisational change, *Organisational Dynamics,* 22–35, Autumn 1987.

Bartlett, C.A., Building and managing the transnational firm: The new organisational challenge. *In* M.E. Porter (Ed.), Competition in Global Industries. Boston: Harvard Business School Press, 1986.

Bartlett, C.A. and Ghoshal, S., Matrix management: Not a structure, a frame of mind, *Harvard Business Review,* 138–45, July–Aug. 1990.

Bates, R.J., Toward a critical practice in educational administration. *In* T.J. Sergiovanni and J.E. Corbally (Eds.), Leadership and Organisational Culture. Urbana (Illinois): The University of Illinois Press, 1984.

Becker, E., The Denial of Death. New York: Free Press, 1973.

Beckhard, R., Organisation Development: Strategies and models. Reading (Mass.): Addison-Wesley, 1969.

Beer, M., Eisenstat, R.A. and Spector, B., Why change programs don't produce change, *Harvard Business Review,* 158–66, Nov.– Dec. 1990.

Bell, D., Thinking ahead, *Harvard Business Review,* May-June 1979.

Bennis. W.G., The coming death of bureaucracy, *Think,* 30–35, Nov.–Dec. 1966

Bennis, W.G. and Slater, P.E., The Temporary Society. New York: Harper & Row, 1968.

Bennis, W.G., Organisation Development: Its nature, origins, and prospects, Reading (Mass.): Addison-Wesley, 1969.

Bernstein, B., Class, Code and Control: Towards a theory of educational transmissions, Vol. 3. London: Routledge & Kegan Paul, 1975.

Bhattacharya, S.K., Achieving Managerial Excellence. New Delhi: Macmillan, 1989.

Blake, R.R., Shepard, H.A. and Mouton, J., Managing Intergroup Conflict in Industry. Houston: Gulf Publishing, 1984.

Blau, P.M., A formal theory of differentiation in organisations, *American Sociological Review,* **35,** 201–18, 1970.

Blauner, R., Alienation and Freedom: The factory worker and his industry. Chicago: University of Chicago Press, 1964.

Boissevain, J., Friends of Friends: Networks, manipulators and coalitions. London: Basil Blackwell, 1974.

Boje, D.M., Fedor, D.B. and Rowland, K.M., Myth making: A qualitative step in OD interventions, *The Journal of Applied Behavioural Sciences,* **18,** 17–28, 1982.

Bolman, L.G. and Deal, T.E., Modern Approaches to Understanding and Managing Organisations. San Francisco: Jossey-Bass, 1984.

Boulding, E., Further reflections on conflict management. *In* R.L. Kahn and R. Boulding (Eds.), Power and Conflicts in Organisation. New York: Basic Books, 1964.

Bower, J.L. and Winberg, M.W., Statecraft and corporate leadership, *California Management Review,* **31**, 38–55, 1988.

Brass, D.J., Being in the right place: A structural analysis of individual influence in an organisation, *Administrative Science Quarterly,* **39,** 518–39, Dec. 1984.

Bresser, R.K. and Bishop, R.C., Dysfunctional effects of formal planning: Two theoretical explanations, *Academy of Management Review,* **8,** 588–99, 1983.

Bruner, J.S., On Going Beyond the Information Given. Cambridge (Mass.): Harvard University Press, 1957.

Burgleman, R.A., A model of interaction of strategic behaviour: Corporate context and the concept of strategy, *Academy of Management Review,* **8,** 61–70, 1983.

Burke, W.W. and Hornstein, H.A. (Eds.), The Social Technology of Organisation Development. Washington DC: NTL Learning Resources Corp., 1972.

Burns, T. and Stalker, G.M., The Management of Innovation. London: Tavistock, 1961.

Business Today, Managing tomorrow, 50–63, April 22–May 6, 1992.

Cameron, K.S. and Whetten, David, Perceptions of organisational effectiveness over organisational life-cycle, *Administrative Science Quarterly,* **31,** 525–44, Dec. 1981.

Campbell, J.P., On the nature of organisational effectiveness. *In* P.S. Goodman, J.M. Pennings, and Associates (Eds.), New Perspectives on Organisational Effectiveness. San Francisco: Jossey-Bass, 1977.

Carlzon, J., Moments of Truth. Cambridge (Mass.): Ballinger, 1987.

Chandler, A.D. Jr., Strategy and Structure: Chapters in the history of industrial enterprise. Cambridge (Mass.): MIT Press, 1972/1973.

Channon, D.F., Corporate industry and organisation structure in British industry, *Journal of Business Policy,* **3,** 60–72, 1972.

Chattopadhyay, G.P., Covert group dynamics, organisational insights and diagnosis. *In* G.P. Chattopadhyay, Z.H. Gangjee, M.L. Hunt, and W.G. Lawrence (Eds.), When the Twain Meet. New Delhi: A.H. Wheeler & Co., 1986.

Chaudhury, S., Corporate strategy: Concept and its relevance in Indian context, Vikalpa, **4,** 27–38, 1979.

Child, J., Organisational structure, enviornment and performance: The role of strategic choice, *Sociology,* **6,** 1–22, 1972.

Child, J., Predicting and understanding organisation structure, *Administrative Science Quarterly,* **18,** 171–85, 1973.

Chin, R. and Benne K., General strategies for effecting changes in human system. *In* W.G. Bennis, K. Benne, R. Chin, and K.E. Corey (Eds.), The Planning of Change. New York: Holt, Rinehart & Winston, 1976.

Chopra, B.S.K.S., Cases in Corporate Planning, Pune: The Times Research Foundation, 1989.

Chowdhry K. and Kakar S., Understanding Organisational Behaviour. New Delhi: Tata McGraw-Hill, 1971.

Clark, K.B., What strategy can do for technology, *Harvard Business Review,* 94–98, Nov.–Dec. 1989.

Clark, P.A., Organisational Design: Theory and practice. London: Tavistock 1972.

Cohen, D., Confidence comes before a crash, *Business Administration,* Jan. 1973.

Covin, J.G. and Slevin, D.P., The influence of organisational structure on the utility of an entrepreneurial top management style, *Journal of Management Science,* **25,** 217–34, 1988.

Cummings, T., Self-regulating work groups: A socio-technical synthesis, *Academy of Management Review,* **3,** 625–34, 1978.

Cyert, R.M. and March, J.G., A Behavioral Theory of the Firm, Englewood Cliffs (NJ): Prentice-Hall, 1963.

Daft, R.L., Sormunen J. and Parks, D., Chief executive scanning, environmental characteristics and company performance: An empirical study, *Strategic Management Journal,* **9,** 123–40, 1988.

Dalton, D.R., Todor, W.L., Spendolini, M.J., Fielding, G.J. and Portor, L.W., Organisational structure and performance: A critical review, *Academy of Management Review,* **5,** 49–64, 1980.

Davis, S.M., Managing Corporate Culture, Cambridge (Mass.): Ballinger, 1984.

De Geus, A.P., Planning as learning, *Harvard Business Review,* 70–74, Mar.–April 1988.

De, N.R., India. *In* New Forms of Work Organisations. Geneva: International Labour Organisation, 1979.

Deal, T.E. and Kennedy, A.A., Corporate Cultures: The rites and rituals of corporate life. Reading (Mass.): Addison-Wesley, 1982.

Denton, D.K. and Wisdom, B.L., The learning organisation involves the entire work force, *Quality Progress,* 69–72, Dec. 1991.

Derr, C.B., Managing organisational conflict: Collaboration, bargaining and power approaches, *California Management Review,* **21,** 76–83, 1978.

Despande, R. and Parasuraman, A., Linking corporate culture to strategic planning, *Business Horizons,* 28–37, May–June 1986.

Dhuru, J., Project management in government and joint sector organisation, Unpublished doctoral dissertation. Ahmedabad: Indian Institute of Management, 1987.

Drucker, P.F., Management: Tasks, responsibilities, practices. New York: Harper & Row, 1974.

Drucker, P.F., Innovation and Entrepreneurship. London: Pan Books, 1986.

Duncan, Robert B., What is the right organisation structure?, *Organisational Dynamics,* Winter 1979.

Dyas, G.P. and Thanheiser, H.T., The Emerging European Enterprise: Strategy and structure in French and German industry. London: Macmillan, 1976.

Dyer, W.G., Jr., Cultural Change in Family Firms. San Francisco: Jossey-Bass, 1986.

Dyer, W.G., Jr., Tracking cultural evaluation in organisations: An historical approach. Working Paper, MIT, Sloan School of Management, 1984.

Earl, P., The Corporate Imagination. New York: ME Sharp, Inc., 1984.

Erikson, E.H., Identity: Youth and crisis. New York: W.W. Norton, 1968.

Farrell, D. and Petersen, J.C., Patterns of political behaviour in organisations, *Academy of Management Review,* **7,** 403–12, 1982.

Fiol, C.M. and Lyles, M.A., Organisational learning, *Academy of Management Review,* **10,** 803–13, 1985.

Floyd, S.W. and Wooldridge, B., Managing strategic consensus: The foundation of effective implementation, *Executive*, **6,** 27–39, 1992.

French, W.L. and Bell, C.H., Jr., Organisation Development: Behavioral science interventions for organization improvement, 4th Ed., New Delhi: Prentice-Hall of India, 1991.

Galbraith, J., Organisation Design. Reading (Mass.): Addison-Wesley, 1977.

Galbraith, J.R., Strategy Implementation: The role of structure and process. St. Paul, Minnesota: West Publishing Co., 1978.

Gamson, W.A., A theory of coalition formation, *American Sociological Review,* **26,** 273–82, 1961.

Gerwin, D., Relationships between structure and technology at organisation and job levels, *Journal of Management Studies,* **16,** 70–79, 1979.

Glueck, William F., Business Policy: Strategy formation and management action. New York: McGraw-Hill, 1972.

Gold, K.A., Managing for success: A comparison of private and public sectors, *Public Administration Review,* 568–75, Nov.–Dec. 1982.

Gray, B. and Ariss, S.S., Politics and strategic change across organisational life cycles, *Academy of Management Review,* **10,** 707–23, 1985.

Gray, D.H., Uses and misuses of strategic planning, *Harvard Business Review,* Jan.–Feb. 1986.

Greiner, L.E., Patterns of Organisation Change, *Harvard Business Review,* 119–30, May–June 1967.

Greiner, L.E., Evolution and revolution as organisations grow, *Harvard Business Review,* 37–46, July-Aug. 1972.

Greiner, L.E., Senior executives as strategic actors, *New Management,* **1,** 11–15, 1983.

Hackman, J.R., Power and centrality in allocation of resources in colleges and universities, *Administrative Science Quarterly,* **30,** 61–77, 1985.

Hackman, J.R. and Oldham, G.R., Development of job diagnostic survey, *Journal of Applied Psychology,* **60,** 159–70, 1975.

Hage, J., An axiomatic theory of organisations, *Administrative Science Quarterly,* **10,** 289–320, 1965.

Hage, J. and Aiken, M., Relationship of centralisation to other structural properties, *Administrative Science Quarterly,* **12,** 79–80, 1967.

Hage, J. and Aiken, M., Routine technology, social structure and organisational goals, *Administrative Science Quarterly,* **14,** 366–77, 1969.

Hall, R.H., Professionalisation and bureaucratisation, *American Sociological Review,* **34,** 92–104, 1968.

Hammer, M., Reengineering work: Don't automate, obliterate, *Harvard Business Review,* 104–12, July–Aug. 1990.

Harari, O. and Mukai, L., A new decade demands a new breed of manager, *Management Review,* **79,** 20–24, 1990.

Harrison, R., Role negotiation: A tough minded approach to team development. *In* W.W. Burke and H.A. Hornstein (Eds.), The Social Technology of Organisation Development. Washington, DC: NTL Learning Resources Corp., 1972.

Hart, C.W.L., Heskett, J.L. and Sasser, W.E., Jr., The profitable art of service recovery, *Harvard Business Review,* 148–56, July–Aug. 1990.

Harvey, E., Technology and structure in organisations, *American Sociological Review,* **33,** 247–59, 1968.

Harvey, J.B. and Albertson, D.R., Neurotic organisations: Symptoms, causes and treatment, Parts I & II, *Personnel Journal,* 694, 770, Sept.–Oct. 1971.

Hax, A.C., Building the firm of the future, *Sloan Management Review,* **30,** 75–82, 1989.

Hedberg, B.L.T., How organisations learn and unlearn. *In* P.C. Nystrom and W.H. Starbuck (Eds.), Handbook of Organisation Design. New York: Oxford University Press, 1981.

Hedberg, B.L.T., Nystrom, P.C. and Starbuck, W.H., Camping on see-saws: Prescriptions for a self-designing organisation, *Administrative Science Quarterly,* **21,** 41–65, 1976.

Heller, F.A. and Wilpert, B., Competence and Power in Managerial Decision Making. New York: John Wiley & Sons, 1981.

Hickson, D.J., Hining, C.R., Lee, C.A., Schneck, R.E. and Pennings J.M., A strategic contingency theory of inter-organisational power, *Administrative Science Quarterly,* **16,** 216–29, 1971.

Hickson, D.J., Pugh, D.S. and Pheysey, Diana, C., Operations technology and organisation structure: An empirical reappraisal, *Administrative Science Quarterly,* **24,** 378–97, 1979.

Hodgetts, R.M., Modern Human Relations. Hinsdale: Dryden Press, 1980.

Hoefstede, G., Culture's Consequences: International differences related to work values. Beverley Hills (California): Sage Publications, 1980.

Hornstein, H.A., Bunker, B.B., Burke, W.W., Gindes, M. and Lewicki R.J., Social Intervention: A behavioral science approach, New York: Free Press, 1971.

Huber, G.P., The nature and design of post-industrial organisations, *Management Science,* **30,** 928–51, 1984.

Hunt, R.G., Technology and organisation, *Academy of Management Journal,* **13,** 235–52, 1970.

Isenberg, D.J., How senior managers think, *Harvard Business Review,* 81–90, Nov.–Dec. 1984.

Janis, I.L., Victims of Group Think. Boston: Houghton Mifflin, 1982.

Jaques, E., Work, Creativity and Social Justice. London: Heinemann, 1970.

Jefferson, M., Economic uncertainty and business decision making. *In* J. Wiseman (Ed.), Beyond Positive Economics? London: Macmillan, 1983.

Kaipa, P., Rethinking organisational productivity, *Newsletter of Mithya,* 14–19, Spring/Summer 1992.

Kanter, R.M., Power failure in management circuit, *Harvard Business Review,* 65–75, July–Aug. 1979.

Kanter, R.M., The new managerial work, *Harvard Business Review,* 85–92, Nov.–Dec. 1989.

Kanter, R.M., When Giants Learn to Dance. London: Unwin Hyman, 1990.

Kast, E. and Rosenzweig, J.E., Contingency Views of Organisation and Management. Chicago: Science Research Associates, 1973.

Katz, D. and Kahn, R.L., The Social Psychology of Organisations. New York: John Wiley & Sons, 1978.

Kelly, G., The Psychology of Personal Constructs. New York: W.W. Norton, 1955.

Kets de Vries, M.F.R., Organisational Paradoxes. London: Tavistock, 1980.

Kets de Vries, M.F.R. and Miller, D., The Neurotic Organisation. San Francisco: Jossey-Bass, 1984.

Kets de Vries, M.F.R. and Miller, D., Unstable at the Top. New York: New American Library, 1987.

Khandwalla, P.N., Organisational design for change. *In* S. Chattopadhyay and U. Pareek (Eds.), Managing Organisational Change. New Delhi: Oxford & IBH, 1982.

Khandwalla, P.N., Organisational Design for Excellence. New Delhi: Tata McGraw-Hill, 1992.

Kibel, H.R., How to Turn Around a Financially Troubled Company. New York: McGraw-Hill, 1982.

Kilmann, R.H., Getting control of the corporate culture, *Managing,* **2,** 11–17, 1982.

Kim, W.C. and Mauborgne, R.A., Cross-cultural strategies, *Journal of Business Strategy,* **7,** 28–35, 1987.

King, A.S., Expectation effects and organisational change, *Administrative Science Quarterly,* **19,** 221–30, 1974.

Kirkpatrick, J., Here comes the payoff from PCs, *Fortune,* 43–48, Mar. 1992.

Kornhauser, A., Mental Health of Industrial Worker, New York: John Wiley & Sons, 1965.

Kotter, J.P., What leaders really do?, *Harvard Business Review,* 103–11, May–June 1990.

Kotter, J.P. and Heskett, J.L., Corporate Culture and Performance. New York: The Free Press, 1992.

Kotter, J.P. and Schlesinger, L.A., Choosing strategies for change, *Harvard Business Review,* 106–14, Mar.–April 1979.

Krafcik, J.F., Triumph of the lean production system, *Sloan Management Review,* **30,** 41–52, 1988.

Kumar, U. and Singh, K.K., Interpersonal construct system of Indian Managers: A determinant of organisational behaviour, *Management International Review,* **18,** 49–59, 1978.

Lawler, E.E., The Ultimate Advantage: Creating the high-involvement organization. San Francisco: Jossey-Bass, 1992.

Lawrence, P.R. and Lorsch, J.W., Organisation and Environment: Managing differentiation and integration. Boston: Harvard University Press, 1967.

Lee, J.A., Leader power and managing change, *Academy of Management Review,* **2,** 73–80, 1977.

Lewin, K., Frontiers of group dynamics, *Human Relations,* **1,** 5–41, 1947.

Lewin, K., Field Theory in Social Science. New York: Harper & Brothers, 1951.

Likert, R. and Likert, J.B., New Ways of Managing Conflict. New York: McGraw-Hill, 1976.

Loasby, B.J., Long-range formal planning in perspective, *Journal of Management Studies,* 1967.

Loasby, B.J., Knowledge, learning and enterprise. *In* J. Wiseman (Ed.), Beyond Positive Economics. London: Macmillan, 1983.

Lorsch, J.W., Managing culture: The invisible barrier to strategic change, *California Management Review,* **23,** 95–109, 1986.

Louis, M.R., Organisations as culture-bearing milieux. *In* L.R. Pondy et al. (Eds.), Organisational Symbolism. Greenwich (Connecticut): JAI Press, 1980.

Lundberg, C.C., On the feasibility of cultural interventions in organisations. *In* P.J. Frost, *et al.* (Eds.), Organisational Culture. New Delhi: Sage Publications, 1985.

Lurie, G.D. and Ahearn, J.M., How companies in trouble get there, *Journal of Business Strategy,* **11,** 25–29, 1990.

Lynch, R.P., Building alliances to penetrate European markets, *Journal of Business Strategy,* **11,** 4–8, 1990.

MacMillan, I.C., Strategy Formulation: Political concepts. New York: West, 1978.

Madsen V. and Polesie, T., Human Factors in Budgeting: Judgement and evaluation. London: Pitman Publishing, 1981.

Maheshwari, B.L., Decision Styles and Organisational Effectiveness. New Delhi: Vikas Publishing House, 1980.

Mahoney, T.A. and Frost, P.J., The role of technology in models of organisational effectiveness, *Organisational Behaviour and Human Performance,* 122–38, Feb. 1974.

Malone, T., et al., Electronic markets and electronic hierarchies, *Communications of the ACM,* **30,** 484–97, 1987.

March, J.G. and Simon, H.A., Organisations. New York: John Wiley & Sons, 1958.

Maslow, A.H., A theory of human motivation, *Psychological Review,* **50,** 370–96, 1943.

McGill, M.E., Slocum, J.W., Jr. and Lei, D., Management Practices in learning organisations, *Organisational Dynamics,* 5–17, Summer 1992.

McGregor, D., The Human Side of Enterprise. New York: McGraw-Hill, 1960.

Medcof, J.W., The power motive and organisational structure: A macro-micro connection, *Canadian Journal of Administrative Science,* 95–113, June 1985.

Menzies, I., A case study in the functioning of social systems as defense against anxiety, *Human Relations,* **13,** 95–121, 1960.

Miles, R.E. and Snow, C.C., Organisational Strategy, Structure, and Process. New York: McGraw-Hill, 1978.

Miles, R.H., Macro Organisational Behavior. Santa Monica (California): Goodyear Publishing, 1980.

Miller, D. and Friesen, P.H., Strategy making in context: Ten empirical archetypes, *The Journal of Management Studies,* **14,** 253–80, 1977.

Miller, D. and Friesen, P.H., Momentum and revolution in organisational adaptation, *Academy of Management Journal,* **23,** 591–614, 1980.

Miller, D., Common syndromes of business failure, *Business Horizons,* 43–53, Nov. 1977.

Miller, D. and Mintzberg, H., The case for configuration. *In* D. Miller and P.H. Friesen (Eds.), Organisations: A quantum view. Englewood Cliffs (NJ): Prentice Hall, 1984.

Miller, G.A., The magic number seven plus or minus two: Some limits on our capacity for processing information, *Psychological Review,* **63,** 81–97, 1956.

Mills, P. and Moberg, D.J., Perspectives on technology of service organisations. *Academy of Management Review,* **7,** 467–78, 1982.

Mintzberg, H., Strategy-making in three modes, *California Management Review,* **16,** 44–53, 1973.

Mintzberg, H., The manager's job: Folklore and fact, *Harvard Business Review,* 49–61, July–Aug. 1975.

Mintzberg, H., Planning on the left side and managing on the right, *Harvard Business Review,* 49–58, July–Aug. 1976.

Mintzberg, H., Structures in 5's: A synthesis of the research on organisation design, *Management Science,* **26,** 336–38, 1980.

Mintzberg, H., Organisation design: Fashion or fit? *Harvard Business Review,* 103–16, Jan.–Feb. 1981.

Mintzberg, H., Structures in Five: Designing effective organisations. Englewood Cliffs (NJ): Prentice Hall, 1983.

Mintzberg, H., Power in and around organisations. Englewood Cliffs (NJ): Prentice Hall, 1983(a).

Mintzberg, H., Opening up the definition of strategy. *In* J.B. Quinn, H. Mintzberg, and R.M. James (Eds.), The Strategy Process: Concepts, contexts, and cases. Englewood Cliffs (NJ): Prentice Hall, 1988.

Mintzberg, H., Mintzberg on Management. New York: The Free Press, 1989.

Mohrman, S.A. and Cummings, T.G., Self-Designing Organisations. Reading (Mass.): Addison-Wesley, 1989.

Morgan, G., Images of Organisation. Beverley Hills (California): Sage Publications, 1986.

Nadler, D.A., Feedback and Organisation Development: Using data based methods. Reading (Mass.): Addison-Wesley, 1977.

Nadler, D.A., Managing organisational change: An integrative perspective, *Journal of Applied Behavioural Science,* **17,** 191–211, 1981.

Nadler, D.A. and Tushman, M.L., Managing Strategic Organisational Change: Frame bending the frame breaking. New York: Delta Publishing Group, 1986.

Naisbitt, J., Megatrends. London: Futura, 1984.

Naisbitt, J. and Auberdene, P., Reinventing the Corporation. New York: Warner Books, 1985.

Narayanan, V.K. and Fahey, L., The Micro-politics of strategy formulation, *Academy of Management Review,* **7,** 25–34, 1982.

Newman, D., Organisational Design. London: Edward Arnold, 1973.

Newman, W.H., Strategy and management structure, *Academy of Management Proceedings,* 8–24, Aug. 1971.

Ohmae, K., The Mind of the Strategist. New York: McGraw-Hill, 1982.

Ohmae, K., How Japanese managers manage. *In* A.A. Thompson, Jr., A.J. Strickland III and W.E. Fulmer (Eds.), Readings in Strategic Management. Plano (Texas): Business Publications, 1987.

Ohmae, K., The Borderless World. London: Fontana, 1991.

Oldham, G.R. and Hackman, J.R., Work design in organisational context. *In* B.M. Staw and L.L. Cummings (Eds.), Research in Organisational Behaviour, Vol. 2. Greenwich, Connecticut: JAI Press, 1980.

Ott, J.S., The Organisational Culture Perspective. Chicago: Dorsey Press, 1989.

Ouchi, W.G. and Dowling, J.B., Defining span of control, *Administrative Science Quarterly,* **19,** 357–65, 1974.

Owens, H., The business of business is learning, *Newsletter of Mithya,* Summer 1990.

Pacanowsky, M.E. and O'Donnell-Trujillo, N., Organisational communication as cultural performance, *Communication Monographs,* **50,** 126–47, June 1983.

Pareek, U., Managing Conflict and Collaboration. New Delhi: Oxford & IBH Publishing Co., 1982.

Pareek, U., Organisational learning diagnostic (OLD): Assessing and developing organisational learning. The 1988 Annual—Developing human resources, University Associates, 1988.

Paterson, T.T., Management Theory. London: Business Publications, 1969.

Pauchant, T.C. and Mitroff, I.I., Transforming the Crisis-Prone Organisation. San Francisco: Jossey-Bass, 1992.

Payne, R.L. and Mansfield, R., Relationship of perception of organisational climate to organisational structure, context, and hierarchical position, *Administrative Science Quarterly,* **21,** 515–26, 1976.

Perrow, C., A framework for comparative analysis of organisations, *American Sociological Review,* **32,** 194–208, 1967.

Perrow, C., Organisational Analysis: A sociological view. Belmont (California): Wadsworth, 1970.

Perrow, C., Complex Organisations: A critical essay. Glenview (Illinois): Scott, Foresman, 1972.

Peters, T.J., Thriving on Chaos. New Delhi: Tata-McGraw Hill, 1987.

Peters, T.J. and Waterman R.H., Jr., In Search of Excellence. New York: Harper & Row, 1982.

Pfeffer, J., Organisational Design. Arlington Heights (Illinois): AHM Publishing, 1978.

Pfeffer, J., Power in Organisations. Marshfield (Mass.): Pittman, 1981.

Popkerwitz, T.S., Educational reform as the organisation of ritual: Stability as change, *Journal of Education,* **164**, 5–29, 1982.

Porter, M.E., Competitive Strategy: Techniques for analysing industries and competitors. New York: Free Press, 1980.

Pucik, V., Strategic alliance, organisational learning and competitive advantage, *Human Resources Management,* **27,** 77–93, 1988.

Pugh, D.S., The measurement of organisation structure: Does context determine form? *Organisational Dynamics,* 19–34, Spring 1973.

Pugh, D.S., Hickson, D.J., Hinings, C.R. and Turner, C., The context of organisation structure, *Administrative Science Quarterly,* **14,** 91–114, 1969.

Quinn, J.B., Strategic change: Logical incrementalism, *Sloan Management Review,* **20,** 7–21, 1978.

Quinn, J.B., Managing strategic change, *Sloan Management Review,* **21,** 3–20, 1980.

Quinn, J.B., Strategies for Change: Logical incrementalism. Homewood (Illinois): Richard D. Irwin, 1980(a).

Quinn, R.E., Applying competing value approach to leadership: Towards an integrative framework. *In* J.G. Hunt et al. (Eds.), Managerial Work and Leadership: International perspectives. New York: Pergamon Press, 1984.

Quinn, R.E. and Anderson, D., Formalisation as crisis: A transition planning program for young organisations. *In* J.R. Kimberly and R.E. Quinn (Eds.), New Futures: The challenge of transition management. New York: Dow Jones-Irwin, 1984.

Quinn, R.E. and Cameron, K.S., Organisational life cycles and shifting criteria of effectiveness: Some preliminary evidence, *Management Science,* **29,** 33–51, 1983.

Quinn, R.E. and Hall, R.H., Environments, organisations and policy-makers: Towards and integrative framework. *In* R.H. Hall and R.E. Quinn (Eds.), Organisational Theory and Public Policy. Beverley Hills (California): Sage Publications, 1983.

Quinn, R.E. and Kimberley, J.R., The management of transition. *In* J.R. Kimberly and R.E. Quinn (Eds.), New Futures: The challenge of transition management. New York: Dow Jones-Irwin, 1984.

Quinn, R.E. and McGrath, M.R., The transformation of organisational culture. *In* P.J. Frost et al. (Eds.), Organisational culture. Beverley Hills (California): Sage Publications, 1985.

Quinn, R.E. and Rohrbaugh, J., A spatial model of effectiveness criteria: Towards a competing value approach to organisational effectiveness, *Management Science*, **29,** 263–77, 1983.

Reddin, Effective Management. New Delhi: Tata McGraw-Hill, 1987.

Reichheld, F.F. and Sasser, W.E., Jr., Zero defection: Quality comes to service, *Harvard Business Review,* 105–11, Sept.–Oct. 1990.

Reimann, B.C., Dimensions of structure in effective organisations: Some empirical evidence, *Academy of Management Journal,* 693–708, Dec. 1974.

Rico, L., Organisational conflict: A framework for reappraisal, *Industrial Management Review,* Fall 1964.

Robbins, S.P., Organisation Theory: Structure, design and applications. Englewood Cliffs (NJ): Prentice Hall, 1987.

Robbins, S.P., Organisational Behavior: Concepts, controversies, and applications. New Delhi: Prentice-Hall of India, 1989.

Ross, G.B.H., Revolution in management accounting, *Management Accounting,* 23–27, Nov. 1990.

Rue, L.W. and Fulmer, R.M., Is long range planning profitable? *Academy of Management Proceedings,* 66–73, Aug. 1973.

Savage, C.M., 5th Generation Management. New Delhi: Prentice-Hall of India, 1992.

Saxena, G., Organisational Change, *Management Review,* **1,** 9–16, 1985.

Schein, E.H., Organisational Culture and Leadership. San Francisco (California): Jossey-Bass, 1985.

Schein, E.H., Reassessing the "divine rights" of managers, *Sloan Management Review,* **30,** 63–68, 1989.

Schmenner, R.W., The merit of making things fast, *Sloan Management Review,* **30,** 11–17, 1988.

Schmuck, R.A., Developing teams of organisational specialists. *In* R.A. Schmuck and M.B. Miles (Eds.), Organisational Development in Schools. Palo Alto (California): National Press Books, 1971.

Schoeffler, S., Buzzel, R.D. and Heany, D.F., Impact of strategic planning on profit performance, *Harvard Business Review,* 137–45, Mar.–April 1974.

Scully, J., Odyssy: From Pepsi to Apple. London: Fontana, 1987.

Seiler, J.A., Diagnosing Inter-departmental conflict, *Harvard Business Review,* 121–32, Sept.–Oct. 1963.

Senge, P.M., The Fifth Discipline. New York: Doubleday/Currency, 1990.

Senge, P.M., The leader's new work: Building learning organisation, *Sloan Management Review,* **31,** 7–22, 1990(a).

Senge, P.M., How to build a learning organisation, *World Executive's Digest,* 48–51, May 1992.

Sergiovanni, T.J. and Corbally J.E., Preface. *In* T.J. Sergiovanni and J.E. Corbally (Eds.), Leadership and Organisational Culture. Urbana (Illinois): University of Illinois Press, 1984.

Shapiro, Benson P., Can marketing and manufacturing coexist?, *Harvard Business Review,* 104–14, Sept.–Oct. 1977.

Sherif, M., In Common Predicament: Social psychology of intergroup conflict and cooperation. Boston: Houghton Mifflin, 1966.

Sherif, M. and Sherif, C., Social Psychology. New York: Harper & Row, 1969.

Shetty, Y.K., Managerial power and organisational effectiveness: A contingency analysis, *Journal of Management Studies,* **15,** 178–81, 1978.

Shukla, M., Demythifying corporate innovativeness, *Business India,* 67-68, June 30–July 13, 1986.

Siehl, C. and Martin, J., The role of symbolic management: How can managers effectively transmit organisational culture? *In* J.G. Hunt, D.M. Hosking, C.A. Schriesheim and R. Stewart (Eds.), Leaders and Managers: International perspectives on managerial behaviour and leadership. New York: Pergamon Press, 1984.

Simon, H.A., Making management decision: The role of intuition and emotion, *Academy of Management Executive,* **1,** 57–64, 1987.

Singh, P., Chief Executive: Role and profile, *Indian Management,* 3–11, Mar. 1985.

Singh, P. and Bhandarkar, A., Corporate Success and Transformational Leadership. New Delhi: Wiley Eastern, 1990.

Singh, P. and Parthasarthy, Kokila, Conflict management strategy—A scenario of avoidance, *Abhigyan,* 57–84, Autumn 1985.

Skaria, G., Corporate *perestroika, Business World,* 10–23, April 1991.

Smircich, L. and Morgan, G., Leadership: The management of meaning, *Journal of Applied Behavioural Science,* **18,** 257–73, 1982.

Smith, R.A., Corporations in Crisis. New York: Doubleday, 1966.

Starbuck, W.H., Greve, A. and Hedberg, B.T., Responding to crisis, *Journal of Business Administration,* 111–78, Spring 1978.

Stevenson, W.B., Pearce, W.B. and Porter, L.W., The concept of "coalition" in organisation theory and research, *Academy of Management Review,* **10,** 256–68, 1985.

Stewart, T.A., The search for the organisation of tomorrow, *Fortune,* 53–58, May 18, 1992.

Strauss, G., Work-flow frictions, interfunctional rivalry and professionalism: A case study of purchasing agents, *Human Organisation,* 137–49, 1964.

Tannenbaum, R. and Davis, S.A., Values, man and organisations, *Industrial Management Review,* **10,** 67–86, 1969.

Thomas, K.W., Conflict and conflict management. *In* M.D. Dunnette (Ed.), Handbook of Industrial and Organisational Psychology. Chicago: Rand McNally, 1976.

Thompson, J.D., Organisations in Action. New York: McGraw-Hill, 1967.

Thune, S.S. and House, R.J., Where long range planning pays off, *Business Horizons,* **13,** 81–87, 1970.

Tichy, N.M. and Devanna, M.A., The Transformational Leader. New York: John Wiley & Sons, 1986.

Tichy, N.M. and Ulrich, D.D., The leadership challenge: A call for the transformational leader, *Sloan Management Review,* **26,** 59–68, 1984.

Toffler, A., Future Shock. New York: Random House, 1970.

Toffler, A., The Third Wave. London: Bantam Books, 1981.

Torbert, W., Learning from Experience. New Work: Columbia University, 1973.

Trist, E.L., The sociotechnical perspective. *In* A.H. Van de Ven and W.F. Joyce (Eds.), Perspectives on Organisation Design and Behavior. New York: John Wiley & Sons, 1981.

Turnstall, W.B., Cultural transition at AT & T, *Sloan Management Review,* **25,** 1–12, 1983.

Van de Ven, A., Delbecq, A. and Koenig, R., Jr., Determinants of coordination modes within organisations, *American Sociological Review,* **41,** 322–28, 1976.

Van Maanen, J., Breaking in: Socialisation to work. *In* R. Dubin (Ed.), Handbook of Work, Organisation and Society. Chicago: Rand McNally, 1976.

Vancil, R.F., The accuracy of long range planning, *Harvard Business Review,* 98–101, Sept.–Oct. 1970.

Walter, G.A., Culture collisions in mergers and acquisitions. *In* P.J. Frost et al. (Eds.), Organisational Culture. New Delhi: Sage Publications, 1985.

Walton, R.E., Managing Conflict. Reading (Mass.): Addison-Wesley, 1987.

Walton, R.E. and Dutton, J.M., The management of interdepartmental conflict: A model under view, *Administrative Science Quarterly,* **14,** 522–42, 1969.

Wanous, J.P., Organisational Entry: Recruitment, selection, and socialisation of newcomers. Reading (Mass.): Addison-Wesley, 1980.

Waterman, Robert, H., Jr., The seven elements of strategic fit, *The Journal of Business Strategy,* **2,** 69–73, 1982.

Weber, Max, The Theory of Social and Economic Organisation (Ed. T. Parsons). New York: Free Press, 1974.

Weick, K.E., The significance of corporate culture. *In* P.J. Frost et al. (Eds.), Organisational Culture. New Delhi: Sage Publications, 1985.

Wofford, J.C., Gerloff, E.A. and Cummins, R.C., Organisational Communication: The keystone to managerial effectiveness. New York: McGraw-Hill, 1977.

Woodward, J., Industrial Organisation: Theory and practice. London: Oxford University Press, 1965.

Wrapp, E.H., Good managers don't make policy decisions, *Harvard Business Review,* 91–99, Sept.–Oct. 1967.

Wrong, D.H., Power: Its forms, bases and uses. New York: Harper & Row, 1980.

Yuchtman, E. and Seashore, S.E., A systems resource approach to organisational effectiveness, *American Sociological Review,* **32,** 891–903, 1967.

Zaleznick, A., Managers and Leaders: Are they different? *Harvard Business Review,* 67–78, May–June 1977.

Zaleznik, R., Power and politics in organisational life, *Harvard Business Review,* 47–60, May–June 1970.

Zaltman, G. and Duncan, R., Strategies for Planned Change. New Delhi: Wiley, 1977.

Zammuto, R.F. and O'Connor, E.J., Gaining advanced manufacturing technologies' benefits: The role of organisational design and culture, *Academy of Management Review,* **17,** 701–28, 1992.

Zand, D.E. and Sorensen, R.E., Theory of change and the effective use of management science, *Administrative Science Quarterly,* **20,** 532–45, 1975.

Zuboff, S., In the Age of the Smart Machine. New York: Basic Books, 1988.

Weick, K.E., The significance of corporate culture, in P.J. Frost et al. (Eds.), *Organizational Culture*, New Delhi: Sage Publications, 1985.

Wofford, J.C., Gerloff, E.A. and Cummins, R.C., *Organizational Communication: The keystone to managerial effectiveness*, New York: McGraw-Hill, 1977.

Woodward, J., *Industrial Organisation: Theory and practice*, London: Oxford University Press, 1965.

Wrapp, E.H., Good managers don't make policy decisions, *Harvard Business Review*, 91–99, Sept.–Oct. 1967.

Wrong, D.H., *Power: Its forms, bases and uses*, New York: Harper & Row, 1980.

Yuchtman, E. and Seashore, S.E., A systems resource approach to organizational effectiveness, *American Sociological Review*, 32, 891–903, 1967.

Zaleznik, A., Managers and Leaders: Are they different? *Harvard Business Review*, 55, 67–78, May–June 1977.

Zaleznik, A., Power and politics in organizational life, *Harvard Business Review*, 47–60, May–June 1970.

Zaltman, G. and Duncan, R., *Strategies for Planned Change*, New Delhi: Wiley, 1977.

Zammuto, R.F. and O'Connor, E.J., Gaining advanced manufacturing technologies' benefits: the role of organizational design and culture, *Academy of Management Review*, 17, 701–28, 1992.

Zand, D.E. and Sorensen, R.E., Theory of change and the effective use of management science, *Administrative Science Quarterly*, 20, 532–45, 1975.

Zuboff, S., *In the Age of the Smart Machine*, New York: Basic Books, 1988.

Author Index

Organisation Index

Subject Index